I0894264

ADVANCED PRAISE FOR *IN THE PRESIDENT'S HOME*

A wonderful read filled with factual and historically accurate details of the times and events in the day-to-day lives of Dr. Norman Auburn, his charming wife Kay, their children, and assorted family members. Written almost to the point of diary entrees, so precise yet filled with colorful details of events, bringing new life into the business community and the excitement of life in a growing town.

The Auburns were an integral part of Akron, beloved and respected. They represented Akron to all guests not only as a lively and beautiful college town on the move but as an industrially motivated town growing and thriving in the aftermath of war.

—Patricia Graves, University of Akron Trustee Emerita

To open the pages of Mark Auburn's book is to open the front door of the president's home and enjoy all they had to offer in an age of tremendous growth and opportunity for The University of Akron under the leadership of a remarkable man. President Norm Auburn and his wife Kay Auburn made it clear for the duration of Dr. Auburn's presidency that their home was a welcoming place to all university family—faculty, staff, and students.

I was inspired by the energy and dedication Norm Auburn had for all his endeavors. The scope of President Auburn's professional activities is remarkable and Mark's accounting of his dad's many faceted career is historically significant not only to the Auburn family, but to the entire Akron community.

—Renée Sandefur Pipitone, daughter of Ray Sandefur, founding Dean of The University of Akron College of Fine and Applied Arts

In the President's Home is a tapestry of family history and numerous memories of what it was like to grow up in the Midwest during and after the Second World War with a father who achieved his American Dream of being a college president and a charming, bright, and extroverted wife who was at his side along the way with their four children.

Under Dr. Auburn's steady hand the university grew in stature and importance and became the center of activity for our community, while the president's home was continuously alive with students and their parents, community leaders, visiting dignitaries, extended Auburn family gatherings, and Kay's famous teas. It was an era in our community, generally speaking, of growth, prosperity, and culture, with the American Dream just around the corner, in which Dr. Auburn played an important role.

—Frances Seiberling Buchholzer

Series on Ohio History and Culture
Kevin Kern, Editor

Joyce Dyer, *Gum-Dipped: A Daughter Remembers Rubber Town*
Melanie Payne, *Champions, Cheaters, and Childhood Dreams: Memories of the Soap Box Derby*
John Flower, *Downstairs, Upstairs: The Changed Spirit and Face of College Life in America*
Wayne Embry and Mary Schmitt Boyer, *The Inside Game: Race, Power, and Politics in the NBA*
Robin Yocum, *Dead Before Deadline: . . . And Other Tales from the Police Beat*
A. Martin Byers, *The Ohio Hopewell Episode: Paradigm Lost and Paradigm Gained*
Edward C. Arn, edited by Jerome Mushkat, *Arn's War: Memoirs of a World War II Infantryman, 1940–1946*
Brian Bruce, *Thomas Boyd: Lost Author of the "Lost Generation"*
Kathleen Endres, *Akron's "Better Half": Women's Clubs and the Humanization of a City, 1825–1925*
Russ Musarra and Chuck Ayers, *Walks Around Akron: Rediscovering a City in Transition*
Heinz Poll, edited by Barbara Schubert, *A Time to Dance: The Life of Heinz Poll*
Mark D. Bowles, *Chains of Opportunity: The University of Akron and the Emergence of the Polymer Age, 1909–2007*
Russ Vernon, *West Point Market Cookbook*
Stan Purdum, *Pedaling to Lunch: Bike Rides and Bites in Northeastern Ohio*
Joyce Dyer, *Goosetown: Reconstructing an Akron Neighborhood*
Robert J. Roman, *Ohio State Football: The Forgotten Dawn*
Timothy H. H. Thoresen, *River, Reaper, Rail: Agriculture and Identity in Ohio's Mad River Valley, 1795–1885*
Mark Auburn, *In the President's Home: Memories of the Akron Auburns*

Titles published since 2003.
For a complete listing of titles published in the series, go to www.uakron.edu/uapress.

In the President's Home

MEMORIES OF THE AKRON AUBURNS

Mark Auburn

The University of Akron Press
Akron, Ohio

ISBN: 978-1-629221-35-9 (paper)
ISBN: 978-1-629221-33-5 (ePDF)
ISBN: 978-1-629221-34-2 (ePub)

A catalog record for this title is available from the Library of Congress.

∞The paper used in this publication meets the minimum requirements of ANSI/NISO z39.48–1992 (Permanence of Paper).

Cover: Photo by Lou Tobias, from the Norman Auburn Papers. Courtesy of Archival Services, University Libraries, The University of Akron. Cover design by Amy Freels.

In the President's Home was designed and typeset in Adobe Caslon Pro by Amy Freels and printed on sixty-pound white and bound by Bookmasters of Ashland, Ohio.

The excerpt on page 183 is reprinted with permission of the *Akron Beacon Journal* and Ohio.com.

For Rebecca and Nora

Contents

Introduction

My father, Norman Auburn, served as President of The University of Akron from 1951 to 1971, the longest period of any person before or since. Under his leadership the university moved from municipal to state status. It added community college and doctoral missions, consolidated and expanded its research capacities, adopted a law school and joined in creating an affiliated medical university, physically expanded and built onto its downtown Akron hilltop location, organized a regional campus, completed its first public fund-raising campaign, and quadrupled in enrollment from 4,500 to 20,500 students. By 1990, it was the third-largest university in Ohio.

Auburn was a forty-six-year-old father of four when he became president. His wife, Kathleen Montgomery Auburn, was the daughter of a Presbyterian minister and three-time college president. Their backgrounds and early experiences in Cincinnati help explain why Norm was chosen to lead the small municipal university in northeast Ohio. When they came to Akron, their children included a college sophomore, a high school sophomore, a first-grader, and a handicapped four-year-old. They lived first in their own Tudor-style four-bedroom home but in 1956 relocated to a much more spacious seven-bedroom five-bath Georgian colonial donated to the university by the former Chairman of Goodyear Tire and Rubber Company, Paul W. Litchfield.

Conceiving their service to the university and the community like that of a minister and his family living in a manse, they entertained extensively and lived in the public eye while raising their three oldest children to adulthood and marriage and guiding their youngest to a comfortable lifelong custodial situation. Seen through the eyes of their third-born child, how they entertained, what they ate, how they exercised, when and where they vacationed, the things they acquired and used reflect day-to-day life in America and Akron in the 1950s and 1960s from behind the public faces of a well-known servant-leader and his family. In retirement from his Akron presidency, Norm became an itinerant "rent-a-president" for six other colleges and universities, was widowed and remarried, and extended a private-sector banking career which moved him from the genteel sufficiency of public service to a comfortable plenty that assured the lifelong maintenance of his handicapped child.

These memories of the Akron Auburns are arranged in three sections.

TOWARD THE PRESIDENT'S HOME—HOW THEY GOT THERE

Through his life's work as an architectural draftsman, my grandfather Joe Auburn raised his two sons into the managerial-professional class a notch beyond his own. My grandmother Hulda Grossman Auburn solidified the family's values of hard work and self-sufficiency which formed Norm's character. But it was to his wife and her family that my father cleaved.

My grandfather R. Ames Montgomery led a professional and personal life which my father took as a model for his own aspirations. Norm was welcomed into the Montgomery family and lived in harmony with its values for much of his life.

My father and mother met at the University of Cincinnati, a municipally funded comprehensive institution in the heart of Ohio's second largest city, and they never really left UC until they moved to the municipal University of Akron in 1951. In order to expedite winning Dr. Montgomery's approval to marry Kay, Norm eschewed graduate study and began a career as the publicity manager for a building trades association. The Depression ended that career path five years later. But Norm parlayed his active volunteer contributions with the UC Alumni Association into a full-time job just eight days before President Roosevelt closed the banks in March 1933.

Twice during his eighteen years at UC, outside offers came to my father. Senator Robert A. Taft asked him to become the first salaried Executive

Director of the Hamilton County Republican Party. When he had risen to second-in-command of UC, he was offered the Senior Vice Presidency of First National Bank of Cincinnati. He used both job offers to strengthen his prospects in higher education instead of changing careers. Meanwhile, during the first two decades of their marriage, Norm and Kay bore four children: that is the family unit that came to support his presidency of Ohio's tenth-largest college in the one-industry town of Akron.

IN THE PRESIDENT'S HOME—WHAT THEY DID THERE

The accomplishments of Norman Auburn's presidency at The University of Akron have been chronicled in George Knepper's *New Lamps for Old* (1970) and his *Summit's Glory* (1990). There are multiple articles in Akron's alumni magazine and in the newspapers of the period. His professional papers are publicly available in the University Libraries Archival Services. Together with John R. Buchtel and Parke R. Kolbe, he is honored as a founder of the university. These memories deal with the personal rather than the public, the day-to-day observation rather than the measured assessment, the person rather than the persona. They are memoirs, not biography or history. They are my memories, not those of my siblings or cousins or contemporary friends. I am responsible for this portrait.

Norm and Kay and their children led a public life. As the third-born child of their early middle years, I remember how they entertained and the behind-the-scenes arrangements that supported them. I connect my family's eating habits to the food traditions in which they were raised, and I write about breakfasts, lunches, dinners, and even snacking because of what they reveal about their personal habits, choices, and values. The Auburn family in the mid 1950s and 1960s lived in America's dietary plenty as it was being enriched through technology, transportation, innovation, and changing sociology, so how and where they dined when they went out and the prepared foods they chose to bring home play a part in defining them, too.

Exercise and recreation characterize a family and its members. I add a memory of bowling (which I did not experience personally) because of what it suggests about the President Auburn of Buchtel Hall as seen by his close subordinates. My father's one hobby, I thought, was photography. In fact, his photography was not so much a hobby as a means of publication for his scholarship.

We took some vacations as a family when I was a child, but they were circumscribed because my father traveled extensively for professional reasons and because he was possessed of a physical and emotional resilience which did not seem to require periods of tranquility or changes of activity like other CEOs. Norm loved cars: who would have ever suspected given his succession of sober blue Chevrolet sedans?

My mother brought friends to the President's Home, friends from her youth, friends who grew closer, friends she managed to make in Akron even as the President's spouse, friends of true intimacy. My father's friends—well, his intimacy was limited to two of his wives and was compartmentalized in relationships with a few others.

FROM THE PRESIDENT'S HOME—LIFE AFTER THE PRESIDENCY

After leaving the President's Home, Norm Auburn lived for thirty-two years, and though he retired from full-time service to The University of Akron, he never completely retired from higher education or from his second longest career, banking. He served six acting presidencies and three other extended university assignments, and he solidified a banking career which helped him create an estate to assure his handicapped child's lifelong comfort. He was widowed soon after he left UA, entered a second marriage which was annulled within months by mutual consent, and married for a third time. This third marriage lasted until his death twenty-seven years later, and just as his marriage to my mother Kay had made his UA presidency possible, so his marriage to Virginia made his careers as a banker and a "rent-a-president" possible.

My father loved to repeat Ralph Waldo Emerson's observation that "an institution is the lengthened shadow of one man." If his father-in-law R. Ames Montgomery cast a shadow by which Norm Auburn measured and prepared himself for fatherhood and a presidency, his handicapped son Davey had a second shaping presence in his adult life. Davey lived almost all his life in Jonesville, Michigan, where the children of R. Ames Montgomery operated The Manor, though he was a regular visitor to the President's Home.

THE FAMILIES OF THESE MEMORIES

Norm Auburn's Family

Walter Joseph Auburn (né Angebrandt) Sr. (1868–1958)
"Joe," "Granddaddy"
Norm's father, an architectural draftsman who lived his entire life in Cincinnati

Hulda Suzannah Carolina Grossman Auburn (1871–1949)
Norm's mother, a homemaker and Christian Science Practitioner; native of Cincinnati

> **Walter Joseph Auburn (né Angebrandt) Jr. (1897–1985)**
> "Walter," Norm's older brother and only sibling
> m. **Mildred Perkins**, children **Walter Joseph III** ("Wally"), and **Corisande**
>
> **Norman Paul Auburn (né Angebrandt) (1905–2003)**
> "Norm," "Normy," "Daddy II" to his grandchildren and daughters-in-law

Kay Auburn's Family

Richmond Ames Montgomery, DD (1870–1950)
"Ames," "Big Daddy" to his grandchildren
Kay's father, a Presbyterian minister and three-time college president, founding President of The Manor Foundation, resident of Cincinnati 1926–1932

Mary Frances O'Reilly Allhands Montgomery, MD (1868–1940)
"Fanny," "Maman" to her grandchildren
Kay's mother, a homemaker (she never practiced medicine)

> **Mary Frances Montgomery (1898–1943)**
> "Mary," Ames and Fanny's oldest daughter; an invalid
>
> **Lillian Josephine Montgomery (1901–1985)**
> "Jo," Ames and Fanny's second daughter
> From 1943 onward, Corporate Secretary of The Manor Foundation, where she taught and pursued a music ministry.

Elizabeth Ames Montgomery (1905–1993)
"Betty," Ames and Fanny's third daughter
From 1943 onward, chief teacher and later Vice President of The Manor
m. **William Blacklock Clark (1906–1975)**
"Bill," an architect. Vice President (1943–1950), President (1950–1971) of The Manor Foundation

Betty and Bill's children
Jane Clark Swinehart (1937–)
"Jane," "Janey"

Robert Montgomery Clark (1939–)
"Rob," "Mr. Rob," "Bob," President of The Manor, 1971–2005

Jane Clark married **Bob Swinehart**; **Rob Clark** married **Jane Huber**, "Miss Jane," who with Rob owned a condominium in St. Thomas, VI.

Kathleen O'Reilly Montgomery (1908–1974)
"Kay," "K-K" to her grandchildren
Ames and Fanny's fourth daughter

Norm and Kay's Children
Ames Montgomery Auburn (1932–2011)
m. **Merron L. Latta Jr.** "Rusty" **(1930–2001)**
children **Lucretia, Kathleen, Elizabeth**
"Ames," "Amesie," "Gran Ames" to her grandchildren
Primarily a homemaker, Ames supported Rusty's career as a diplomat with postings in Europe and southeast Asia and Washington, DC. She earned an MA in English and taught at Montgomery Community College, worked for O. B. Hardison at the Folger Library, and sold real estate.

Richard Paul Auburn, MD (1937–2006)
"Dick," "Dickie"
m. **Mary Elizabeth Sanford (1938–)**
children **Jennifer, Cynthia**
Dick was a general surgeon and partner in the physician-owned Hammond Clinic in northwest Indiana. He retired in 2002.

Mark Stuart Auburn (1945–)
"Mark," "Markie"
m. **Sandra Ray Korman (1945–)**
"Sandy," "Miss Sandy"
children **David, Benjamin (1972–2000)**

David Bruce Auburn (1947–2009)
"Davey" Handicapped by cerebral palsy, resident of The Manor from 1952 to his death

ASSOCIATES OF THE AKRON AUBURNS

Caroline J. Pardee (1911–2003)
"Caroline," "Miss Pardee"
Executive Assistant to Norm at UA from 1953 to 1971, godmother of Norm and Kay's grandchildren Kathleen and Benjamin, subject of 1994 UA dissertation by Charmaine Streharsky, "Caroline Pardee at The University of Akron"

Dolores Martin Skinner White (1935–)
"Dolores," "Dee"
m. 1 **Bill Skinner** (children **Billy, Pammy**)
m. 2 **Bill White**
Housekeeper in the President's Home, 1961–1971, companion and retainer to Kay and Norm in retirement

To the President's Home

Family Origins

THE AUBURNS

Norm Auburn's father, Walter Joseph Angebrandt, was born February 16, 1868, in Cincinnati, Ohio, and died almost ninety-one years later in Akron. He was known as Joe. The oldest of thirteen children, he left school after fourth grade to support his family during a time of diphtheria and worked with one interruption until 1950. With Hulda Suzannah Carolina Grossman he fathered two long-lived sons, Walter Joseph Jr. (1897–1985) and Norman Paul (1905–2003). Like Joe, Hulda was a native Cincinnatian. Her family manufactured paper bags and boxes, but if she brought a dowry to their marriage, it provided less security than their mutual habits of frugality and self-reliance.

Sometime after my father neatly signed his birth name "Norman Angebrandt" on a sixth-grade paper, Joe and his surviving brothers went together to the US Courthouse in Cincinnati and changed their surname to "Auburn." I think their act took place in 1917, about when America entered the Great War and anti-German fever peaked. Cincinnati had a thriving German community marked by *Biergärten*, and choral societies, and *Turnvereinen* (gymnastics clubs), and Oktoberfests, and opera, and four German-language newspapers. Fifty-seven percent of the 1890 Cincinnati population was either born in Germany or had German parents. To folks who knew of Cincinnati's "Mt. Auburn" neighborhood, "Auburn" sounded like a good American name. It even captured something of the "burnt" meaning of "Angebrandt."

Joe, Walter, Hulda, and Norman Angebrandt in 1916, a year before the surname change. *From the author's collection*

Uncle Walter

Norm had one sibling, an older brother who completed high school and served stateside in the army during World War I. He met and married Mildred, a Virginian, during his service and brought her home to Cincinnati. They had two children—Walter III, called "Wally," and Corisande. Uncle Walter spent fifty years as a writer and editor, producing the in-house magazine of a major manufacturer and relocating with it to Chicago by 1922, later publishing an independent version and operating a small public relations consultancy with Mildred.

There was not much interaction between our families during my childhood. I recall meeting Uncle Walter only once, at Joe's funeral in 1958. My sister Ames (thirteen years older) became reacquainted with her childhood playmate, Wally, when they were in their sixties. Kay and Mildred never related well. Mother had formed antipathy for Southerners from her teenage years in Danville, Kentucky, and by her family's alienation with the Louisville Allhands, who were thought to have stolen and squandered her mother's patrimony.

But though their families did not comfortably mesh, the brothers kept in touch, and in their senior years when each widower had remarried, they

Norm, Kay, Mildred, and Walter Auburn celebrate Joe and Hulda's fiftieth wedding anniversary, April 26, 1945. *Pogue Studio, from the author's collection*

established cordial couple relations including exchanged Florida visits, Fort Lauderdale to Dunedin and back. In our Akron years I remember seeing my father with multi-page single-space typed letters from Uncle Walter, and I knew that Dad answered them by hand. Mom would quietly repeat to me phrases like "your little college" or "your fat-cat friends."

Joe and Hulda

For more than fifty years as a draftsman for a Cincinnati manufacturer of ornamental ironwork, Joe worked ten-hour days, five days a week, with a half day on Saturday. He walked to work each day, rain or shine, and he walked home for the lunch which Hulda served him, and those eight miles a day must have strengthened his always firm constitution: Well into his forties he was a member of the North Cincinnati Turners, which gave public gymnastics programs in the Music Hall. His sons were proud of his work: Dad pointed to the ornamental iron around the Ohio Statehouse lawn and accenting the flat round cupola on its roof as his father's design, and once in Richmond, grandson Wally identified to cousin Ames the fencing around the statue of native Virginian George Washington as our grandfather's work. It was a subordinate's job, not an architect's, but he wore a suit and tie to work every day, and not for him the blue-collar workingman's relaxation of the Biergärten, no, he went on Saturday afternoons to the opera, and according to my brother Dick, the grandson who inherited both his spatial-motor and his musical talents, he could sing several operas (or at least their principal arias) straight through from memory. (His granddaughter Corisande got the musical gene, too.)

Joe and Hulda had married on April 28, 1895. Hulda, born September 30, 1871, was two-and-a-half years his junior. Until my father's adolescence, Hulda was a fulltime homemaker. She pickled, preserved, and canned, delighting her granddaughter Ames with the neatly arranged treasures of her pantry and her cooking and the spotless dust-free atmosphere of her home, and after work and on weekends Joe was expected to beat carpets, sterilize jars, tote and seed and peel fruits and vegetables, and wash the windows and storms. That home economy helped to sustain a family of four living from pay envelope to pay envelope in rented apartments. Though he never said it to me, my mother hinted that my father had known times of hunger in his youth.

Walter left home when my father was ten, and with only one child Hulda began training to qualify as a Christian Science Practitioner, which she achieved in 1919 and practiced for thirty years until her death. In this paid, nonordained, church-approved capacity, she visited the sick and prayed with them for God's intervention or for patience under His providence. Among other tenets, Christian Scientists believe that God will heal all bodily ills. They preach a lifestyle of vigorous exercise and moderation in food and drink and no nonnatural substances, and when they fall sick, they seek in prayer, scripture, and the writings of founder Mary Baker Eddy relief from present ills or acceptance of God's will. Practitioners bring comfort to the home; they, rather than nurses or physicians, are called to the sick. For some Christian Scientists, even the use of eyeglasses is forbidden by faith. Hulda held that eyeglasses were mechanical, not medical, interventions.

One measure of her success as a Practitioner showed in the scores of floral arrangements sent to the funeral home in 1949. Tiers were built up along the walls of the viewing room to array in four or five shelves the overflowing vases and planters, floor to ceiling. In addition to paying the stated fee, a grateful congregant or grieving family might also give a personal token, and Hulda's bureau was stuffed with worked linen and cambric handkerchiefs and figured silk and wool and cashmere scarves. Joe adopted, or at least countenanced, his wife's faith.

I never had a conversation with my father about his mother's faith. When I came along, he'd been a Presbyterian for most of his adult life. To an adolescent, his abstemious habits seemed idiosyncratic rather than faith-based or familial. I saw that he brought his father to live with him, an act of love and faith in family, so I grew up with the notion that such was natural. I never heard Dad speak any German, in which his parents were fluent. I have an infant's dim memory of a tickling game chanted to "*Hier kommt die Maus, Und raus die Haus, Der Alter kommt, Zu* tickle *die Maus*," but nothing else except a recipe or two remains of my German heritage. It would be to my mother's Scots-Irish family that Norm Auburn cleaved.

THE MONTGOMERYS

Kay's father was born in Hendricks County, Indiana, on July 16, 1870, and died eighty years later on his birthday, July 16, 1950, in Jonesville, Michigan. The fifth of seven children, he was baptized Richmond Ames Montgomery but was always called "Ames." He graduated from Miami University in Oxford, Ohio, in 1892 and earned the Doctor of Divinity from McCormick Theological Seminary in Chicago in 1896. In Chicago he met Mary Frances Allhands, a recent MD graduate of the Northwestern College of Medicine. They would be married forty-four years and raise four daughters before her death in 1940. The daughter of physician David Allhands and his wife Mary Ann O'Reilly, she was always called "Fanny." Family lore holds that her parents advised against her marrying Ames because he complained of digestive disorders, but she was twenty-eight and willing to take love's chance.

The couple's first twelve years of marriage brought four babies and three jobs. Ames had pastorates in Duluth (Minnesota), Edgerton (Ohio), and Xenia (Ohio). Their first daughter, another Mary Frances (Mary), was born in 1898. Lillian Josephine (Jo) was born November 23, 1901, in Duluth. Elizabeth Ames (Betty) was born July 18, 1905, in Xenia. And Kathleen O'Reilly (Kay) was born May 25, 1908, also in Xenia, in her mother's forty-first year.

Big Daddy holding Dick Auburn and Maman holding Jane Clark at Chalmers Place, 1938. *From the author's collection*

Fanny devoted herself to her husband's career and her children's education. While she used her medical training informally among their congregations, she did not practice. She probably sensed that something was wrong with Mary, her first born, long before the *grande mal* epileptic seizures presented, for she decided early to oversee her children's education at home. Fanny always had help in the home, usually a cook-housekeeper, often an additional heavy cleaner. But whether there was enough money to employ specialist tutors I do not know: both Betty and especially Jo became deft pianists, and her three youngest children completed baccalaureate and master's degrees. Jo, Betty, and Kay survived the normal round of childhood maladies, though Kay was born like many children of older mothers with a visible anomaly, a deformed pinna and no functional hearing on the right side. Jo grew to be as tall for a woman at 5'11" as Ames was for a man at 6'3". Betty at 5'3" was taller than her mother's 4'11" and plump like her. Kay's 5'7" height made her tall among her peers but not too tall for most men, and she split the difference between Jo's slenderness and Betty's plumpness.

I never knew "Maman" personally. She died five years before I was born. "Big Daddy" lived until I was four. I can't find the picture of him holding me as a baby in 1946, at his seventy-sixth birthday celebration: the family is standing on the lawn at the west front of the Manor, the boarding school for handicapped boys which from 1943 he operated with all his daughters (except my mother) and his son-in-law in Jonesville, Hillsdale County, Michigan, and he is erect, strong, stern, kindly, and confident, cradling a plump eight-month-old towhead just as he must have held hundreds of babies for the Sacrament of Baptism.

Ames Montgomery's Career

Ames preached the Gospel for fifty-four years. He gave his first sermon in 1893 and his last in 1947. He was pastor of the Glen Avon Presbyterian Church of Duluth from 1894 until 1904, then every summer from 1905 to 1933 he returned to preach there as "pulpit supply." Sometime during his decade's full-time service to Glen Avon he also ministered to a congregation in Edgerton, Ohio, about fifty miles on US 6 east of Lake Wawasee, where he would rent a summer cabin for many years, and about thirty miles south of Jonesville. From 1904 to 1909 Ames and Fanny led the First Presbyterian Church of Xenia, where both Betty and Kay were born and where many family papers and photographs were lost in a fire in the parsonage. In March 1909, Ames became the sixth minister of the First Presbyterian Church of Ottumwa, Iowa. In a history of the congregation published on its centennial in 1953, Dr. Montgomery is remembered for his "attractive personality, his originality, his literary ability, and his deeply spiritual character [which] made a deep impression on all with whom he came into contact. His custom to speak to at least one person daily, in regard to his personal relation to Christ, resulted in the salvation of many souls." He was pastor for four years before being called downriver to the Taylor Place Presbyterian Church of St. Louis in 1913.

Four years later in 1917, Ames was elected President of Parsons College in Fairfield, Iowa, twenty-five miles east of Ottumwa. He served five years before being elected President of Centre College in Danville, Kentucky, in June 1922, where he inherited responsibility for an athletics program which was overshadowing the strong liberal arts tradition for which the Presbyterian college is still known today. Parsons College was a quarter the size and focused mostly on Iowans; Centre College had national aspirations and students from many states. On March 9, 1926, he resigned after a student-initiated petition called for his removal: his opposition to the football craze, which had seen Centre play and beat Harvard and had brought the Middle States Association to threaten its accreditation, doomed his presidency.

Without a job or a home (Ames and Fanny lived in parsonages or academic manses for all but two of their forty-four years of married life) for several months, later that year he was appointed President of Lane Theological Seminary in Walnut Hills, Cincinnati, an institution still remembered for its active support of abolition, where he oversaw the sale of its assets and the transfer of its students, records, and traditions to his alma mater, McCormick Theological Seminary, six years later in 1932. He was appointed Professor of Homiletics at McCormick (there was some talk of his being made President there when the position opened, but that did not happen) and moved into a faculty home on Chalmers Place on its Lincoln Park campus in Chicago. Betty had married William B. Clark on September 12, 1927; Kay had married Norm on June 28, 1930. Jo, whose one serious romance had been discouraged by her parents, lived with Ames, Fanny, and Mary at Chalmers Place, working and studying at Northwestern University, and Betty and Bill lived in Chicago while Bill pursued his career as an architect with Armour and Company.

Ames Montgomery's Scholarship

While he was pastor in Duluth, Dr. Montgomery published his first book, *The Secret Place: Studies in Prayer* (1901). While minister of First Presbyterian in Ottumwa he brought out *The Triumphant Ministry* (1914) under the pseudonym Timothy Kilbourn. At Centre College he published his Monday-morning sermons about the balance of academics and athletics as the pamphlet "The Winning Team at Centre College" (1925–1926). While presiding at Lane Seminary he completed the biography of his former parishioner *Thomas D. Foster, 1847–1915* (1930). Reaching a primarily teaching position at McCormick in 1932, he completed three books in less than a decade, *Expository Preaching* (1939), *Preparing Preachers to Preach* (1939), and *Reality in Religion: Studies of the Atonement of Jesus* (1941). Shortly before his crippling strokes in 1948, he sent for safe keeping to his son-in-law Norm the typescript of a collection of sermons, "Listen to the Angels Sing," which he planned to publish privately

R. Ames Montgomery at his desk. *From the author's collection*

* * *

Norm and Kay both came from stable families and were younger siblings of their parents' mature years. Neither was born to a silver spoon, and both survived the thousand natural shocks of childhood and young adolescence to become healthy, vigorous, intelligent, diligent young adults. Norm's family was working class, father and then mother employed outside the home, native to Cincinnati, upstanding and self-sufficient. Kay's family was highly educated and professional and a bit peripatetic, and her father's employment as a minister and a college president conferred higher social status than monetary compensation: there would be few salons which she would enter at a disadvantage, whereas my father by birth was always an aspirant.

How They Met
Norm Auburn's Early Career

Norm Auburn entered the University of Cincinnati as a freshman in September 1923, the first in his family to attend college. He had graduated from Norwood High School, where he had been President of the Senior Class. In college he majored in economics with minors in political science and economic geography. He graduated in 1927 with a Bachelor of Arts. He had won the Law School Scholarship from the College of Liberal Arts, which would cover his first year (1927–1928) in the University of Cincinnati College of Law.

CO-CURRICULAR ACTIVITIES

He was a member of Lambda Chi Alpha, as were two of his Auburn cousins. He participated in intramural athletics, worked both backstage and onstage in dramatics with two different student organizations, was an officer in the Glee Club, a class officer and committeeman and member of Student Council, and in December 1927 he was sent to the annual convention of the National Student Federation in Lincoln, Nebraska, as the official UC delegate. He was elected to the legal honorary Phi Alpha Delta, the journalism honorary Pi Delta Epsilon, and the senior-class honorary Cincinnatus.

Throughout his UC career, Norm reported, wrote, and edited for the *University News* and the *Cincinnati Bearcat*, two semi-weekly newspapers sharing a common staff. In his senior year 1926–1927, he rose to the office of Associate Editor-in-Chief, and with his plan to remain on campus

Norm Auburn as a student at UC, about age twenty. *From the author's collection*

and start law school in the fall, he became Editor-in-Chief for 1927–1928. These were paid positions; I believe he was on his own financially from the time he turned eighteen. (During high school he delivered newspapers, bagged groceries, and assisted in the Norwood Branch of the Cincinnati Public Library.)

My mother said that she got to know my father in the *Bearcat* offices. Three years his junior chronologically, she was two years behind him in school, which she entered as a sophomore during his senior year. While they worked on plays together, they would not have shared many classes given the gap in their academic progression. But in the *Bearcat* offices, she could smoke, something she could not do in her Chi Omega fraternity house, her parental home on the grounds of Lane Theological Seminary, or (as a woman, the custom then being) while walking or standing outside. So, she took news assignments and hung around with the other reporters and editors to type and file her copy and smoke cigarettes.

My father must have known that he did not want or could not afford to continue law school, for by the close of academic 1927–1928 he had applied for and won the Strietman Fellowship to research for the Resource Survey of the Commercial Club of Cincinnati. It bore a $1,000 stipend. He had done some work much like it studying the Cincinnati rapid transit system in summer 1927. It could lead him toward an advanced degree in economics and political science. But the transition from law school to graduate study did not take place. My mother, writing to him from Ann Arbor where she was visiting Bill and Betty in July 1928, expressed dismay that he had resigned this fellowship and wouldn't be around for her senior year in 1928–1929.

FIRST JOB, ACTIVE ALUMNUS

Instead of completing law school or beginning political science graduate study, he launched a career based upon his co-curricular journalism experience and his economics major. He became Assistant Manager of the Cincinnati Chapter of the Associated General Contractors of America, which shortly before January 1929 merged with the Associated Building Industries to form the Allied Construction Industries. With that merger and six months experience, he was named Publicity Director, and his duties expanded beyond writing and publishing a trade journal, *The Cincinnati Constructor.*

In his new role, he managed local and national publicity. He made personal appearances before civic, fraternal, and political entities. He assisted in executing membership campaigns among contractors, builders, and supply dealers (principal source of income for the alliance). And he served as the confidential secretary to the groups, boards, and committees which the alliance facilitated. Such groups included, for instance, the Wage Board, which set the wage scales for the building trades and resolved jurisdictional disputes, and the Joint Conference Committee of Architects and Contractors, which lobbied for public and private works projects. He represented the alliance at state and national meetings, was elected secretary of the All-Ohio Safety Congress, testified at numerous municipal, county, and state hearings on legislation and policies, and designed (as the Great Depression deepened) a major "Build Now" campaign with the Cincinnati mayor and city manager. The writing and editing of an industrial journal was the base, but the nuanced public representation, image management, and confidential execution of trust provided the real challenges. On the strength of this well-paid growing career, he and my mother married (June 28, 1930), and two years later she bore their first child, my sister Ames (October 25, 1932).

As Norm was developing this career with the Allied Construction Industries, he continued his relationship with the University of Cincinnati. He had been invited to join the "Alumnal [*sic*] Committee of One Hundred" upon his graduation in June 1927, the youngest person yet elected. He served prominently on the "Seventh Annual Homecoming Committee" for June 1929 and became vice-president of the "Liberal Arts Alumnal Association." In September 1929, he was appointed first Editor of *Cincinnati Alumnus*, the initial publication of a newly established alumni magazine which by early 1935 had a circulation of 10,000.

In this unpaid volunteer role he got something else valuable to him professionally: the right and responsibility to attend meetings of the Executive Alumni Council. The University of Cincinnati was a loose confederation of professional colleges—medicine, law, pharmacy—with a liberal arts college and a dominating College of Engineering and Commerce. Herman Schneider, Dean of Engineering and Commerce from 1906 to 1928, brought from Lehigh University the concept of cooperative education, and UC had become a world-wide leader in what today is sometimes called "service learning," and what at UC meant that engineers and apprentice business people alternated semesters between classes and practical on-the-job experience, both paid and unpaid. (Schneider served as President of the University of Cincinnati from 1928–1932, then returned to his deanship.) Many of the people whom Norm lobbied during the day for Allied Construction Industries were the UC alumni engineers, architects, and accountants with whom he watched Bearcat basketball games or served on the Executive Alumni Council at night.

Just as his co-curricular activities led to the first job of his working career, so his avocational activities supported his vocation. Most everywhere I look in my father's life, I find this kind of symbiosis.

COURTSHIP AND MARRIAGE

Neither my father nor my mother told me much about their courtship more than "I could smoke in the *Bearcat* offices." Only four letters from their

Kathleen Montgomery as a student at UC. *From the author's collection*

prenuptial lives remain, all from my mother to Dad. I know that in July 1928, writing from Ann Arbor, Kay asked to have her regards passed on to Norm's parents: he must have taken her home on approval. I never asked him if he were already thinking of marrying. But his change of school plans look to me as if they were about burnishing his case for marriage.

In June 1928, finishing law school would have taken him two more years and establishing a career in law with a good salary at least a couple more. In June 1928, completing a master's program even with the Strietman Fellowship could have cost two years and left him with uncertain employment opportunities. By going to work for industry in public relations, in only a year or two he might have the resources to support a wife. He was a boy from a lower-middle-class family, both parents working, who could not make much of a case to a potential father-in-law for the hand of his youngest daughter without better prospects. If that were his motivation, he didn't hint anything of it to my mother before she wrote in July 1928, for she was perplexed by his throwing over the fellowship.

The next letter that Norm saved for seventy-three years was written in April 1930, by which time they were formally engaged. Kay wrote to him from the courthouse in Louisville, Kentucky, where her whole family had gone to testify in a probate court trial pitting my grandmother Fanny against her older sister Lillian over their father's estate. Kay called him "Dearest Normy," and "Sweetheart" and "dearest" and "darling" and struck a rhetorical posture of intellectual dependency—the legal instruction going on with her family and its lawyer was "getting too technical for me to get much from it." This posture conflicts with one of the earlier letter from Ann Arbor in 1928, where she is an independent operator, one who complains about gender exclusion rules that require her being accompanied to take a swim at the University of Michigan natatorium. I know one more detail about their courtship—this one not from a letter—which my mother always cited in a posture of self-effacement and pride in her family: my father fell in love with her only after he had seen her father's library.

Kay started her higher education at Western College for Women in Oxford, Ohio, in 1925, when she was seventeen. (Western began as an outpost of Mount Holyoke in 1853 and merged with Miami University, Dr. Montgomery's alma mater, in 1974.) Following her father's resignation from Centre College in March 1926, his five months of unemployment, and then his appointment as President of Lane Theological Seminary, she enrolled at the University of Cincinnati in fall 1926 and took her baccalaureate degree in sociology in 1929. She earned the Cincinnati-Wesleyan Fellowship to support her study toward the Master of Arts, which was granted in June 1931. For her master's degree she switched from sociology to English literature, and she wrote her thesis on the Restoration poet-dramatist-statesman-rake Sir Charles Sedley, author of *The Mulberry Garden* and subject of entries in Pepys's diaries recording his public lascivious obscene drunken behavior. (I suspect that the clergyman's daughter chose this subject at the suggestion of a professor who had seen the just-published 1928 edition of Sedley's works edited by the British poet-scholar Vivian de Sola Pinto.)

Through Chi Omega at UC she made two friends who remained faithful all her life: Peggy Armstrong Schaefer and Blanche Rule Huss. The three contemporaries married about the same time and bore their first and second children within months of each other. Peggy and Kay would follow husbands away from Cincinnati, but Blanche lived there into the 1980s until Wes Huss's death: it was to her home our family came when we buried my mother next to her parents in the Lane Seminary plot at Spring Grove Cemetery in 1974.

A MARRIAGE MADE AT UC

A great public university, operated then as a municipal trust, brought together two young people of different classes and backgrounds. Norm's folks were working-class, ethnic Germans. Neither his father nor his mother had gone to high school. Kay's folks had Scots-Irish and Irish and probably Huguenot roots but were fully assimilated, and she was the third generation to attend college and the second generation to continue into post-graduate education. Norm's elder brother could not consider college: stateside US Army service during the Great War and an early marriage made it necessary for him to launch his career as an editor, writer, and publicist for industry on his own. Norm's father wore a suit and tie to work every day, but he was a draftsman taking orders from the architects who worked for the owners. Kay's older siblings were in or through college when she met Norm. Her father had been principal pastor of churches since 1894 and president of colleges since 1917 and in 1926 had begun his third career, this time as a seminary president. That position allowed Dr. Montgomery to rub shoulders with all but the innermost power brokers of Cincinnati: he led prayer at UC's 1928 Commencement ceremonies. I never saw that library which my mother thought made Norm decide to love her, but I have saved a few of the books from it—the half-calf-bound set of Dr. Johnson, some early nineteenth-century biographies—which suggest the atmosphere of serious inquiry and luxurious resources it might betoken to a young man whose parents' apartment home had few. Norm Auburn was marrying up.

When they married in June 1930, times were still somewhat optimistic, despite the stock market crash of October 29, 1929. My father had a good job. My mother was studying with the help of a fellowship. He was twenty-five, she twenty-two. The Montgomerys were living in the fieldstone presidential manse of the Lane Seminary buildings, but they knew they would be moving on to the home campus of McCormick Theological Seminary in the Lincoln Park neighborhood of Chicago within twelve to eighteen months where Dr. Montgomery would teach, write, and perhaps assume the presidency of his *alma mater* when the incumbent retired. The young married couple lived in Clifton, near the university, up the hill from downtown, and the university focused their social lives. When they were not watching football and basketball games or attending lectures or performing in community theatre, they took meals at his or her parents' homes or visited the apartments of former UC classmates. But the Great Depression deepened, and in February 1933, my mother wrote news to her folks in Chicago which alarmed them.

NORM CHANGES CAREER PATHS

In his first six months with Allied Construction Industries, Norm had more than doubled his starting salary so that, in September 1929, he was earning $325 a month. That was more than three times the amount he had lived on during his five years at UC. On the strength of that salary he married. He continued to enjoy the sum for two years more after Black Tuesday, but in November 1931, his salary was reduced to $225, in July 1932 to $175, in December 1932 to $125, and in February he learned of imminent layoff. I imagine that Norm was angry at Kay's having told her parents that he might lose his job; he was always diligent in shaping the narrative of his life to emphasize the positive. But he kept for some seventy years Dr. Montgomery's sweet February 25, 1933, "Dear Son" letter of condolence, good cheer, and veiled offer of financial support calculated so as not to insult the young father of his first grandchild and namesake.

As it happened, on the same day he received his father-in-law's loving letter, Norm wrote to Mr. Raymond Walters, the relatively new president of UC. He had managed to visit President Walters in his office some days before, and now he sent a five-page typed single-space invited follow-up to that conversation, a letter containing his résumé with a proposal that UC create a new position for an Executive Secretary of an "alumnal association" for the

1. *Maintanance [sic] of the cultural and social prestige of the institution and an active furtherance of its interests in the life of the city and the country.*
2. *Support of bond issues.*
3. *Development of extension work in education.*
4. *Enlistment of financial benefactions.*

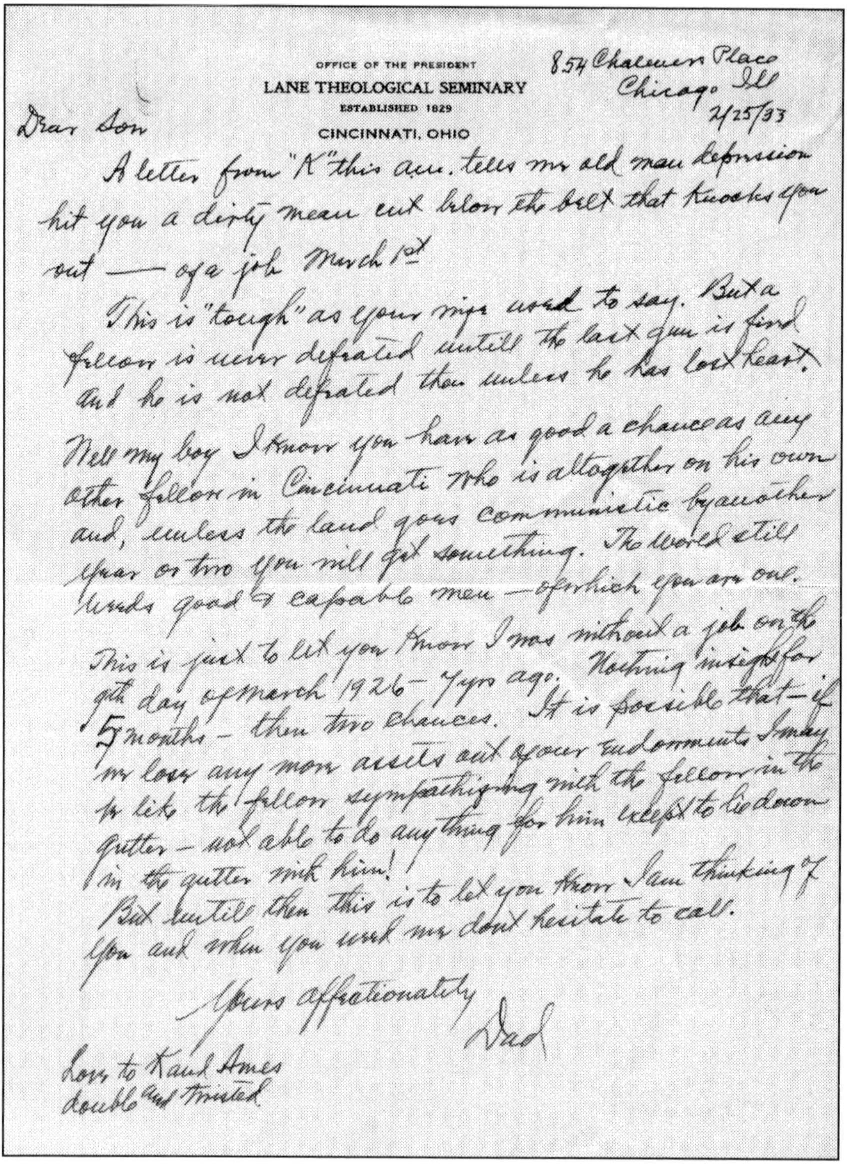

OFFICE OF THE PRESIDENT
LANE THEOLOGICAL SEMINARY
ESTABLISHED 1829
CINCINNATI, OHIO

854 Chalmers Place
Chicago Ill
2/25/33

Dear Son

A letter from "K" this a.m. tells me old man depression hit you a dirty mean cut below the belt that knocks you out — of a job March 1st.

This is "tough" as your nips used to say. But a fellow is never defeated until the last gun is fired And he is not defeated then unless he has lost heart.

Well my boy I know you have as good a chance as any other fellow in Cincinnati who is altogether on his own and, unless the land goes communistic by another year or two you will get something. The world still needs good & capable men — of which you are one.

This is just to let you know I was without a job on the 9th day of March 1926 – 7 yrs ago. Nothing in sight for 5 months – then two chances. It is possible that – if we lose any more assets out of our endowments I may be like the fellow sympathizing with the fellow in the gutter – not able to do anything for him except to lie down in the gutter with him!

But until then this is to let you know I am thinking of you and when you need me don't hesitate to call.

Yours Affectionately
Dad

Love to K and Ames
double and twisted

Message of encouragement and love from Dr. R. Ames Montgomery to his son-in-law Norm, February 25, 1933. *From the author's collection*

5. *Encouragement of the matriculation of high caliber students.*
6. *Support of athletic events and undergraduate productions.*

To accomplish such ends UC needs to build an "Alumni Association" to enlist its graduates' aid through

1. *Publication of a monthly alumni magazine to serve as a direct medium of contact.*
2. *Maintenance of complete and accurate records of graduates.*
3. *Apprisement [sic] of alumni of the manifold extra-curricular activities of the University which offer stimulating cultural and intellectual opportunities.*
4. *Establishment of a placement bureau for graduates.*
5. *Organization of alumni clubs in principal cities.*
6. *Continuance of social contacts through group meetings, homecoming celebrations, etc.*
7. *Organization of an undergraduate vocational guidance bureau comprised of prominent alumni.*

He proposes funding these activities through "a dues-payment plan." He does not remind President Walters that UC is already getting that monthly alumni magazine edited for free. He defines the posture of the founding Executive Secretary as neither "a high-pressure promoter nor a superficial salesman but the directing force of a unified, long-range program. It demands a personality with staying power, consummate tact[,] and diplomacy."

RAYMOND WALTERS: START OF A PARTNERSHIP

Raymond W. Walters, AM, was forty-seven (born August 24, 1885) when twenty-seven-year-old, soon-to-be-laid-off Norm Auburn got into his office. It was the third time they had met there. Walters had assumed the UC presidency earlier that academic year from Herman Schneider, architect of the Cincinnati Plan of cooperative education. Those two shared a Lehigh University connection, though they were never there together: Walters was an English professor, registrar, and assistant to the president of Lehigh before becoming professor and Dean of Swarthmore College seventy miles to the south. He had been a stateside artillery instructor during the Great War, he published a book-length history of the city of Bethlehem, Lehigh University's home, just as he left for Swarthmore, and he is remembered today in part for his astute, learned collection of Stephen Foster memorabilia.

Norm Auburn had interviewed the new President Raymond Walters for a feature story in an autumn 1932 *Cincinnati Alumnus* soon after he arrived. Walters would preside at UC longer than anyone in its history, twenty-three years from 1932 to 1955, through the Great Depression, through World War II, through the crush and demand of the GI Bill, and well into the growth of UC's research mission. He aspired to make UC a "national institution" as well as a municipal university, and by compiling and sharing annual collegiate enrollment surveys he became well known among practitioners of higher educational administration, doing useful statistical aggregation that national associations and the federal government would take over in less than a generation.

But that distinguished career was still in the future when Norm visited President Walters in his office for a second time later in fall 1932, when his Allied Construction Industries salary was down to $125 a month. Dad told him that he would like to work for UC, and Walters said (my father recorded in a discarded autobiographical fragment), "Mr. Auburn, there are only two avenues for work at the University—teaching or business affairs. You don't have any advanced degrees, so teaching is out. You don't have any accounting or business experience, so that is out." Norm was not discouraged from yet another attempt in late February 1933, still looking for work at UC and watching his Allied Construction Industries job die, but this time he came with talking points that quickly turned into the detailed proposal quoted above. My father's 1933 pitch led to more than two decades of close ties between these leaders. Raymond Walters gave Norm Auburn the job of Executive Secretary of the Alumni Association, and he would add to Dad's duties and salary or promote him at least six times in their eighteen years as mentor and disciple.

My father always had a contingency plan for every life event. When he contemplated not being able to continue law school, he sought and won the Strietman Fellowship, essentially a service-learning research project, which he resigned to accept far better prospects with Allied Construction Industries. When President Walters offered him the position of Executive Secretary in April 1933, Dad was holding an offer to edit *Fire Protection*, a monthly magazine published by the National Underwriter Company of Cincinnati. He accepted the UC position at $150 a month, scarcely more than his four-time reduced salary with his disappearing ACI job, and he continued his volunteer editing of *Cincinnati Alumnus*. Within a year he had been elected to UC's chapter of Omicron Delta Kappa leadership honorary, by which he had been passed over as an undergraduate. His election as a nonstudent proves an influence on campus beyond the alumni association, a stature which student leaders want to embrace. By June 1934, he had obtained a salary increase to $2,000 a year, plus bonus ($250 to $500). He could raise his toddler daughter and support his wife on about $200 a month.

LEVERAGING AN OUTSIDE OFFER

I know my father was a lifelong Republican. As a student Dad had been a member of the Executive Committee of UC's "Hoover-For-President" club, and he remained friends with fellow Republicans. In 1932, local attorney Robert A. Taft suffered the only ballot-box defeat of his long career, for reelection to the Ohio Senate. His law partner John B. Hollister was representing the First Congressional District of Ohio, one of two in Cincinnati. Another fellow Republican William E. Hess represented the Second Congressional District. Then in 1933, the adjacent Eighth Congressional District elected Thomas B. Fletcher, a former Democratic State Representative.

A firm party loyalist, personally less conservative than those he supported, Taft was crafting a run for US Senate, at which he would be successful in 1938. And after the fall 1933 election, he was looking for energy and drive to shore up the local party, and he began discussions with the UC alumni secretary to serve as founding Executive Secretary of the Republican Committee of Hamilton County. Dad had been on the job for about a year. The flirtation went by fits and starts and left letters and carbons indicative of reluctance to be seduced. By August 1934, Dad had turned the conversation into a firm offer of $3,750 annually. While he never had a bad word to say about the Senator (not even of his grandson Governor Bob Taft), the way he handled the offer cannot have endeared him to party loyalists.

My father promptly showed the offer to President Walters.

Walters couldn't match it, but he appointed Norm to an additional position, Secretary of the UC Department of Physical and Health Education, today's equivalent of associate director of athletics, for an additional $1,000 a year. Among his duties was announcing home football games, and Walters sent him one of two handwritten notes that Dad saved all his life praising his sports announcing. Together with his alumni secretary position, Dad had a guaranteed annual salary of $3,000 plus bonus, not as much as Taft had offered but without having to leave the university to which he had first come eleven years before. By June 1935, Norm had raised his total salary to $3,850, exceeding the future senator's offer. He would coordinate these three positions (alumni secretary, athletics secretary, *Cincinnati Alumnus* editor) until March 1936.

INSTEAD OF TENURE AND PROMOTION

In the seven years from leaving the university in June 1928 through matching the outside offer in June 1935, Norm's professional accomplishments resemble what would be expected of starting faculty or law or accounting associates. Apprentices prove by the increasing scope and complexity of their work that they are worthy of being made journeymen, worthy of tenure and promotion or of partnership in the firm. Norm thought of these seven years as being spent in two different arenas, private business and the public academy, and his official biographies emphasize the difference of the arenas rather than the consonance of the tasks.

Working to publicize a trade association exercises the same talents as organizing and growing an alumni association or assisting an intercollegiate athletic program to interface with the public. The constituents were a generation older and possessed of more power than the suppliant, so the youngster seeking their aid accommodated, maybe truckled, but persisted, seeking to enlist support, be it membership in Allied Construction Industries or in the Cincinnati Alumni Association or paid advertisements in his publications. The youngster serving as secretary for their private meetings heard and kept secrets and observed the powerful in guarded and unguarded moments. He would learn quickly that keeping confidence was the most important aspect of his job. He would also learn that by ordering and inscribing the written records of their business he could shape it.

The apprentice representing either Allied Construction Industries or the University of Cincinnati before subcommittees of city council or statewide conventions of business or political associations learned to come knowledgeable about the subject at hand, possessed of responses to anticipated or unanticipated queries and objections, and prepared both to tell

UC Board Chair Frank Dinsmore and his wife Mary, 1934. *From the author's collection*

the truth and not to tell everything he knew. He learned to plan his costume, how he would look. He wanted to appear at least as formally clad as the most formal person in the room. But he did not wish to appear more expensively clothed, or more flashy than, the attendees. A few years later, a reporter described him as always "immaculately dressed" with his reddish-tinged sandy hair shown to advantage by tan or brown suits.

The publicizing, selling, lobbying, and confidential advising common during these first seven post graduate years overlay the daily administrative and managerial duties of publishing and writing large parts of two monthly publications, from June 1928 through February 1933 *The Cincinnati Constructor* and from its inception in September 1929 through all of 1936 *The Cincinnati Alumnus*. A 1932 article called "A Twentieth Century Siege of Troy" (mostly my mother's, I think) won a national trophy from the American Alumni Council. Articles signed by Raymond Walters and Mrs. Frank Dinsmore (wife of the Chairman of the UC Board of Directors) were largely written by Norm and Kay. The permanence of print perpetuates both excellence and error, as any lawyer filing a brief or accountant submitting an opinion or university scientist publishing a paper learns quickly.

In these precomputer days, the publishing steps from notes to longhand to typed copy to composed proofs to laid-out pages to published magazine involved others whose opinions should be weighed, whose work costs must be estimated and met, and whose time constraints affected the ability to correct or to improve their own work. Editors exercise tact and diplomacy and retain good reporters and writers by those skills more than by overt command and control. Everyone who would lead an organization must learn the human consequences of decisions large and small. And the position of editor, like that of department chair or managing partner, teaches much about the behavior of people, the keys to their character, the things by which they are motivated, the conditions in which they can excel, the true consequences of earning their loyalty or their enmity.

LESSONS OF THE GREAT DEPRESSION

And in the first seven years of post-collegiate adulthood with marriage and fatherhood magnifying the responsibilities of breadwinner, what were the costs to my father's character and personality of the economic cataclysm that forced the change of employers and laid the groundwork for a life in higher education? As a child of Great Depression parents, I saw only a few habits of frugality. My mother kept a generous table but expected me to eat what I took—"Children are starving in China, Markie"—yet there were no parental struggles of will over the last green peas. Dad and Mom had shoes resoled and repaired, but then didn't everyone throughout the mid-twentieth century when the primary materials permitted repair and skilled artisanal service was still inexpensive? Dad repurposed the clothes he wore to work into play clothes, so that yesterday's suit trousers became today's lawn-mowing pants. As soon as they were able they employed household help at competitive rates, and the servants once hired tended to stay until a life change came along. Dad always kept tight personal control over the family finances, but I rarely observed Mom stinting because she'd exceeded her household allowance.

Some people were mildly surprised at Dad's insistence at getting a check into the bank as soon as possible to earn interest. When he was acting president of Salem College and a million-dollar check arrived from Pittsburgh's Benedum Foundation on a Friday morning, he watched its progress through administrative offices until late in the afternoon he finally inquired as to why no one had deposited it. The answer was that the college had no interest-bearing accounts with their local bank, so what did it matter? The knowledge permitted him to correct a serious old-boy-network exploitation.

There was always a minor theme of financial foreboding in my father greater than my own, child that I was of his financially comfortable years, affected as I was by the "genteel poverty" of my mother's family, which always could afford a cook though it never owned a home until very late. But that foreboding didn't cripple him emotionally, didn't lead to an excess of caution, and didn't destroy a breadth of spirit and imagination for others' circumstances and a willingness to help others, so that I was taught active charity from my earliest days by example. It could be traumatizing, almost losing a job when he was a driven twenty-seven-year-old with two dependents, but preparations for disaster didn't characterize my father's future planning thereafter.

A NEW CAREER TRAJECTORY AT UC

Raymond Walters at first opposed the new direction which Norm Auburn took in March 1936: to become Assistant Director of Evening and Extension Courses and Assistant Professor. Walters wanted him to stay as Alumni Secretary. Dad had flanked him. Before broaching the subject with the president, Dad had gotten Herman Schneider's recommendation for this move from public relations to academic affairs. Schneider and his deputy had mentioned a salary of $4,250 for this job. When Walters took a recommendation to the Board of Directors, the same salary which had been guaranteed by the alumni-secretary/athletics secretary combination of $3,850 was written in. In a few months, Walters advanced the salary, but he had in effect warned the young man to be cautious about manipulating a sitting CEO.

What a brilliant move! But what a risky move. Just thirty years old, possessed of no advanced degree, no credential to serve in teaching or business at UC, without any experience in the classroom, Norm Auburn achieved academic rank and administrative responsibility two steps below that of a dean. He reported to Director V. H. Drufner, who reported to Herman Schneider, the Engineering and Commerce Dean and former

UC President beloved by the UC governors. Schneider had initiated evening courses. Twelve years later, now representing other university divisions such as liberal arts, the academic offerings and their support services were still reporting to the University's biggest academic unit.

Dad agreed to continue editing *Cincinnati Alumnus* for the rest of the year, and President Walters sent him a second, more personal "sincere note of appreciation and thanks" for his "excellent" and "splendid contribution" as alumni secretary and his cordial wish for "all success... in your new field" accompanying his formal letter of appointment. Norm replied with a note of "deep appreciation" for President Walters's "unfailing kindliness" and made an "assurance of continued loyalty and devotion to the University."

The academic rank qualified Norm to serve as faculty advisor to evening student clubs, newspapers, government, yearbook, and to serve the evening faculty as secretary. I never heard of his actually teaching courses. His skill in publicity transferred to speaking to high schools, "downtown" executives (to sell workplace credit and noncredit programs), and recruiting or business development travel out of town (Hamilton, Middletown). He coordinated radio advertising and lectures. He staffed the office from six to ten p.m. weeknights. He assembled materials for the catalogue, gathered syllabi for office files, recruited part-time faculty from within and from outside the university, operated the placement office (proposed for alumni support a few years earlier), and arranged dinners and ceremonies for faculty and students. In two years he was promoted to Associate Professor, and he'd become a second-time father with the birth of my brother Richard (February 6, 1937).

Freed of the day-to-day responsibilities of editing an alumni magazine and of the travel required to establish alumni clubs in more than a dozen other cities, Dad turned the skills which had greatly increased paid alumni association memberships to expanding the Evening College. In 1937 he started an evening lecture-discussion series featuring faculty. In 1938 he launched "The World at Your Door" series of illustrated lectures bringing luminaries such as H. G. Wells, Sinclair Lewis, Eve Curie, Clare Booth Luce, Thomas Mann, and Edna St. Vincent Millay to campus. In two more years, the Evening College had become a freestanding unit and the position of director had grown into a deanship.

A DEATH, A DEANSHIP

Then, Dean V. H. Drufner died of a heart attack at age forty-nine (July 1940).

While just thirty-five years old, Norman Auburn became acting Dean and Professor at the second-largest municipal university in the country, serving a city with 450,000 people. Walters forced a national search, but in May 1941, Norm became permanent. He would henceforth be known in and around Clifton Avenue and downtown in the Queen City as "Dean Auburn." (Visitors to Akron in the 1950s and 1960s with Cincinnati ties would use that honorific instead of "President Auburn" or his own preferred "Dr. Auburn.")

The UC Evening College was the fifth largest in the nation after those of the City College of New York, New York University's at Union Square, Northwestern University's in the Loop, and Western Reserve University's University Circle campus. Everyone in 1940 knew that the Selective Training and Service Act covered men just up to age thirty-five, so when a headline writer archly commented that this "live wire" was "Probably Only Dean in Nation to Own Draft Registration Card" readers learned the upper limit of his age. William Lyons Phelps, Yale literature professor and Methodist minister, syndicated columnist, radio personality and "incandescent speaker" whom Norm had featured in the "World at Your Door" series sent him a handsome note of congratulations signed "Billy." And in a newspaper profile soon after my dad cited handball, tennis, and sailing as his past-times—and the only place he had ever sailed was at Lake Wawasee at his in-laws' summer cabin.

I never learned clearly why Dad, who was thirty-six when America declared war in December 1941 at a time when draft registration and service was extended to all men through age forty-five, didn't don a uniform. He had two children, nine and four. He had problematic vision in one eye from a childhood injury, but he was otherwise fit. His brother-in-law Bill Clark, two years his junior, had tried repeatedly via three service branches to overcome medical objections to his enlistment, and the desire to serve motivated the Clarks and the Montgomerys to leave Chicago on the mission which created the Manor Foundation for the education of handicapped boys. Perhaps Norm's stateside wartime activities may have counted as national service, for he was Director of Education for the Cincinnati-area Civilian Defense Corps and supervised the training of hundreds of instructors. Dad (or was it Mom?) told me that he thought some of his wartime advancement at UC was due to others' service abroad.

THIRD PROMOTION: SECOND IN COMMAND

In June 1943, longtime Executive Vice President Daniel Laurence was approaching mandatory retirement at age seventy. President Walters divided his job responsibilities rather than replace the only vice president on his slate. Ralph W. Miller, a former Engineering and Commerce faculty member, served as Comptroller. Effective September 1943, Norm became "Dean of Administration," which the press (but not Walters) declared to be "second in command," and thus my father's third major promotion and third area of emphasis at UC went into effect. At thirty-eight, fifteen years after graduation, he was the same age as the fast-track associate professor reaching full professor or the hard-driving junior partner of a law or accounting firm being made an equity stakeholder. He did this without benefit of an academic or professional credential—no MA or PhD, no JD, no CPA.

A measure of the trust Norm had earned was a second concurrent appointment as Secretary of the Board of Directors, reporting not just to President Walters but also to the Board. Frank Dinsmore was still chair. The chair of the Board Committee on Alumni Affairs was Director Jane DeSerisy Earley, Liberal Arts 1929, wife of a prominent Cincinnati physician, and former fellow member of the Executive Committee of the student "Hoover-For-President" Club with him. And there was a third role, as well, in which Walters entrusted his fondest hopes for UC's achievement of national status to young Norman: Executive Secretary of the University of Cincinnati Research Foundation. My father would hold paying jobs in banking, foundations, associations, and government over the next sixty years of his ninety-eight-year life, but he never thereafter left higher education.

Leaving Cincinnati

In 1950–1951, municipal universities in Akron, Toledo, and Louisville were all looking for new presidents. The municipal University of Cincinnati was enjoying the eighteenth year of leadership from President Raymond Walters. But he would be forced to retire at age seventy in another four years. Norm wanted at least one of these presidencies.

In 1951, my father might have changed careers again. The array of skills that he had honed as a leader of university administrators and faculty and the range of contacts among political, industrial, and financial executives positioned him for very different extramural advancement. In spring 1951, he was offered the senior vice presidency of Cincinnati's largest bank. Two earlier events, however, make me believe that Norm was positioning himself to become a college president—receipt of an honorary degree, and three months' service as acting president of his *alma mater*.

AN HONORARY DEGREE

On August 15, 1945, Parsons College in Fairfield, Iowa, awarded Norm the LLD, the Doctor of Laws, *honoris causa*. He gave the commencement address. He was just forty. He had been elevated from Dean of Administration to Vice President at the University of Cincinnati on April 7, 1945, four months earlier. After receiving this honorary doctorate, he always called himself "Dr. Auburn." That title sought to compensate for the shortcoming Raymond Walters had pointed out in their first professional development conversation in fall 1932, Dad's lack of an academic credential. How did a small Presbyterian college in Iowa choose to honor my father, a university administrator with no earned advanced degrees and no obvious connections to Parsons, to Fairfield, even to Iowa?

From 1917 to 1922, the Reverend Doctor Richmond Ames Montgomery was President of Parsons College. He had become a familiar figure in nearby Ottumwa as pastor of the First Presbyterian Church from 1909 to 1913. After service to a large church downriver in St. Louis, he returned to Iowa to preside over the college in 1917. Still revered by the children of his original parishioners, he would be called back to Ottumwa's First Presbyterian at Christmas time 1945 for a three-month interim pastorate.

Big Daddy was present on August 15, and he must have delighted in the honor to his son-in-law. He had another spiritual child at that commencement, for also receiving an honorary degree was T. Henry Foster, Parsons College '97, the retiring president of John Morrell and Company, the great international meat-packing firm headquartered in Ottumwa. Foster's father was Thomas Dove Foster (1847–1915), the first president of John Morrell and Company after its eponymous founder (of whom he was a cousin), and a lay pillar of the First Presbyterian Church of Ottumwa. Big Daddy published a biography of Thomas D. Foster in 1930.

One doesn't apply for an honorary degree. One doesn't matriculate and take courses. One is nominated by a third party who has contacts and authority with a granting institution. Undoubtedly, Big Daddy proposed Norm to Parsons.

Newspaper reports welcomed back Kay Montgomery Auburn with her father and her husband and her children Ames and Dick and noted that they visited their cousin, fellow townsman John Montgomery, while staying at the Hotel Turner in Ottumwa. Kay hadn't been back for twenty-three years. Norm had never been there. (He used his time in Iowa also to visit his counterparts at Iowa State and the University of Iowa, rather than "chew the fat" with Kay's relatives and Big Daddy's friends.) Important as Norm was as the sole vice president of a great municipal university with the fifth largest evening college in the nation and a collection of distinguished professional schools, folks in and around Parsons College knew him mostly as Dr. Montgomery's son-in-law.

ACTING PRESIDENT OF THE UNIVERSITY OF CINCINNATI

My father's commitment to a career in higher education must have been further cemented by his service as Acting President of the University of Cincinnati from January to April 1949. Raymond Walters was asked by the US Army to advise postwar Japan on restructuring its system of higher education, and President Walters and his board felt confident in Norm's handling any problems during his absence, even in this period of struggling to accommodate returning GIs. Over the years, Dad would remind me that *vice* is a preposition stemming from the Latin meaning "in place of." A "Vice" President is someone who should be able to serve in place of the President. And someone who serves in the place of a president can get used to wielding sole executive authority. (Could that be why my father arranged later in life, when he served two year-long sabbatical appointments while continuing to preside at The University of Akron, to retain the title and the powers of his presidency?)

NORM'S RELATIONSHIP WITH RAYMOND WALTERS

When my father drafted some abandoned autobiographical notes, he shared this backstory of how he reached the position "Dean of Administration." In 1942, Norm had been Dean of the Evening College for a couple of years and was serving in visible national positions as President of the Association of Evening Colleges and of the American Platform Guild. With the long-time UC Vice President and Business Manager Daniel Laurence nearing mandatory retirement age of seventy in 1943, Raymond Walters asked Norm to conduct a study for him and the Board of Directors on reconstituting the vice president's position. Walters didn't want to know how smaller or less famous universities organized their administration; he selected a group of aspirational peers in which he thought the University of Cincinnati belonged.

Walters arranged appointments for Norm with the presidents and their top associates at the University of Chicago and Northwestern University; Harvard and Boston Universities; Yale University; Columbia and New York Universities. Dad found several weeks to make these visits while still running the Evening College. As he prepared to draft his report, the chairman of the Board of Directors subcommittee took him aside to confide that one purpose of the study was "to tailor-make a new administrative position to shore up areas in which President Walters had little interest or expertise." Consequently, Dad wrote, he found himself overloading in a single position responsibilities for financial and business administration with fund raising, community relations, intercollegiate athletics, and all academic budgeting, including representing the president to the deans and directors and Faculty Senate—a blend my father had not found combined by a single vice presidential position anywhere in the dozens of interviews he had conducted. It was a kind of executive vice presidency with chief operating officer scope and key external affairs concerns grafted on.

In this instance, my father records being trusted like an independent consultant. A director shares confidential information designed to influence the results of a study: "help us shore up a beloved leader's weaknesses in your conclusions." Norm was a subordinate of this leader, not a third-party neutral. It broke the proper chain of command, but the trust was not misplaced, because this young dean—thirty-seven at the time—used the information to strengthen rather than to undermine the leadership of Raymond Walters. And when he was permitted to fill this proposed position, he used the experiences to qualify himself for a college presidency.

Eight years later, in 1951, when Directors of the municipal University of Akron came to town to recruit him, my father justified to himself leaving his home and his *alma mater* as an act of loyalty to President Walters. By accepting Akron's offer, he was preserving Walters's chance to work until mandatory retirement age. He spurned, he confessed, a proposal by one UC director for him to accept the presidency while Walters was made chancellor. "I could not be part of the movement which would put my friend Ray Walters on the shelf five years before his scheduled retirement," he wrote in that abandoned autobiographical fragment.

HOW RAYMOND WALTERS SHAPED NORM'S CAREER

Raymond Walters certainly was a friend and mentor to Norm. He was twenty years older; he had worked and studied at many colleges and universities; he had served in the military during the Great War; he had earned an advanced degree, written a scholarly book, and earned tenure

Raymond Walters, UC President, 1932–1955. *From the Norman Auburn Papers. Courtesy of Archival Services, University Libraries, The University of Akron*

as a teaching professor. He hadn't done public relations work, but he had done the kind of confidential executive assisting at which Norm excelled and many other jobs to help an organization prosper. And he had a vision for UC which he pursued tenaciously. My father was lucky to be able to work for him and to be brought closer and closer into his confidence.

But Norm never forgot what he took to be the slights of their relationship. The warning about being under-credentialed for university service; the delay in fully matching Taft's financial offer to lead the Hamilton County Republican Party; the initial opposition to Dad's moving from alumni affairs to academic and administrative leadership in the Evening College; the year-long search for Dean Drufner's successor culminating in Norm's appointment to the position he'd been fulfilling and advancing all that time (proof that the search was a waste of time); and the granting of the responsibilities for the Dean of Administration role but the delaying of the title of vice president for two years: Dad resented these.

But these same decisions could be cast as a wise leader's judicious nudges to the growing career of a "live-wire" administrator with a non-traditional entrée into the academic world. Under credentialed? Norm saw instance after instance during his fifty-five-year higher education career in which the lack of an advanced degree or earned tenure as a professor hindered his advancement. Meeting an outside offer? If an employee seeks to advance his career by showing a telegram, he should not chafe when the answer isn't the complete acquiescence that he desires. A power play works both ways. How generous was Raymond Walters not to put Norm on the street when he found himself flanked with a recommendation from his unassailable senior dean to move an accomplished PR man from alumni to academic affairs, a recommendation which the canny brash thirty-year-old clearly orchestrated. Walters greatly admired Norm's energy, talents, and loyalty, but he had reason to fear that faculty would not see them as virtues, that faculty might need time to get used to the outsider.

At every step in his relationship with Raymond Walters at UC, my father was as likely to attract a veto group for himself as to gain respect for his ability to attract the support of the "town" for the work of the "gown." I don't think my father ever thought of this interpretation. I don't think he thought until too late that his strong identification with the Republican Party might have hurt him with faculty, and that Walters had done him a favor in keeping quiet that offer from Taft. But I do think he admired and even revered Raymond Walters.

He recognized how Walters's trust during the six years that he was UC's only vice president gave him learning opportunities which burnished his case for promotion to a presidency. During the post-war physical expansion to accommodate returning GIs, Walters made Norm chair of the campus construction committee. Dad coordinated the building campaign from assembling the financing through certifying the punch list. Walters sent Norm downtown to raise both public and private monies. Walters let Norm design the first annual fund campaign for UC, years before such appeals became a standard marketing strategy at public universities. Walters assigned Norm to creating UC's research foundation. Walters made Norm "clerk" of the Board of Directors, its Secretary, the official point of contact between the publicly appointed governors and all the rest of the university, except for the CEO. The route to a university presidency from the time of Walters's appointment in 1932 well through the late 1980s lay through the academic side, with deans of faculties and vice presidents for academic affairs being the majority of persons promoted. Even while directors sought such traditional leaders, they highly valued the kinds of experiences Norm gained, which few deans or provosts have encountered before becoming presidents.

THE FAMILY SUPPORT SYSTEM FOR A PRESIDENT

Directors seek a certain maturity and stability in the lives of presidential candidates, and that includes in their personal circumstances. By the spring of 1951, Norm and Kay had the maturity and self-knowledge to adapt to life-changing events, personally and as a family. They had become the senior generation. Only one of their own parents remained, eighty-three-year-old Joe. Mary Frances Allhands Montgomery had died of congestive heart failure at the Lake Wawasee cottage in 1940, before the war. Hulda died after a lingering two-month illness in late January 1949. R. Ames Montgomery had suffered nearly two years, bed-ridden, stroke-paralyzed, before dying in summer 1950.

Norm turned forty-six in May 1951 just as Kay turned forty-three, and their family was complete. My mother had had eight pregnancies. After Dick was born in 1937, she had miscarried four times before the full-term pregnancy of which I was delivered in late 1945. Eighteen months later, near her thirty-ninth birthday, my little brother David was born. Although it would be many months until a diagnosis of cerebral palsy would be attached and several years until its consequences and limitations were fully understood, she had quickly detected cause for concern. By the time Norm was appointed Acting President of the University of Cincinnati for those three months in 1949, the two young parents were beginning to understand that their responsibilities to one of their children would always include his custody, that he would never be able to live independently.

My father liked to cite Emerson's aphorism that "a great part of courage is the courage of having done the thing before." In this case, Kay had always lived in a family with a handicapped child. Her eldest sister Mary, whose epilepsy then had no effective medical intervention, grew increasingly incapacitated by her condition and never lived independently. As a new widower at seventy, Big Daddy needed to plan his life around hers. Norm had not experienced permanent disability in his own family, and Davey's condition was harder for him to accept. (To his very last months, some fifty-two years after this cusp in his career, my father held Davey near to his thoughts and part of his plans.)

Four babies and eight pregnancies in twenty years of married life define anybody's full-time job, especially if you're married to a man who works outside the home seventy to ninety hours, week in, week out. My mother ran her household with hired help from very early. There was a "cleaning lady" even in the mid-1930s, once a week or so, and she believed she understood how to supervise and what to pay such servants. By the time I was born, there was also a "girl of all work," a young, sketchily educated, live-in, good-hearted mother's-helper who combined child-rearing duties with light housework. I remember crying when we left Cincinnati to learn that eighteen-year-old Mary Harris wouldn't be coming with us to Akron. Mom did most of the family cooking in those days, arising with Norm, seeing that a hot lunch was on the table for him many days of the week, and always having a family meal ready for what was another break, but not an end, to his work days. She accompanied him to many evening University events—lectures, plays, concerts, sports contests—and she entertained out-of-town guests, especially distinguished lecturers, in the home overnight for some of these events.

But she also had time to serve extensively outside the home, though never (to my knowledge) as a paid employee. She was active in Chi Omega alumnae affairs. She served on the Women's League of Immanuel Presbyterian Church and in the Girl Scouts. Her book reviews sparked many literary parties in her lady-friends' homes. She was an officer with the Queen City League of Women Voters and a participant with the local United World Federalists, an organization of which her rock-ribbed Republican husband didn't approve. After Davey's diagnosis, she participated locally in United Cerebral Palsy, forming a Cincinnati chapter. She was president of the statewide organization, and by 1951 she was Secretary of the national United Cerebral Palsy.

Before her marriage, Kay had never lived in anything but a pastor's manse or a president's home. By nurture, she understood how a servant-leader met and cultivated the constituents. In the only significant cache

Ames and Dick stand behind our mother, holding Davey, and our father, holding me, 1947. *From the author's collection*

of letters to remain from their forty-four-year marriage, she advises her husband. She is visiting her parents in Chicago with my toddler big sister Ames in January 1935. She tells Norm where he ought to take dinner while she's gone for a month, not with his nutritional needs but his political advantage at issue. She advises him to call on Mrs. Frank Dinsmore, wife of the chairman of the UC Board of Directors (presumably, her responsibility while in town). She focuses him on the latest issue of the *Cincinnati Alumnus* and reminds him of its importance to his expanding portfolio. She seems to know better than he where the next rungs on his ladder of advancement are fixed. When he makes his second trip to Akron in spring 1951 to meet with the directors, she is at his side.

This was the partnership and the family that supported Norm's career in early 1951. He was the sole breadwinner, neither could expect inheritances, and they had the added responsibility of a third life in any plan of retirement. One had been born and bred to the gown, and the other learned to aspire to a college presidency.

LEVERAGING ANOTHER OUTSIDE OFFER

Every two or three years in his first eighteen professional seasons in higher education, Norm got a raise or a shift in duties and usually a promotion. This pattern would continue right on through his last position as Acting President of Lincoln University of Missouri from 1987 to 1988, the end of his fifty-fifth season. He did not remark on this fact of frequent job reclassifications or promotions. He did not draw attention to his plans in assuring it. He never described himself with the mid-twentieth-century phrase "on the make." He sought to obscure his rainmaking role in his advances and changes. Sometime in spring 1951, with those three municipal universities seeking presidencies and his "well-meaning friends" having suggested his name to all three of them, and with the University of Cincinnati watching its long-time President Raymond Walters advancing toward his sixty-sixth birthday, First National Bank of Cincinnati, then the largest bank in town, offered Norm the position of Senior Vice President.

Dad was president of the Cincinnati Rotary Club from 1950 to 1951. In those days, Rotary membership was limited to males who held chief executive or chief operating officer positions in their businesses or organizations. I suspect Dad became eligible when he advanced to Dean of Administration in 1943, which everyone in Cincinnati knew to be second-in-command. Persons serving a large Rotary club like Cincinnati's progress through several chairs before assuming the presidency for a single year. In the vice presidency, their most important duty is recruiting their successor to the presidential rotation. From 1950 to 1951, the vice president of the Cincinnati Rotary Club was Reuben B. Hayes, President of the First National Bank of Cincinnati. The person who offered Norm the senior vice presidency of his bank in the months while the presidencies of three municipal universities were open had been recruited by Norm to serve under him in Rotary.

Lee R. Jackson, President of the Firestone Tire and Rubber Company, as chair of the UA search committee flew himself and three other directors into Cincinnati on Tuesday, June 26, 1951, to complete due diligence in hiring my father. They conferred with President Walters and others on campus and in the community and negotiated the final terms of the offer. On my parents' twenty-first wedding anniversary, Thursday, June 28, my dad brought home twenty-one red roses (as was their custom) and the offer they had known to expect and had decided to accept. The evening papers had the news, and when President Walters made the announcement on campus, "the slim, reddish-haired UC vice president received a thundering ovation Friday at a UC summer school convocation."

The Cincinnati *Enquirer*, the Cincinnati *Times-Star*, and the Cincinnati *Post* published positive editorials about a favorite son's promotion. It was newsworthy to the Cleveland *Plain Dealer*, the Dayton *Daily News*, and the *New York Times*. The *Akron Beacon Journal* sent a twenty-eight-year-old reporter named Fran Murphey, and she filed two "color" stories by July 1 with a couple more by the Fourth. She spoke to "his boss, secretary, students, townspeople, and even reporters" who all declared Norm a "nice man." In a front-page story Murphey characterized him as "a slim man of average height with blue eyes and reddish hair," and on the sports page he became "the handsome slightly built administrator." My mother's first public description to her new home town was if anything even warmer: "a slender, graceful woman with graying hair, observant eyes and a friendly smile," "she seems like a refreshingly frank and genuinely sincere person."

When my father retired in 1971, UA was on its way to becoming the third largest university in Ohio, after Ohio State and Cincinnati. When he took the job in the fall of 1951, UA was much smaller, the tenth largest of Ohio's four dozen colleges and universities; Cincinnati was second in size to the land-grant in Columbus. The town of Akron was a gritty, smelly, dirty, one-industry city half the size of cosmopolitan Cincinnati. On his visits Dad must have learned that President Hezzleton Simmons was paid $12,500, just what Dad was already making as the second-in-command at UC.

Then as now in public higher education, the largest jumps in compensation occur upon initial hires. Once in place, particularly for the chief executive, large salary increases are politically difficult and cause public relations problems. Norm showed his bank offer. UA started my father at $16,000, thirty percent more than they were paying their eighteen-year veteran president, but less than the offer Norm had from First National Bank of Cincinnati. It was a big reach for the tax-payer-funded 4,500-student hometown college. Dad helped by keeping confidential the size of the bank offer. His long-time boss Frank Dinsmore, Chairman of the UC Board of Directors, told him, "Dean Auburn, it is apparent that you would rather be captain of a Cunard Freighter than First Mate on the Queen Elizabeth." Late in his life, Dad told the Rotary Club of Akron, "I'd made that freighter the Queen Mary by the time I left."

THE TRANSITION TO AKRON

President Walters let Dad out of his duties almost immediately. To pick up the slack he appointed a business faculty member as the Dean of University Administration, and he elevated Dad's longtime assistant (who earlier had been Secretary of the Alumni Association) to Assistant Dean of University Administration. The vice president title lapsed. Dad had two months to prepare for his new job, but even as he began the transition, local forces gathered to try to make his stay in Akron short and his triumphal return to Cincinnati inevitable. On July 25, 1951, the Cincinnati *Times-Star* told its readers to expect Norman Auburn to return soon to replace Walters, who was sixty-six and had to retire at seventy. My father made no public comment on this gossip.

There was a family drive to Colorado for a vacation. There must have been trips to Akron to buy the four-bedroom Tudor home with semi-attached three-car garage at 344 Merriman Road. Ames found a living situation for her second year at UC in her Kappa Alpha Theta sorority house. Dad started work on September 1, staying in Akron's Mayflower Hotel with Dick, who started tenth grade at Buchtel. When the house became ours on October 1, Mom and Davey and I followed, and I continued first grade at King School.

We left Cincinnati.

DANGEROUS FLIRTATIONS

Dad had a great first year at Akron, using the good will generated by his appointment to raise millions of dollars from the voters for capital support and from industry as well, enough for two new buildings, which would be completed in 1954 and in 1955, Memorial Hall and Kolbe Hall.

We returned to Cincinnati on June 6, 1952, when Raymond Walters awarded Norm his second LLD, this time on behalf of his *alma mater*. The family scrapbook includes a news picture of the stage party honorees with Cincinnati Mayor Carl W. Rich, UC '23, Lambda Chi Alpha member in Norm's "big brother" generation. In his political role as mayor, Rich appointed the UC directors.

The Auburn family was back in Akron for six weeks before the Cincinnati *Enquirer* published a reminder that Dr. Norman Auburn was likely to return to replace President Walters, who would turn sixty-seven in August. My father made no public comment on this gossip.

But a front-page story in the November 10, 1952, Cincinnati *Times-Star* required a reply. Dad's picture was published under the front-page headline "City Manager to Retire Soon" with the subhead "W. R. Kellogg Indicates Desire to Leave Job He Held Since 1944: Utilities Director Robert White and Dr. Norman Auburn Mentioned as Successors." Since 1925, Cincinnati was governed by a nine-member Council elected at-large via proportional preference-ranked voting. The councilman with the most votes usually served as Mayor. Mayor and Council employed a City Manager, and this article cited the facts of his $25,000 annual salary and of Dr. Auburn's $16,000 salary at UA. Carl Rich was mayor. He had mentioned Norm's name. Dad told the local press in Akron that he had not applied and had not spoken with the search committee. Three months later in February 1953, Manager Kellogg said that he would delay his retirement as long as he was needed.

In the November 1953 election, the Republican majority headed by Carl Rich was turned out, and Manager Kellogg retired. On January 13, 1954, Norm just happened to be in Cincinnati to deliver a speech to the Association of American Colleges. While there, he hand-carried a letter to Mayor Edward N. Waldvogel, asking that his name be dropped from consideration for city manager—for which he had never formally applied—because he wanted to devote his energies to higher education, an event reported in Cincinnati and in Akron. The Cincinnati papers reported that Council might pay as much as $35,000 for the next city manager and that UC President Raymond Walters would retire soon. The same day the *Akron Beacon Journal*'s "Behind The Front Page" column reprinted much of Norm's letter to the Cincinnati mayor. The timing assures that Norm was its source.

It so happened that a few days before Norm delivered his letter, Mayor Waldvogel had reappointed Mrs. Daniel E. Earley, née Jane DeSerisy, to the UC Board of Directors. Two months before, following Waldvogel's upset election, the new mayor had announced a plan to replace her because she was a party Republican. Pressure from some sitting board members that she was their only female director may have played a part in her reappointment. The Cincinnati *Enquirer* wrote "It was reported, also, that Mrs. Earley had indicated to the Charterites [Waldvogel's majority Council party] that she was in no way committed to support Dr. Norman Auburn, president of The University of Akron, for the UC presidency when Dr. Raymond Walters should retire early next year." Jane and Norm had been fellow officers of the UC "Hoover-For-President Club" in 1927.

In November 1954, Carl Rich won the votes to return as mayor, and on November 17 it was reported that "Rich's return to the major's office enhances the chances of Dr. Norman Auburn to become president of the University of Cincinnati when Dr. Raymond Walters retires next spring.... The City Charter Committee, which now loses any influence in board appointments, has been lukewarm toward Dr. Auburn, but the Republicans right along have favored him." That drumbeat forced my father to make a statement in Akron to the Associated Press about the UC presidency: "I have not applied for the job.... I have not been approached about it nor have I been called to Cincinnati to meet with the board or a committee of the board." In Cincinnati, the new UC board chair reacted by saying that it didn't matter if Auburn hadn't applied, he knew he would be considered: that was the nature of such executive searches. That boxing-in remark must have hurt. It bore an edge of condescension. It showed that the tide of support was turning. Mayor Carl Rich, Lambda Chi Brother Rich, made a lukewarm statement including "it would be presumptuous of me to even think about making any such suggestion" about Norm Auburn for UC president. Insiders said that the UC faculty wanted a "real academic" with earned degrees and that Norm's "Republican activities gained him opposition."

The last trimmed and pasted stories in the family scrapbook were those of the city manager flurry, not a careful documentation of all stages of the UC presidential search. There are plenty of pictures and reports of Ames's wedding in summer 1954 and several pictures and stories about Paul W. Litchfield's gift of the spacious home at 856 Mayfair Road in summer 1956 folded and shoved between leaves. But all the stuff about the UC presidential search through spring 1955 didn't get pasted, and reports of the endgame in spring 1955, leading to the appointment of Walter Langsam to the office, did not even get saved. Langsam earned a PhD from Columbia University in 1930, taught there and at Union College until 1945, and served as president of Gettysburg College and Wagner College before coming to UC. He was the author of fifteen books. He was one year younger than Norm. UC would grow and prosper during his presidency. It would maintain its stature as the state's second largest comprehensive research and teaching institution even while millions upon millions poured into the land-grant campus at Ohio State and its home city of Columbus eclipsed Cincinnati as the second-largest metropolis. He would serve UC until 1971, the same year Norm retired from UA.

In Mother's interpretation, the villain was Jane Earley. Her treachery in stepping away from Dad's candidacy provided cover for a minority that became a majority, particularly under the leadership of the new chairman, a Proctor and Gamble vice president prone to credit faculty opinion. I never heard the name of Carl Rich at home, though the record shows his centrality in Norm's life and in these machinations. Neither my mother nor my father spoke warmly of Walter Langsam. And I don't think they ever looked back to Cincinnati from that time forward. The strategic silences and tactical candidacy-buffing denials had been for naught. Akron was truly now their home.

In the President's Home

Entertaining

My parents conceived the President's Home as a manse and University constituents as a congregation. They believed that every congregant should have access to the parsonage. When we moved into the Georgian-style red-brick seven-bedroom five-bath house (which Dad persuaded former Goodyear Chairman Paul W. Litchfield to donate to the University in 1956), they worked out a plan whereby nearly everyone associated with the University would be invited to visit the home at least once a year, and they held to that scheme for fifteen years, even as the University grew from about 4,500 to 20,500 students.

Invitations to Sunday afternoon teas held early in the fall or late in the spring went at least once a year to every salaried employee (faculty, administrators, staff) and to every full-time student; later the student list was pared with the advice of the Dean of Students. Members of the Board of Directors were invited to sit-down dinners at least twice a year. Buffet dinners mixing Directors, faculty, alumni, and townspeople might bring 300 at a time to the house and tents on the grounds in good weather. Speakers for the Town and Gown lectures and the World at Our Door series were invited to stay at the President's Home, and their visits were marked by sit-down luncheons or dinners and post-lecture desserts or receptions. Honorees at Commencement and military officials present for Commissioning Exercises stayed in the house, and their presence provided similar opportunities to honor University friends with intimate time in the company of these celebrities. After Dad built an extension on the Gardner Student Center, the larger dinners and all-

Kay and Norm Auburn on the steps of the President's Home, 1956. *Photo by Lou Tobias, from the Norman Auburn Papers. Courtesy of Archival Services, University Libraries, The University of Akron*

campus receptions were held there; A-Day, Founders' Day, prefootball game buffets, and the occasional prebasketball event were held on or close to campus, but this entertaining did not relax the plan to extend to all the yearly invitation to visit the President's Home.

LARGE RECEPTIONS

Invitations to Sunday teas were staggered in two-hour intervals: 2:00 to 4:00 p.m., 3:00 to 5:00 p.m., and 4:00 to 6:00 p.m., so that at most 200 of the 300 invitees were present at any one time. Mom and Dad would stand at the threshold of the house, and generally Mom would be the first greeter: Dad was expected to know everyone by sight, and while between them they could recall and name most of their guests, this positioning allowed my mother the opportunity to ask and to repeat the identity of the few neither of them immediately recognized so that the myth of Dad's Presidential omniscience was strengthened or maintained.

Past the threshold, guests were invited to take their coats upstairs and to the master bedroom on the right, the large one with twin beds, mirrored bureau and highboy, en suite bathroom, and walk-in-closet-dressing-room. The entire upstairs was open; guests could wander through the master bedroom into Dad's study, or they could pass the top of the two-flight reversing main staircase unobserved from below westward to peek into the sewing room, the formal guest bedroom (where Mother slept many nights; her snoring was persistent and stertorous) and adjoining bath, or even further into the upstairs library (which Mom used for her study) and through it and down a step into the two back bedrooms and bath over the garage. In practice, most guests left their coats in the master bedroom and returned downstairs directly, but Mom and Dad encouraged everyone to "look at the house," and many enjoyed the impression that they were exploring the private lives of their public leaders. I know that Dad locked his desk, and even when no one was around he rarely kept papers visible; but otherwise, we took no particular security precautions, and only once or twice in fifteen years did something go missing after one of these receptions. There was a back staircase adjacent to the main stairway which provided access to the attic above, to the landing of the main staircase, to the kitchen through the butler's pantry, and to the basement, and the doors to this staircase were closed during receptions. During my late high school and college years when I lived in the attic apartment, I could seal myself off entirely from the entertaining. Otherwise, all rooms were open.

I never tired of the party fare. Sturdy caterer Flossie Lewis, whose ready smile showcased her missing incisors, and two or three helpers would arrive laden with three-by-four-foot single-layer waxed cardboard boxes crammed with finger sandwiches and *petits fours*. Egg, chicken, and ham salads, and pimento-laced cream cheese were spread on good crumb white bread with the crusts removed, cut into four squares or triangles or three rectangles, and decorated open-face with thin slices of green or black olive, sweet pickle, and cucumber. I remember half-dollar-sized cream-puffs, squares of brownies or gingerbread, inch-cube iced white-cake boxes with a squiggle of pink decoration, crisp wafers, and thin slices of fruitcake like blurry stained-glass rectangles. Bowls of salted mixed nuts (no peanuts at all) and small trays of mints supplemented the sandwiches and cakes; the mints were half-inch-thick nickel-sized sandwiches of two creamy, pastel-colored meltaways enclosing a thin dark chocolate lozenge, and I regret to this day the passing of their maker, Blossom Shop Candies.

Flossie brought multi-gallon coffee percolators and tea urns, ice, and punch, with which she filled and refilled my mother's various silver pots and her big five-gallon silver punch bowl. In addition to a couple dozen silver-plate pots and trays, my parents had accumulated about fifteen dozen china cups, saucers, bread-and-butter plates, glass punch cups, and silver-plated teaspoons and salad forks. Flossie's staff kept circulating to collect the dirty utensils and clean them for the next guests. At some point, we acquired many dozen footed glass coffee cups and coordinated bread-and-butter plates, which obviated the need for a separate saucer. The sandwiches, *petits fours*, nuts, and candies were arranged on my mother's silver trays and dishes and displayed in the dining room on the buffet, the half-moon punch table, and the dining table. Only two chairs remained in that room; on these perched in shifts the faculty and administrative wives who felt privileged (Mother said) to be asked to pour for the afternoon and to come early to chat with their host and hostess.

These receptions were hard work for the President and the President's wife. They were on their feet at the doorway, or in the vestibule when the crowd turned to leave, steadily from 2:00 until 4:30 p.m., then, until the last guest left at 6:00, they would circulate. My mother might find time for a cigarette at three-quarters past the hour, but Dad didn't want her smoking when people were arriving, though when she mingled it was less objectionable. (Except at cocktail parties, women rarely smoked standing up those days.) Dad would take a little punch but no coffee or tea; he wanted to manage his urine output. Neither of them ate during the party.

For some events, they might be joined at the door by the Dean of Faculty and his wife or, for student-predominant receptions, by the Dean of Men and the Dean of Women, to create a four-person receiving line. My mother felt it was important for all guests, no matter their level of sophistication, to learn to greet and meet, as she called it, and everyone had to pass this gauntlet coming and going. She was gracious, warm, and charming; her laugh sparkled as much as her eyes, and she never seemed to tire; she was adept at a grasp-and-pass maneuver that kept everyone, even the momentarily tongue-tied, moving through the line and into or out of the house. But they would both get tired, and Mom would retire to the solarium-television room "to put her feet up" after the reception, even before Flossie and her crew had gone, where she'd stay drinking Coca-Cola long past my bedtime, while Dad would start reading in his bed by 9:30 p.m. rather than the usual 10:30.

In addition to a social formality unusual in the experience of many guests, visitors faced a long walk from where they left their cars on the neighborhood streets. The concept of valet parking didn't reach Akron for a few more decades. At the height of the receptions, people would have to park out of sight of the house, and there were two four-step flights in the twenty yards from sidewalk to front door to be negotiated under the eyes of their hosts, not unlike a model's runway or a graduate's platform. Only two or three regular visitors with mobility challenges ever arrived at the backdoor, and I don't recall seeing anyone who used a wheelchair coming to the house. Worldly faculty muttered that they weren't about to walk three or four blocks, possibly in the rain, for a lousy sandwich and a cup of tepid tea and nary a drink at the cocktail hour. But the yield per invitation was so high and the novelty of seeing the President's Home so special that these receptions were always crowded and usually reported in the *Buchtelite* and in the society pages of the *Akron Beacon Journal*, and they continued as a UA tradition in some form right into the mid-1990s.

A SPACIOUS HOME

The red brick Georgian colonial house at 856 Mayfair Road was sited on a large corner lot with six large trees (two were felled by Dutch Elm disease in the sixties). The north lawn sloped upward from east to west by about one foot per twenty, and the lot was 120' broad. The east side yard extended ninety feet from Mayfair Road in the front along Ridgecrest Road on the side to the straight driveway in the rear, which was planted in lilac and rose of Sharon on either side from thirty feet beyond the curb. The main entrance faced north. Four Doric columns held a triangular pediment above the middle three of five second-story windows in the central structure, creating a spacious covered front porch.

The Georgian Colonial house given to UA in 1956. *Photo by Lou Tobias, from the Norman Auburn Papers. Courtesy of Archival Services, University Libraries, The University of Akron*

Stepped back a dozen courses or about four feet on either side of the five-window-broad main building were two other room-broad two-story rectangular wings under a common roof: solarium and Dad's study above on the east, breakfast room in front of kitchen and butler's pantry with library above on the west. (The large basement extended under the main portion but not the wings.) On the west side, a three-car garage with two bedrooms and bath above stepped back behind the kitchen, not visible from the Mayfair Road prospect. The garage extension formed an ell at the back of the house, sheltering a poured concrete patio on its east side. A sidewalk beside this patio led through tall lilacs from the driveway to a formal rear door with covered portico which opened onto a vestibule co-extensive with the front entrance, creating a hallway under the landing of the main staircase. The rear façade of the house rose to the full-sized windows of the double-wide dormer of the attic apartment, and off the solarium a twelve-foot-high trellised brick arbor extended southward to the lilacs and pachysandra along the driveway, creating an enclosed backyard. Open stairs parallel to the house's rear façade led from the formal rear door to the basement. Around the base of the arbor were four well-drained triangular rose beds, each with a dozen or more tea-rose bushes.

The grounds were broad, and the house was spacious, particularly good for overnight and extended-stay visitors. There was an attic suite with two rooms, a full bath, walk-in-closet, and a storage room reached by an enclosed stairway, which could be accessed from a rear door or through the butler's pantry without going through public space. The two bedrooms and full bath above the garage had a separate entrance from the garage side as well. Either of these could be configured as bedroom-sitting room suites for visiting couples or families. Later the basement was remodeled to include beyond the laundry room and utility room another full bath (the fifth), a playroom, and bedroom.

Mother oversaw one initial decoration in 1956, then in the late 1950s or early 1960s as the house's usefulness for entertaining became clear, managed another set of improvements. She chose a single color and a single style and installation of neutral wall-to-wall carpeting in the four large first-floor public spaces, solarium and living room on one side of the hallway and vestibule, dining room on the other, brought together by the wall and floor treatments. Her perennial complaint, however, was that the layout did not permit continuous circulation: if only both the solarium and the living room had had two entrances each, then the crowds could make circuits rather than turning back on themselves. With the solarium-living room a *cul de sac*, serving a meal to more than three dozen at a time was problematic.

OUTDOOR BUFFETS

In late spring, summer, or early fall, perhaps twice a year my folks would host large buffet lunches or dinners. A day or two before, the roustabouts from Akron Tent and Awning would throw up one or two eight-foot high white canvas tents over the side or front lawns. Miller Rental followed with scarred plywood-topped round metal tables and flimsy wooden folding chairs, which by means of table cloths and thick linen covers became clean white settings. Someone would run electrical lines from the basement and cover them with rubber plates. And a couple

Buffet meal in a tent on the grounds of the President's Home, 1971. *From the Norman Auburn Papers. Courtesy of Archival Services, University Libraries, The University of Akron*

of hours before the party, the caterers would arrive with all the food, drink, plates, cups, and linen to lay out buffet tables with steaming chaffing dishes while my mother would pray for weather which would allow the tent sides to be kept rolled up. I was always surprised by how the span covered by the tents seemed so much larger on the inside than the lawn and by how the tents seen from the outside shrunk the broad grounds and by how the house seemed taller in the descended cloud of the tents. Perhaps 300 guests would sit down for the meal, and my father would always find a moment after everyone was eating to call for attention and make some remarks about how grateful he, Kay, and the University were for their presence and their support. By evening of the following day only trampled grass and stake-holes witnessed the party's physical effects, and those disappeared by the next mowing. We might also have a day or two of leftover party food, and I would have increased my private stash of salted nuts and mint sandwiches.

FLORAL DECORATIONS

Mom took pleasure in preparing flowers for all the parties at the house. A day before a party she'd bring home an oblong white cardboard box or two of cut flowers and greens and tramp around the rose garden, taking the most promising buds and blossoms, then commandeer the kitchen and breakfast room as her staging area. From the butler's pantry would come vases and bowls, from beneath the sink desiccated crumbly-foamy chunks of Oasis, raveled and rewrapped rolls of thin stretchy green floral tape, fagots of green bamboo, and where-are-my-clippers-Markie-I-told-you-never-to take-them! I tried to absent myself when the *furor botanica* overtook her, but after I could drive I'd be sent for more baby's breath and tall fern if I appeared inopportunely or responded in my attic to her second or third call or the furious peal of the cowbell when words failed her.

Mom's arrangements were quite nice. She had good taste, a good eye, just enough patience, and an expanding knowledge of materials available and seasonally appropriate. By the late 1950s she had regular professional help from Phil Burkhalter of Townhouse Florists in Highland Square, who would swoop in before receptions or large dinners dressed in a tight shirt that emphasized his muscular torso, beefy arms, and narrow waist with a dozen arrangements and help her place them and praise or adjust the one or two she'd done herself (for even when she ordered the flowers, she still did her own) and root around in the butler's pantry to recover vases and bowls from the last party before he dashed away. The house would smell sweet and look lovely, and once or twice I took an arrangement back to my room after a party. Years later when I prepared my own home for company, the only thing that I added to her model was a bud vase in the powder room.

DINNER PARTIES

In cold weather, perhaps monthly, Mom and Dad would host forty people for buffet meals, one plate of three or four choices which could be eaten without a knife from the lap in the living room and solarium and later, after Dad caused the University to remodel it, in the basement. A dessert course and coffee would follow, and Dad might have to visit two locations to make his customary remarks of welcome, thanks, and reminders about the University. My mother's favorite dinner party was for a dozen around the federal-style golden oak dining table, occasionally enlarged to sixteen or twenty by the addition of one or two tables of four just within earshot of one another in the front hall and north side of the living room.

Dinners were usually catered meals, although Mom herself cooked breakfasts and lunches served in the dining room for overnight guests. Flossie would add a couple of waitresses and a bartender for the dinner and offer hot cheese boxes or skewered meatballs to supplement drinks to order served on a silver tray. Salad would be on the table when guests were called; my dad's favorite was cottage cheese on pineapple, but he had to put up usually with dressed greens (his own would be plain). Flossie's waitresses would remove the empty salad plates (I don't think we used chargers), distribute dinner plates, and stand passing three or four dishes—a silver tray with thick slices of beef tenderloin cooked until the pink was gone, a broad seashell dish of asparagus spears followed by a boat of lemony dip-your-own hollandaise in summer or a head of cauliflower reassembled with buttered toasted breadcrumbs surrounded by green peas accented by sautéed mushrooms in winter, and another tray of miniature fluted pyramids of potatoes mashed with cream and cheddar and browned with a sprinkle of paprika under the broiler.

Mother would preside at the west (or kitchen) end, Dad at the east with the hall at his back, and I think Mom loved encouraging general conversations and being seated with the male guests of honor flanking her. She taught me my responsibility to converse at least once, through a course of several exchanges, with the person on my right and then the person on my left. Wine was not served at dinners until very close to their retirement in 1971, and other than sherry, we kept no wine in the house; but it was the house's supply of hard liquor on which Flossie's bartender called to mix drinks, and he would arrange to replace those supplies. Second-time hard-drinking guests knew to bring their cocktails to the table where another round would be offered in lieu of wine. Dad's formal greetings would occur after everyone's plate was full. Dessert and coffee would be served while we were still seated, and guests withdrew generally to the living room and solarium for their second post-dinner cigarettes (their first having been taken at table), mints, and nuts. For certain guests, Dad himself saw to another cocktail after dinner, but I do not remember general canvassing or the offer of cordials or brandies, though Mom did keep some crème de menthe in the butler's pantry.

Mom's gaiety permeated the evening. She would move from group to group with her Tareyton in its short tar-reducing holder. If someone present could play the piano, she'd always encourage singing, and many times when the last four or five were gathered round the piano and the time had advanced past 10:30 p.m., Dad would say goodnight and climb the stairs to his bedroom. Mom could rarely keep the party going more than half an hour after this point, even with the addition of Coca-Colas, but she'd do her best, and some nights ended at twelve or later, especially evening receptions begun after a lecture, concert, play, or ballet. Indeed, on those evenings my father's post-event participation was so minimal (never a formal speech of welcome that I recall) that his exit went unnoticed or at least did not serve to dampen the more convivial.

Mom herself hosted small sit-down and larger buffet luncheons for the University Women's Committee, her PEO chapter, bridge groups, book clubs, or later, the organizers of the Chamber Ballet. And she encouraged my giving parties for the sons and daughters of UA Directors and rubber executives who lived in the neighborhood. For dances I'd wash and dry the larger garage and throw wax on the floor and snake out extension cords to run a record player. For bridge parties I'd muster the tables and chairs and cards and score pads and pencils and Cokes and beg Blossom Shop nuts and mints, and if it didn't interrupt Dad's evening eating schedule, we might even drive over to State Road in the Falls to bring home the pizzas first available in Akron about 1955—sausage, mushroom, green pepper, and onion.

LIQUOR

Attitudes toward alcohol and entertaining changed considerably during my parents' adult lifetimes. Dad's boyhood home was teetotal because of his mother's Christian Science faith, and although his brother Walter was an early adopter of the daily cocktail, he took nothing stronger than Red Dubonnet on ice, except when traveling abroad, when he would safely hydrate with one or two beers a day in countries where the water supply was doubtful. He didn't even start the Red Dubonnet until the 1960s when it seemed necessary to avoid appearing puritanical among his guests. As a minister's daughter, Mom grew up in parsonages and church-related college president's homes without alcohol. Midwestern Presbyterians prided themselves on attitudes more liberal than the Southern Baptists with whom they coexisted, so the Montgomery girls could go to properly chaperoned dances. And while Big Daddy did not sermonize against a glass of sherry in the house of a latitudinarian parishioner, he and Fanny kept no liquor at home except next to the emetics, laxatives, and tonics.

Mom's sisters Betty and Jo kept no wine or liquor in their houses well into the 1960s; it was Rob who as a young adult introduced beer and distilled spirits first into the basement rec room he built as his bachelor pad and later into the half of the house where he and his new bride Jane Huber Clark made their home. Betty and Jo did drink alcohol, almost ritually, at the July 31 celebratory dinner at Win Schuler's when the Manor closed for a month. And Aunt Jo made a *memento mori* anecdote over having been prescribed three ounces of sherry nightly for insomnia in her seventieth year: "But, doctor, won't I become an alcoholic?" "Well, Miss Montgomery, at your age you don't have to worry about that." By the time I was eighteen or nineteen and liking to take a drink myself, my mother might have a J&B on the rocks of an evening when there was no company. (Doubtless I encouraged, and accompanied, her.) Dad did not approve, and he muttered about it, so that it came to Ames's ear in Europe that he thought Kay was becoming a lush. And certain it is that by her sixties my mother used liquor more freely than before, though I never saw her drunk or wobbly anytime and I can think of only one nonsocial occasion when she took a drink during the day.

But because their guests liked alcohol and because they saw it almost always in other homes in Akron, Norm and Kay began to keep and serve it in the President's Home in the late 1950s. They still ministered to their congregation, but the congregation had become more liberal. While there was almost never wine, there were always a couple of bottles of cold beer in the house after Dick graduated college in 1958, and there was a large selection of hard liquor in the butler's pantry. A drinks table or even two became features of large evening parties, though I hardly remember a time except for family feasts when the bar was unattended. Pitchers of whiskey sours for Jo, Betty, and Bill showed up on Christmas Eve and sometimes needed to be replenished, and Kay made sure there was gin and vermouth in the house for nephew-in-law Bob Swinehart's "silver bullets," the martinis about whose construction the advertising man waxed more eloquent as the family evening progressed.

Mother always said that it was far better to provide alcohol in the home on a controlled basis than to teach hard drinkers to expect none and hence show up with a snootful. And she dated her habit of having speakers stay in her home to the 1930s and 1940s when Norm oversaw the University of Cincinnati lecture series as part of his duties as Dean of the Evening College: they would carefully control alcohol before lectures with the promise of post-lecture lubrication, and she told colorful set pieces about famous visitors—H. G. Wells calling for sliced cucumbers to garnish the Cincinnati Club's hock, or Edna St. Vincent Millay in the car on the way to her lecture saying to her suspiciously young and darkly handsome companion, "For God's sake, Gene! Where's that flask?" (In his autobiography *The World is My Home*, James Michener tells of being escorted, guarded practically, by young assistant professors of English right up to taking the stage for his UC lecture in the early 1960s, then deserted thereafter, so my parents' tradition continued in a degenerated form after their departure for Akron in 1951—all caution, but no hospitality.) At no time was alcohol served when there wasn't food or before 5:00 p.m. or at the teas, and not even beer appeared at student parties. Some people came to the President's Home for cocktail receptions with hors d'oeuvres only, but their invitations specified departure times before the honored guests sat down to dinner (and that tactic worked because they were subordinates who were cautioned to leave promptly). Otherwise, there were no cocktail parties at 856 Mayfair Road.

NOTABLE VISITORS

I shared my home with famous people. African explorer Robert Goddard thrilled me when I was eleven by requesting two raw eggs of Kay at breakfast, breaking one into a cup and gulping it whole then asking for some Worcestershire sauce to douse the second. I believed his tales of living on snakes' eggs in the jungle and extracting a tapeworm from his own stomach by pulling it out through his throat, and I would have debated anyone who claimed that Goddard's filmed wrestle with a crocodile was staged, particularly after watching him stretch those tight steel springs in his fitted T-shirt as part of his morning ritual. Ten years later novelist C. P. Snow came for a Friday lecture and a Saturday morning on the Convocation dais and then announced that he wouldn't be leaving until the following Wednesday. Among my duties with him (while home from graduate school in Chicago) was to procure a second half-gallon bottle of J&B and another carton of my mother's Tareytons, so deeply did he dip into his hostess's supplies. (Though Dad and Mom were happy to keep his whiskey topped off all through the post-dinner hours—one ice cube only, thank you, and drown it.)

I remember publisher Jack Knight flicking his cigarette ashes into the fireplaces of the living room and solarium, and refilling his Scotch took me away from his heated (but not profane: he controlled himself in dear Kay's home) debates once with Ambassador Averell Harriman (they agreed about the Vietnam war) and another time with Joint Chiefs Chairman Maxwell Taylor (they didn't, but Jack looked as ramrod-spined as the taller general). In those days of my heritage Republicanism, the closest I came to questioning authority was when General Taylor the next morning on the tennis courts of Portage Country Club mistook his hosts' son, who was shagging balls during his match with my brother-in-law Rusty, for a club employee and tried to tip me. Tiny Ariel Durant of *The Story of Civilization* ate eggs and bacon with me and Mom and Sandy in the breakfast nook after she had prepared and taken up to her then ninety-year-old husband Will, writing in a bedroom over the garage, a special granola-like porridge, which she whispered guarded against gas. No one can remember which general's wife left a surprise in the wastebasket of the back bedroom: Mom and Dolores fished around with a straightened coat hanger before they prized from the clear Smirnoff pint the scrap of paper with the words "Bet you've never found a note in a bottle!"

Vincent Price at breakfast was not at all sinister; he was amusing and charming. General Curtis LeMay was handsome in his blue Air Force undress uniform, and Dad stayed home for breakfast that day before AFROTC Commissioning: did I know what power his SAC could wield? *Dr. Strangelove* would teach me. Explorer-filmmaker Asa Johnson was actually a quiet little man at table, not the great authoritative presence at the lectern narrating scenes of Acapulco cliff-diving and Filipino vine-bungee jumping. And how was it I missed the evening with musical

Toddler David Auburn with his parents Mark and Sandy at the President's Home, July 4, 1971. *From the author's collection*

playwright Meredith Willson? Mother felt a special bond because in the first draft Marian's little brother Winthrop suffered like Davey from cerebral palsy; Willson sat at our piano and sang all the tunes of *The Music Man* and then ran through the score of his current project, an untitled love story about a Colorado miner's daughter who survived the Titanic. (I must have been at Western Reserve Academy. Mom said that Dad stayed up until midnight.) Lord Harlech (British Ambassador to US 1961–1965) came to review British foreign policy and the Special Relationship but spent his time at dinner fending off the questions of *Beacon Journal* social columnist Betty Jaycox about his relationship with the newly dating Jacqueline Kennedy. I can't remember which general it was who left for Washington directly after Commissioning Exercises on June 13, 1971, skipping the planned lunch at the President's Home with profuse apologies to his hostess, but I do remember how after supper we all pored over a copy of that morning's *New York Times*, whose six-column banner headline announced its publication of secret Pentagon papers, about which until then we had not heard.

OTHER PRESIDENTIAL SOCIAL DUTIES

In addition to the entertaining that I saw at home, the President and his wife had extensive social duties elsewhere. They spent many evenings dining in the homes of University friends and benefactors, which Dad did reluctantly since he was uncertain of meeting his dietary and bedtime preferences. They were honored guests at college-sponsored awards banquets and the annual black-tie military balls. They attended Akron's round of charity cotillions and lent their presence on the dais for community recognition dinners. They came to nearly every University Theatre production and many orchestra concerts and student events like Songfest, May Day, Interfraternity/Panhellenic Council, and ODK/A-Key initiations, and they presided at A-Day, Founders' Day, Christmas luncheons, and receptions.

Dad maintained a high profile as an elder, usher, and member of the Session of Westminster Presbyterian Church and as a Rotarian, and Mom had her role in the ladies' auxiliaries. They supported the new Akron Symphony Orchestra and the venerable Tuesday Musical Club with their presence and patronage, and after being instrumental in the transfer of Stan Hywet to a community trust, they led there as well. In retrospect there were very few evenings of just the three of us at home, so I have no memories of recurring family time around a favorite TV show, no sense that we always watched (say) Ed Sullivan or never missed an episode of *Bonanza*, though I do remember my mother's faithfulness at 11:30 p.m. to Jack Parr and then Steve Allen and finally Johnny Carson, because her evenings would usually be free by then; Dad, of course, had gone to sleep, since he would be poaching his egg, squeezing his glass of orange juice, and toasting one slice of bread at 6:45 the next morning and on his way to the office by 7:30 while Mom slept on.

The Presidency as pastorate was constant work socially, but this PK (president's kid) was only vaguely aware that his parents were always working whenever they were in public. I watched Dad speaking from the field of the Rubber Bowl at halftime and I thought that speech constituted his work for the afternoon. Lunching among sixty others at the University Club and riding with them on a chartered city bus to the game was not work. My mother dressing for the weather with a large yellow chrysanthemum corsage trimmed with blue ribbon on her lapel, walking in two-inch heels over the gravel of the parking lot and the uneven concrete of the stands, and sitting on a narrow wooden folding chair in a cold concrete-sided box on the ground at the fifty-yard-line during three-and-a-half hours of pageantry and football game was not work. Dad's walking up the sixty-five steps to the press box once or twice a game and making us wait afterwards when he stopped at the dressing room was not work, nor was the half-hour ride on the much emptier bus back to the University Club amid the commiserations or postgame quarterbacking or questions about Joe McMullen's contract as head coach. Making conversation with the honored students, alumni, or Directors who sat with us in the box, or taking the greetings from people who walked by our seats must be just fun. For a long time I thought it was great fun to eat dinner quickly and join Dad (still dressed in his suit and tie) for the ride to Memorial Hall and sit beside him in the four seats on the front row of the first mezzanine at midcourt and hang around afterwards in the pungent spearmint-scented locker room with those big sweaty men naked or in jockstraps while Dad shook some hands and said a few words, and only many years later did I figure out that if I accompanied Dad to the basketball game, Mom got a night off. And I was not aware that Dad always went to two or three soccer matches, baseball games, and track meets every year; he just wasn't home many Saturday afternoons.

HOW THEY DRESSED

Often entertaining and always the object of attention, Dad took care about his appearance. Dad habitually wore a suit and tie—indeed, years later one subordinate asserted that he always wore a blue-and-gold tie in UA's colors, though I know that wasn't so. He followed American business fashion closely, so that I remember good quality dark-colored Hart Schaffner Marx double-breasted followed by three-piece followed by single-breasted two-button suits. The few sport coats were muted dark blues and grays, and he didn't own a brown suit while he worked at UA—only one camel-colored blazer. The majority of his shirts were white, but later he admitted blues and blue stripes. He wore button-down collars and experimented only briefly with a collar pin. When we had a laundress for about a year, his shirts were starched and ironed at home; but otherwise they came back folded in a paper ribbon around cardboard stiffeners from

Champlin Cleaners. He completed his shirt-and-Countess-Mara-tie assembly with his favorite tie pin: a looped gold chain around the wider tail of the tie just below his diaphragm, the ends of the chain invisible behind the tie, attached unseen to a paper-clip-like stay that slipped between the fourth and fifth buttons of his shirt front and allowed the tie to move without blousing awkwardly when he stooped or sat. He was always clean shaven, a brush-and-blade man, and he always used an after-shave—Old Spice, though he experimented with the latest expensive scents for his second and third wives. He got his hair cut often enough that I never heard Kay to remark it as too long or as recently cut, and he took a manicure but no polish at the barber shop in the Mayflower Hotel.

Unlike other fathers Norm didn't have leisure clothes—no golf shorts, no polo shirts, no bright sport coats, though he did own a pair of blue jeans which came out exclusively for very occasional horseback rides. Instead of a bowling shirt or a leisure suit, he had a tuxedo, a white evening jacket, and a sumptuous academic robe and mortarboard that he wore for ceremonies. Dressing down meant a blue blazer and tie and maybe a solid light blue or brown cashmere sweater, but not khakis—he always wore dark hard-finished wool trousers except for winter wool flannels and a summer cord suit. He used a belt rather than braces. The lapel buttonhole of his coat invariably held his platinum Rotary pin with a small diamond President's stud. The breast pocket showed the starched pressed horizontal top of a white handkerchief, and he only briefly experimented with color-coordinated silk squares when they became popular in the sixties. He would change his tie shoes for hard-bodied slippers if he were going to be at home for the evening, remove his tie, and perhaps add a cardigan. I don't remember his ever using sports shoes. He wore thin silk ankle-length socks with reinforced toes, heels, and anklets without garters. While he tried nylon socks, he stayed with the silk as long as he could buy them, adopting wool-nylon blends during his seventies and beyond. He wore cotton boxers with strapped undershirts whatever the weather, but he would add long underwear and a sweater under his suit coat when the temperature fell below zero. Dressing for yard work or shooting baskets behind the garage meant changing his suit for a shirt and trousers that he had once worn to the office and now, with the collar open and the sleeves rolled, that he repurposed.

Mother always wore knee-length dresses over a girdle, hose, bra, and half-slip (she adopted pantyhose in her late fifties). She must have had some blouse-and-skirt outfits, but it is in a dress or in a woman's tailored suit that I remember her. She chose many rich fabrics, colors, and textures and had a full range of each for every season, and I do not remember her having any of the print cotton dresses which my aunts Jo and Betty favored. I would guess that she spent a lot of money on her clothes, and I remember that finding them to fit properly occupied a lot of her time, and she had relationships with various dressmakers in Akron. Sandy remembers her creativity in buying flowing lingerie items and refitting them with accessories to serve as cocktail party dresses. She was a colorful Milady Fashion to Dad's Lord Sobersides.

During our University years she depended upon professional hair styling for color and permanents, though like many in the mid sixties she went gleefully through the short era of wigs. "Frivolous Fawn" was a blond coloring she chose to match the hue of her Chevrolet Bel-Air convertibles of the 1960s; her natural hair was brown. Her hair was mostly white by my early teens, and so blond tints over a white base were exotic treats to her. I hardly remember her washing her hair, no memory of that astronaut-like hair dryer humming in the house to which a couple of high school girl friends introduced me. Neither do I have an image of her in hair curlers, nightly facials, nets, caps, and special appliances for sleeping: a brush and some hairspray would prepare her for public presentation in just a few minutes. What is interesting about the somewhat carefree style of her hair is that it always had to cover her ears, for she did not choose to have the misshapen right ear visible.

Unlike Dad she had play clothes and clothes for lounging. She would take the sun on our patio in a bathing suit and add a muumuu cover-up for the rest of the day and even receive informal (and subordinate) visitors in that outfit; and when she was at home for an evening with just family she had a large variety of long warm dressing gowns. She had lots of shoes, mostly low heels of one or two inches (since more than two would overtop her husband), and she was much troubled by ingrown toenails and calluses and wore flats or slippers in the house—even up to the last minute before guests arrived. Eyeglasses were part of her outfits, and in addition to her favorite smoky-gray frames for her bifocals, she had a variety of party frames and sunglasses, and these multiplied further when she adopted contact lenses in her late fifties. I do not remember her wearing trousers or even shorts, except on vacation or for trail-riding. Her flat behind was not attractive in pants, she felt, and she did not wear outfits closely defined at the waist, either. Her sisters, similarly shaped, fulminated against pant suits for years on anti-feminist grounds until Jo (the tallest and slimmest) quietly adopted them in her late sixties and never again wore a dress. It's a pity Mom would not use pants, however, because she hated the marbled and often painful varicose veins in her legs, and she used a variety of colored and support hose to disguise and to relieve them. When hats were in, she wore one of a large collection, and when they were out she wore only her nimbus of white-blond hair, no matter how cold, unless it rained or snowed, in which case she'd add a plastic bonnet. She did her own nails but went for long periods without polish. She always wore scent—Chanel No. 5—but never a lot of it.

Like Dad, Mom had lost many teeth by middle years, and she wore upper and lower plates. Both cherished their remaining molars and the scattered incisors and bicuspids anchoring their dentures, Mom complaining a lot about chewing, Dad mostly stoic. She always claimed the tenderloin piece of a T-bone steak, and she loved to have "my son, the doctor" carve her very thin slices of roast meat.

Kay wore wedding rings and solitaires and party rings; Norm wore no rings. Kay always wore necklaces and brooches and bracelets; Norm wore a leather-banded gold watch with a small rectangular gold case until his third wife set him to collecting Rolexes and gold bracelets. Dad splurged on high quality buttoned overcoats but avoided belted models or Chesterfields; his most common wear was a lined hard-finished cotton or herringbone-textured wool raglan shell with lining, but he had blue cashmere and tan camel-hair square-shouldered midcalf coats at well. He always wore a trilby hat, though a Kongol might substitute at football games, and he always uncovered in greeting or indoors or in elevators. Mom filled the closet with outerwear in all varieties and stored some coats in furriers' vaults. She had rain coats in several styles, lightweight midcalf models and full-length wools, a good quality mink stole and at sixty a full-length mink. But she wore in winter almost always the coat she said kept her warmest, which she'd had made for her in Nepal and which the insurance company and she called snow leopard: Thirty-one years after her death Sandy discovered that it was civet cat.

ALWAYS A PUBLIC COUPLE

Whenever they left the President's Home, Dad and Mom expected to be seen and to have their appearance and behavior reported. If they were at a social event, chances were their names and often pictures would show up in the press. They were recognized and greeted in restaurants, pharmacies, grocery stores, parks, department stores, and gas stations. Rarely could they relax anywhere in Akron. To walk beside either of them in a strange city was to accompany someone lighter, almost carefree, which is one reason why Dad made opportunities for himself to live in New York and Washington, DC, for a couple of semesters each. And Mom made friends in Akron unassociated with the University or with newsworthy society in whose homes she could—as she would say—let her hair down.

What We Ate

"What We Ate" in the President's Home tracks a story of the plentiful American Century after the Second World War. It is also a story about the tastes of Norm, Kay, and the child who remained at home during their presidency. It is a story of preferences without privation. It is a story affected by technological and social change, transportation advances, commercial enterprise, and the rise of a sector of America's service industry. It won't tell you why you can find sushi and salad bars today in The University of Akron Jean Hower Taber Student Union. That's for you to extrapolate.

FAMILY FOODWAYS

At her parents' Chicago home when she arrived with toddler Ames for a three-week visit in January 1935, my mother Kay was served a late Thursday supper of "Montgomery" stew and mince pie, she wrote. (My father kept her dozen letters from this trip for sixty-eight years. It was their first separation since they wed on June 28, 1930.) The next night she helped her mother make cheese soufflé, plain spinach, baked apples, and chocolate pudding with whipped cream and turned down an invitation to dine out with her big sister Jo and some friends so she could enjoy her "favorites." For lunch on Saturday there were buckwheat pancakes, and for Sunday dinner sirloin of roast beef with carrots, potatoes, onions, and cauliflower, hot yeast rolls, and individual butterscotch pies for dessert. Sunday's simple supper was served in the library as tea, and she mentions rolls, cheese, apples, and cranberries. After a winter ice storm early the next week, Kay wrote that the "world outside looked glacéd like a taffy apple in a thick coating of ice." Two days later the Reverend Doctor Montgomery, then Professor of Homiletics at McCormick Theological Seminary (on whose grounds he and his wife and two of their daughters lived), held a subscription dinner for visiting clergy, and my mother took an unclaimed place among them and mailed home the mimeographed menu: oyster cocktail, bouillon with wafers, celery hearts with stuffed and ripe olives, baked beef tenderloin with mushrooms and parsley buttered potato balls, avocado pear and grapefruit salad, and lemon sherbet with light and dark cake, $1.10 per person. (For comparison: on this three-week trip, my mother's whole incidental travel budget was $5.00.) Her second Friday brought another meatless supper at the academic manse, prepared by Maman and Kay on the cook's night off: cheese and macaroni, baked apples, slaw, and gingerbread with butterscotch sauce.

Eighteen months later in July 1936, Mother and Ames visited Maman, Big Daddy, Jo, and Mary at Lake Wawasee where the first midday meal included corn cakes, eggs, bacon, milk, and cupcakes. Supper was macaroni and beef and raspberries. A couple of days later Kay lunched on a hamburger before an afternoon's fishing with her father. When friends arrived for a week's stay they brought two boxes of candy, a big chocolate cake, and a seven- or eight-pound rolled rib roast of beef still warm from the oven. Norm was to train up from Cincinnati after work on Friday: she wrote, will he bring two loaves of Vienna bread, sweet rolls, and a cake that he likes?

It was the height of the Great Depression, but my mother's family knew no dietary privation except of their own choosing: Fridays in the Presbyterian minister's home were always banyan days, not just in Lent. Here are some of the things about my grandparents' foodways that I infer from Kay's letters to Norm. Mostly they ate at home. They ate together. They did not snack. They ate heavier meals in the evening than at midday, except on Sundays. Other than some baked goods or some house presents, they ate foods of their own preparation. Except for canned vegetables (e.g., the "plain spinach" of the Chalmers Place supper), they ate fruits and vegetables of long storage life—apples, cabbage (as slaw), potatoes, carrots, onions, cauliflower, cranberries, raisins (in mince pie)—or in season (raspberries). Avocados, grapefruit, and oysters appeared at banquets, not at the home table. Eggs, butter, cream, milk, cheese, added sugar in cooked

A rare group portrait of the R. Ames Montgomery family nearly complete: only Norm is missing from this Wawasee photograph, summer 1934. Big Daddy and Maman, holding baby Ames, Bill Clark above Betty's shoulder, Mary holding baby Ames's hand, Jo behind, and Kay in front. *From the author's collection*

forms, beef (roasted, stewed, and ground), bacon, and milled grains (wheat and whole wheat, corn meal) provided most of their calories. Macaroni and dairy products were the few prepared or processed foods that came into the home. Fish joined the diet at Lake Wawasee only if they'd caught it. While chicken is never mentioned in the letters, I'm sure it found regular rotation, roasted or stewed but probably not fried. I think that there were pork chops and roasts, hams, and lamb chops in season.

From other facts I can extrapolate more about my grandparents' diet. For instance, I knew the condiment choices made by the Montgomery daughters in their own homes. Unlike others of my mother's generation, they did not keep cruets of vinegar and oil on their tables or always serve a chambered dish of sweet pickles, apple butter, and cottage cheese at lunch or dinner. The condiments for a Montgomery table were butter, salt, and ground black pepper only. The pepper was served from a shaker, already ground.

The times tell me some other things about their diet. In 1935, Charles Birdseye was just experimenting with his process of freezing fish and vegetables, the Heinz family only starting to market their remarkable ketchup and other condiments, and World War II with its great advances in food preservation and prepared canned food was still five years away. The range of food available was much smaller than mine would be eight decades later.

Nevertheless, they would eat some things which we wouldn't ever see except in commercial forms. Consider fruit preserved in the manner of cucumber or watermelon rind pickles. Still repeated ritually at my twenty-first-century festal table is the malicious question posed nine or ten decades earlier by one of Big Daddy's visiting sisters. "My goodness, Fanny," she said to her sister-in-law, surveying the Thanksgiving or Christmas feast of roast turkey, sage-celery-and-onion bread stuffing, mashed potatoes, baked candied sweet potatoes, mashed carrots and rutabagas (a family version of the Scots "clapshot"), (canned) green beans, cranberries thickened and popped open by boiling in sugar and orange zest, hot yeast rolls, butter, and gravy made in the turkey roasting pan by adding and whisking flour and milk over heat, "My goodness," she said as her brother carved the turkey, "you've gone to a lot of trouble for little ole me. Why, this is a feast! But, what about the pickled peaches?"

I know less about the Angebrandt-Auburn foodways than I do about the Montgomery traditions. In their place, I'll cite a couple of Angebrandt-Auburn dishes, but Mother was the cook of our family, and Dad (I would grow to understand) rejected for reasons of preference and perhaps aspiration the diet on which he had been raised for the first couple of decades.

When I began to make my own food choices and develop into a cook during the mid 1950s, frozen vegetables and home storage space for them extended the seasons, canned prepared foods simplified preparations or substituted for dishes once prepared from scratch, almost all baked goods were acquired rather than home produced, Eisenhower's interstate system brought California lettuces, grapes, broccoli, Florida oranges, tomatoes, green beans, and corn to our neighborhood Acme every week of the year, and the milkman delivered pasteurized milk, cream, and cottage cheese to us three times a week. There were Italian and Chinese restaurants within a short drive (though except for a very occasional pizza when Dad was away, we didn't patronize them). We ate most of our meals together, at home, and our evening meal was the largest. Our food was much more varied than my grandparents', and that which came into the house already prepared was fattier, saltier, more sugary, and more processed. Packaged cookies and potato chips supplied a lot of my calories as snacks. Bottled carbonated drinks, especially Coke, Vernor's, root beer, and on some wondrous occasions cream soda, waited in my refrigerator and those of my friends' parents. In hot weather I could access Popsicles and ice cream bars. I learned how to use money before I was nine chiefly for the power it gave me to acquire food. I watched Mom and Dad cook and imitated them and took opportunity to prepare things we all ate or I wanted for myself. Pictures show me as a chubby baby and toddler, and when I entered Western Reserve Academy in September 1959 in my fourteenth year, I stood 5'9" and weighed 180 pounds.

BREAKFAST

In Akron from 1951 until I left for the Academy, there were two or three breakfasts most days: Dad's, mine, and Mother's. Left to myself, I would have dunked graham crackers or Hydrox cookies in milk until I was sated. But under supervision, I drank juice and milk and took toast with peanut butter and jelly or ate cereal or anything else that was presented.

Dad's Breakfast

Dad's breakfast was routinized, and he made it himself. First, while his coffee dripped, he prepared half a glass of freshly squeezed orange juice by pressing and turning orange halves in a manual juicer: a rigid, sharpened, egg-sized stalagmite rising from the middle of a shallow lipped handled glass bowl. Seeds, pulp, and juice were released, and he would pour them through a small hand-held sieve into his glass. Later, perhaps 1960, Mom found him an electric juicer which incorporated a strainer and a rotating pulper but still required his pressing down the orange halves.

As coffee dripped and he reamed his orange halves for juice, his egg would be poaching. He had various stovetop egg poachers, flat two-inch deep covered pans with an insert that rested inside the stepped circumference of the pan with two or three two-and-a-half-inch diameter depressed half-spheres into which he cracked an egg when the water in the pan beneath the insert had reached a rolling boil; two or three holes between the cups permitted steam to escape, and a close fitting lid redirected the steam back down onto the cups, cooking the egg simultaneously from top and bottom. While his egg cooked, he would toast one piece of whole wheat bread, and with a soup spoon he would scoop out the glistening, still jiggling poached egg onto one-half piece of his dry toast. Together with a half glass of milk, a cup of coffee with cream, and a couple of tablespoonfuls of jelly on the other half of his toast, he would break his evening's fast. If I liked, he'd double all the ingredients and feed me, too. Very occasionally he'd agree to scramble eggs for us both, with just a little butter, but never would he fry eggs, because that took too much butter. We'd listen to WAKR radio and the bass voice of Martin Agronsky while he cooked and ate; he'd start his preparations at 6:45, and he'd be upstairs completing his toilet by 7:15 and out the door to work by 7:35 or 7:40, smelling of Old Spice aftershave and Dial soap from his shower.

Eggs and Pancakes

Mother arose usually in time to see him off—or both of us after we moved to the President's Home in 1956 and I would catch a ride to King School. On her own, she rarely took more than coffee and toast. If her and my breakfast eating schedules coincided, she would make us both scrambled eggs. We were a soft scrambled egg family, and we usually incorporated cream with the beaten eggs. We enjoyed other egg preparations as well—fried, coddled, soft boiled—which achieved cooked but still wet runny yolks and soft opaque but glistening whites.

Mom (and very occasionally Dad) made pancakes. By the time I was paying attention, the process started with a cup of commercial mix, either Bisquick or Aunt Jemima, and continued with a dollop of oil, an egg, something less than a cup of milk, and our hand-cranked egg beater. Commercial syrups could usually be found in our cupboards; all I remember is that they were not Karo, which Mom execrated, or molasses, which she thought low class. On occasion I'd get a taste of the pure maple syrup Mom and Dad reserved for themselves. If it were discovered after the batter was prepared that we were out of syrup, Mom took several spoonfuls of brown sugar, some butter, and some water and heated them in a small pan to a rolling boil. This thin concoction never satisfied me as much as the store-bought stuff, and secretly I preferred the commercially thickened syrups.

I preferred pancakes to waffles. We had an electric waffle iron by the mid-1950s, and before the days of Teflon and aerosol food oils, Mom made a batter incorporating enough fat that she could release perfect waffle after waffle from the teeth of the grill. To my tastes, the waffle is all crispness and no cake. I liked French toast, but we didn't make it often.

Cereals

Hot or cold cereals appeared on our breakfast table several times a month. I would eat a bowl of oatmeal with butter, raisins, and brown sugar with pleasure. Dad and Mom and I were content with Akron's own Quaker Oats in the round red-and-blue box with the picture of the smiling fellow with a white page boy haircut, an eighteenth-century neck cloth beneath a flat broad-brimmed blue hat such as parsons wore in the 1700s, who was supposed to represent our image of Pennsylvania's founding sect. Toward the end of life, Mom would relish the slow-cooked, steel-cut or chopped whole grain oat styles her daughter-in-law Mary Liz showed her, but she never went out of her way to acquire them, though she did experiment by cooking rolled oats in milk rather than water or adding raisins to plump up during the cooking. Cream of Wheat we had occasionally, and I won battles at Acme to try specialties like Maypo (heavily, cleverly advertised oatmeal incorporating a maple flavor) and some wheat product with chocolate whose brand name I don't remember.

We tried different kinds of cold cereal mostly because I'd keep asking—corn flakes, Cheerios, Kix, Puffed Rice, Puffed Wheat, Shredded Wheat, Raisin Bran (Dad's favorite), and all their sweetened cousins (mine). Mom and Dad were of the generation to whom the first highly processed cereal products like corn flakes and graham crackers were pitched as technological marvels and nutritional improvements with all the natural vitamins and minerals that were "steamed away" in old fashioned home-cooked porridges. But my parents were market aversive and still believed that real stick-to-your-ribs food involved heat and home preparation. I was predisposed, thus, to consider cold cereals rather an empty food, and so I did not know how to judge an evening ritual I observed as a second-grader in best-friend Johnny Swenson's household: all five of the Swenson children (eight and under) sitting down at seven-thirty at night in their pajamas eating bowls of cereal and milk before tooth brushing, bedside prayers, and lights out at eight-thirty. I knew that Polly Swenson fed her children an early supper soon after school at four-thirty or five (because she and Frank would dine together later, after he returned home from his residency in radiology), but I didn't have nearly enough parenting experience to admire her strategy in assuring a calming period before retirement, a pretty good reason to deny all other requests for post-dinner snacks, and a set of full tummies to encourage sleepiness and a quiet night's rest. Mostly, what bothered me about the Swenson nightly ritual was that no sugar was offered to sprinkle on the cereal.

Meat and Potatoes

We only occasionally had meat or potatoes at breakfast. Mom would dice and fry leftover baked potatoes, jackets and all, in butter, and she'd form leftover mashed potatoes into patties, dip them in beaten egg, roll them in breadcrumbs, fry them in butter, and call them potato pancakes. These I could have eaten daily, but rarely did we have the prime ingredient. I was happily confused by my first restaurant potato pancake, a latke, and then relegated Kay's mashed potato pancakes to the dusty corners of history's butler's pantry. I don't remember Mom's making home-fried or hash-browned potatoes from scratch, let alone latkes.

Bacon was the most frequent meat on our breakfast table, but sausage—sage-flavored breakfast links or patties—might appear for visitors, particularly Uncle Bill. Dad would eat none. So, our breakfast meats omitted a world I would discover which contained casing sausages, pork chops, small beef steaks, ham; or fish of any kind, kippers, Blind Robins, smoked white fish, lox, herring pickled or smothered, freshly fried smelts, cod cakes or salmon patties; never any organ meats, chicken liver or lamb's kidney. But Mom and I and Dick enjoyed one meaty standby and two rarely appearing meaty mixtures which I would have eaten weekly.

Composed Breakfast Meat Dishes

The most popular with me was corned beef hash, made not from scratch with our own leftover corned beef (for we never made any corned beef) but fried to a crispness as dumped from the squat fifteen-ounce Armour and Company can. Canned corned beef hash is an engineered product, like spam: no home cook ever diced potatoes so finely, though some nineteenth-century ship's cooks may have added as much slush (rendered tallow from boiling preserved beef) to their lobscouse as manufacturers do. Served with one or two poached eggs, whose runny yolks form a perfect liaison, crisped canned corned beef hash was my childhood perfect breakfast.

Scrapple and goetta were the two other meaty mixtures which Mom and I enjoyed when we didn't have to consider Dad's tastes. Both are mushes of boiled meats and grain shaped into loaves, cooled to congeal, then sliced into half-inch-thick pieces to be pan fried before being eaten with sweet or savory condiments and often eggs. Scrapple's origin is Pennsylvania Dutch hog slaughtering. Pig's heads and innards, particularly the liver, are cooked in water until connective tissue has dissolved and the bones are clean; the bones are discarded and all the meat finely chopped and returned to the cooking liquid with cornmeal and herbal seasonings and cooked until the slurry thickens, then poured into loaf pans and allowed to set until ready for use or storage. (A cousin of scrapple, panhaus, is made in a similar fashion, except that the chopped meat is not returned to the slurry but reserved for other purposes.) Scrapple bears resemblance to Irish and Scottish white pudding and the spicier West Country hog's-pudding, but it is arguably a New World product of the seventeenth century.

Goetta's origin is northwest Germany—Oldenburg, Hanover, Westphalia—as preserved by their emigrant Cincinnati descendants. My father distanced himself from many foods of his youth and other reminders of the relative poverty from which he sprung, but he would have eaten lots of goetta growing up, I think, just as would my mother during her Cincinnati years. Goetta starts with a pig's head, but no innards, and may add a calf's head or a meaty pork shoulder. Bulk is provided by oats, not cornmeal; onions and other chopped vegetables are sometimes added; and bay and thyme take the place of scrapple's sage, savory, and rosemary. After shaping and congealing, breakfast preparation involves the same frying of slices in fat, sometimes after a dusting of flour. Mom and I would eat store-bought goetta brought from Cincinnati by one of Mom's visiting sorority sisters.

Fruits

Our range of breakfast fruits expanded over the years. My father arranged things so he could always count on that half glass of fresh orange juice. He'd take a dish of stewed prunes, if Mom had made any, and he loved sectioned, seeded oranges and grapefruit, again if Mother were making them. He would add raisins to hot or cold cereals, and if he had a bit of leisure in the morning, he'd spoon his way through half a grapefruit with a sprinkle of sugar. He enjoyed melon, in season (and it was only in his eighth and ninth decades that out-of-season melons reached his price point), but Mother and I both lacked some digestive enzyme for melon and avoided it. Preserved fruits as jams and jellies were always available with strawberry a great favorite. Mom's treat was fresh red raspberries, with heavy cream. Curiously, raspberries could appear at breakfast, but fresh strawberries (another seasonal treat) were for lunch or supper. Of juices we rarely had any other than orange, though I do remember Dad in his high fifties wanting cranberry juice around, and I remember Walt the milkman sampling us with mixtures we never started buying from him.

Breakfast Breads

Instead of or in addition to toast, a great favorite after its mid-1960s creation was Sara Lee's pecan coffee cake. It was a pleasure to watch my disciplined father take a second piece. We rarely had doughnuts in the house, and if we did, Dad wouldn't eat them. I don't remember Mom preparing a coffee cake from scratch. The only breakfast muffins that I had heard of in the 1950s and early 1960s were corn or blueberry and didn't yet come in packaged mix forms, which meant we never had them except from the bakery, and all-in-one fruit-and-fiber muffins weren't marketed out our way before the 1990s. I don't remember breakfast biscuits or hot rolls, even after Pillsbury pioneered dairy-case-measured packages of dough. Bread for toast was white or whole wheat, usually Pepperidge Farm, never rye, never any soft micro-crumb Wonder Bread type, but sometimes raisin bread. When they came along, toaster treats like Pop Tarts or Eggo waffles arrived only once or twice in the house, always through my connivance. We all loved the buttery caramelized bottoms of cinnamon-nut swirl yeast rolls, but take-homes from Kaase's or the Women's City Club rarely were still around at breakfast time. I would devour whole cellophane-wrapped six-piece packages of some mass baker's half-size version of this treat; meant to be oven-warmed before eating (for which I never had time), they had the concentrated chewiness of under-baked cookies, but Mother regarded them with distaste.

LUNCH

Dad's Lunch

If he could make it for himself, as he did many Saturdays when he returned from the office at noon, my father's lunch would always be half a can of Campbell's vegetable beef soup, a piece of toast spread with peanut butter and eaten open faced with a leaf or two of iceberg lettuce, one or two tablespoons of Welch's grape jelly or Smucker's strawberry jam, taken from the spoon, and a glass of milk. The template admitted variations or additions: almost any homemade soup Mom made; four or five saltines or Ritz crackers; two slices of dried chipped beef from Armour's pry-lidded glass jar or one precut slice of boiled ham, on top of the peanut butter and below the lettuce; Jell-O with fruit or a slice of canned pineapple with a scoop of cottage cheese; one or two oatmeal or sugar cookies or graham crackers.

Considered from nutritional and sensory points of view, my father's habitual lunch balanced food groups and fiber, vitamins and minerals, proteins and carbohydrates and fats, warmth and cold, sweetness, saltiness, bitterness (the lettuce), very little sourness (no lemon, no vinegar, no pickles), and some umami or savory sensations (the broth of the meat soup, the flavor additives of the peanut butter), and a nice variety of textures from pasty through crispy and chewy.

He would not have felt satisfied without the soup. Fifty years earlier his father's lunch would almost always have included soup of his wife's making. In his own middle age, my father could open a can of his choosing, dump the contents into a sauce pan, fill the empty can with water and pour it into the pan, heat, stir, and serve. That must have felt like progress, especially to someone who liked to control his environment without putting himself under the obligation of receiving a favor or acknowledging an order obeyed. The range of choice Campbell's provided him in their condensed soups must have felt like progress, too. Many were familiar from amateur provenance, and many he had never tasted before. We sampled Heinz's condensed soups but stuck to Campbell's. We stocked our cupboard with cans of vegetable, vegetarian vegetable, vegetable beef, chicken noodle, chicken with rice, cream of celery, cream of mushroom, cream of chicken, green pea, split pea with ham, tomato, chicken bouillon, and beef consommé. By the 1960s, we would have tried Campbell's cream of asparagus, bean with bacon, cream of potato, Manhattan and New England clam chowder, Scotch broth, shrimp bisque, minestrone, and a few others.

Soup was frequent fare at our home, nutritious and satisfying. Mom encouraged me to make the cream soups with milk instead of water. If several of us were lunching together, she might make one of Dad's favorites, purée Mongol—a can of green pea and a can of tomato cooked with one can of milk and one can of water. I would heat for myself a can of vegetarian vegetable without water and greedily spoon out every bite of the salty, sweet stew, marveling at the occasional unfamiliar green disc-shaped things with the small brownish pink soft seeds (it was sliced okra, a vegetable we never otherwise tasted). I'd also make green pea soup with sliced Vienna sausages. Mom showed me how to mash and mix the cylindrical block of purée from dried peas with water and to dump the gelatin and juices in which the pale pinkish brown soft sausages were preserved, then cut the sausages into half-inch thick lozenges. Dad would take a scant bowl, and I'd finish the pot.

As for the new breakfast cereals, so for condensed soups Dad and Mom were the hard-sell demographic. Soup conjured mother in the kitchen, relief from hunger and cold, the first taste of food after the assembled family had bowed in prayer. With totemic associations like these, it is surprising that my parents were sold. Dried soup mixes, even the pretty good Knorr products like potato-leek or Lipton's French onion (which made a better base of chip dip than soup), couldn't compete. But good though Campbell's was, broader than the home cook's repertory and materials though its range, it wasn't homemade. Mom made three soups frequently—vegetable, lentil, and split pea.

Homemade Soups

Her vegetable soup ranged in character from borscht to minestrone, from tomato-beef consommé to goulash. In it she demonstrated cooking as improvisation, and its substance and style depended upon what remained in the refrigerator and pantry far more than what was written on a recipe card. Every variation had meat, chopped carrots and celery, and canned tomatoes. Most had diced potatoes and a little chopped onion. I don't remember macaroni, rice, beans, or thickeners like rolled oats or breadcrumbs. I'm sure she didn't use green pepper, garlic, canned tomato sauce, basil, oregano, and a little sugar (the flavor builders of Campbell's vegetarian vegetable), but she would throw in a handful of barley. The last heel of Sunday's rump roast on Thursday probably put into her head the idea of a vegetable soup, and she'd start by chopping it up. Leftover green beans or succotash or a package of Birdseye frozen mixed vegetables would join a can of tomatoes, a couple of cans of water, and some cubes of beef bouillon in the pot. Heat, time, and adjustments to taste made it soup. Never were two alike.

A consistent lentil soup she'd make from scratch, probably according to Hulda's recipe; it was a staple of my father's childhood, I think. Mom taught me to peel carrots and turn them into coin-sized slices with a serrated bladed knife (and since she never mastered the art of sharpening a blade or had high quality knives which would hold an edge, she idolized serrated knives and perforce taught me slicing rather than chopping). Mom would slice the peeled onion. Onions, celery, and carrots went into our largest pot (about six quarts) with sizzling butter and were stirred until the onions turned from white to translucent, when she'd open and pour in the one-pound bag of brown lentils and add enough water to fill the pot about two thirds, add a can of tomatoes, toss in a bay leaf and a quick pour of salt, bring the pot to a rolling boil, breaking up the tomatoes with a cooking spoon, then reduce the heat and cover and let it cook for one hour.

(Sometimes she used a pressure cooker. Then, when the lentils began to boil, she'd put on the heavy lid with its complementary die teeth and thick rubber gasket, rotate it until the dogs on the pan's circumference engaged and the handle of the lid joined the handle of the pot with a sealing *cha-clunk*, then place the little heavy round regulator disc [think five stacked half-dollar coins] on the steam vent in the middle of the lid, and adjust the heat under the pot until the rocking regulator made a steady *chugga-chugga-chugga* of about ninety to the minute. Then our soup would be ready in about fifteen minutes rather than an hour, but we couldn't make more than three quarts at a time.)

Halfway through the cooking she'd add diced potato. The soup was ready when the lentil skins were soft, the broth thickened and purplish-brown, the carrots and celery and potato soft, and the onions had mostly disappeared. Mom would fish around for the bay leaf and throw it away, and she'd let me open two cans of Vienna sausages and slice them and add them to the soup. Dad would take seconds of Mom's lentil soup, and he'd skip the peanut butter on his toast.

Split pea soup usually started from a different impulse—to use up a left-over ham bone—and it involved a proved home technology I saw employed for only one other purpose, to make applesauce. My favorite part of the cooking was the miracle of the Foley food mill. I enjoyed turning the handle and watching the pea seed coats rub against the perforations and be macerated as they were pushed through by the pressure of the blade; bits of meat and softened gristle, coins of carrot and crescents of celery slipped beneath the upward curve of the blade and reappeared in the pot as purée. It was an early lesson in mechanical advantage. Our split pea soup often had a distinct clove flavor and aroma from the fugitive hard buds that hadn't been picked off the left-over chunk of our home-baked ham.

I love casseroles to this day, and what are lentil and split pea soups but liquefied casseroles? Blending varieties of foods until their individual characteristics subordinate to a new whole with only one or two flavors or textures predominating strikes me as the great achievement of cookery. I was born at the right time and place to develop this taste, because in post-World War II America the vertically integrated food producing corporations were eager to turn wartime lessons in preparation and preservation into consumer products. Campbell's soups, Armour's processed meats or composed dishes like corned beef hash, new advances in freezing and storage were enlarging tastes. My mother had a full-time unpaid job as a college president's spouse, and though she knew how to can and preserve (I remember pouring warm paraffin on top of jars of her strawberry jam), even her traditional husband recognized the wisdom of eating Smucker's, Welch's, Libby's, or Del Monte's products rather than keeping her in the kitchen, as his mother had chosen.

Composed Luncheon Dishes

We had two composed luncheon dishes fairly regularly, creamed chipped beef, and baked beans. Jarred dried beef is a twentieth-century product of wars, an updating on the tuns of salted or pickled beef that fed Western navies from the sixteenth through the nineteenth centuries. These older cures left the cook needing to leach out preservatives by soaking and boiling before table preparation, during which lots of fat and flavor was lost along with the unpalatable amounts of salt. Drying for jerky achieved long storage life but left connective tissues whole, which then had to be broken down by chewing or by an intervening cooking process before the meat could be combined with other ingredients into something edible. For jarred dried or chipped beef, the meat was cooked, sometimes smoked, and formed into blocks and dried and then shaved; the shaved pieces (connective tissue now easily chewed) kept well preserved in an anaerobic environment and were palatable by themselves or when combined in other preparations. Dad loved a slice or two in a sandwich; I thought the taste strange to the texture. Mom liked creamed chipped beef over toast. She taught me how to make a béchamel sauce of flour cooked in hot butter and thickened with milk, seasoned with nutmeg or dried mustard, into which sliced ribbons of dried beef were quickly warmed. Dad would partake; perhaps he'd even call for it.

One time when Kay was searching for something hot to serve Sandy for lunch early in our marriage, my mother made a white sauce and heated slices of hot dog in it and called it "Pennies from Heaven." Raised in a family which never cooked meat with milk and with a father who had loathed creamed chipped beef on toast during his World War II basic training, Sandy found her store of daughter-in-law patience and tact tested by this novelty.

I like baked beans prepared with onions, bacon, and brown sugar. Canned baked beans had been available most of my parents' lives by the time I saw them made in my home. We bought Campbell's version, navy beans stewed in a sweetish tomato sauce with a bit of pork fat, but instead of serving them straight out of the can, we doctored them with one or two crumbled strips of bacon and a half cup of sautéed chopped onions and two or three tablespoons of brown sugar. It was the first composed luncheon dish that I attempted on my own, taking over from what my big brother Dickie had shown me. Dad always wanted some but never made a complete meal on them. I noticed a half-dozen variations of beans in various sauces by just one manufacturer on a recent trip to Acme.

DINNER

We ate our heaviest meal in the evening, usually at six o'clock, and called it dinner. We ate together as a family, seated at table in the breakfast nook or with company in the dining room. If my aunts or visitors were present, we said grace before Dad served, and for our words we always repeated together the simple prayer of The Manor—"Lord, we thank Thee for this food, for life and health and every good. Amen"—which I imagine Big Daddy wrote for the handicapped boys. We shared conversation as well as food. If Dad were listening to a record on the hi-fi (as he might on a Saturday or Sunday afternoon when he worked in his study), he'd turn it off. Once or twice I remember the radio's playing a Zips basketball or football game, but we never had the television on during a meal even after we acquired a portable in the late 1960s that could come into the breakfast nook, except for one occasion when television trumped dinner: November 22, 1963, when we ate from our laps in the solarium so as not to miss any coverage of our national tragedy.

Meats

One meat, one green or yellow vegetable, one starchy vegetable, and a salad usually involving fruit formed the template of our dinners. Mother and Dad believed that everyone should partake of the same dishes without regard to individual preferences and that Dad's antipathy to foods and preparations highly seasoned or rich in fats should guide the template. Mom's culinary traditions were grounded in the educated affluent Scotch-Irish experience of agrarian Midwest America, enriched by living in Iowa, Kentucky, and southern Ohio. Their household usually had a cook as well as a maid-of-all-work who were directed by a trained physician partnered to a sometimes dyspeptic, gentle authoritarian. Dad adopted most of Mom's culinary traditions, just as he had adopted many of the mores, manners, and attitudes of the Presbyterian servant/leader family into which he married. He had been raised in a second-generation German immigrant Cincinnati household living from pay envelope to pay envelope upon the earnings of a draftsman whose wife helped to assure solvency through domestic economy. While Dad grew up on fruits and vegetables preserved by his mother's hands, many were combined in composed dishes meant to retain most of the fats of the meats she could afford, and he put this tradition behind him as soon as he could. Working longer hours than his fellows, disciplining himself to eat lightly and to hold in check a love of sweets, avoiding the beer and *Gemütlichkeit* and the sausage and schnapps which characterized his contemporaries—Norm believe these habits permitted him to rise above his parents and to maintain his health.

I rarely saw tension in the mixture of my parents' traditions and attitudes toward food. Mom and Dad had spent twenty-five years together by the time I sought to influence dinner choices, and a rich set of compromises and mutual respect led to peaceful coexistence at the dinner table. Dad may not have appreciated the hint of rue in Mother's responses that "Daddy wouldn't like" the exotica I suggested we try, and Mother did not always appreciate the glances he threw her way as she rebuttered her baked potato or sopped up the meat drippings, but I never heard any overt recriminations. Except for the fact that I increasingly felt Dad's choices were more discretionary than he characterized them, it was no worse than living with, say, a diabetic in the family.

Simply prepared meat centered most dinners, and tender cuts of beef predominated. At least once a week, Mother chose T-bone or porterhouse steaks or ground round (90% lean) hamburger patties; one pound of uncooked meat served the three of us generously with leftovers. She broiled the meat in our electric oven—our first outside grill was a small hibachi acquired after a University Classrooms Abroad trip took the President and Spouse to Asia in the late 1960s—until well done and brought the meat in the broiler pan to the table where Dad would share the hamburgers (no buns) or cut the steak into three or four portions, always reserving the tenderloin for Mom, the "dental cripple," as she styled herself. Salt was our seasoning, though when I discovered A-1 sauce in restaurants I lobbied for our having some at home. Mother would soak up the pan drippings with a slice of Pepperidge Farm white bread, and sometimes I would share a few bites and wonder what she valued in it; Dad wouldn't touch it. With steaks Mom would try to convince Dad that he could enjoy his meat cooked medium well or even medium, but he was suspicious of a pink center and would ask her to return his portion to the broiler. (When I could make my own choices, I came to prefer the sirloin portion cooked medium rare, red but not purple. Dick rebelled. He instructed the restaurant chef to heat the grill, place the meat on it, turn it over, take it off, and bring it to him "still mooing," purple and cool in the center and barely marked on the outside.) Dad would cut off and discard any visible fat.

Vegetables

With a steak or hamburger we would usually have a frozen vegetable—green peas, baby lima beans, chopped spinach, French cut (julienned) green beans, chopped broccoli, or occasionally Brussels sprouts—or fresh broccoli spears. Mom would liberally salt just enough water not to evaporate completely in the cooking, so she wouldn't drain away the vitamins, she said; and she always added a small pat of butter to the hot vegetables and shook them in the pan to melt it before turning them into a serving dish. When they became available in frozen form, she would serve mixed vegetables or peas with carrot cubes or lima-bean-and-corn succotash. In my memory, these frozen combinations were not available until the late 1950s, or it could have been that Mom didn't start buying them until we had a refrigerator with a larger freezer compartment after we moved into the President's Home.

I was not as fond of a head of cauliflower as were Mom and Dad, even when sprinkled with toasted buttered bread crumbs, but I learned to prefer Mom's preparation to the flaccid watery frozen florets then available. Occasionally Mom would peel and slice and steam fresh carrots, and a few times she sliced celery, browned it in a bit of butter, then steamed it with salted water. We never had cabbage by itself or hard squash or summer squash. Turnips, parsnips, rutabagas and the like appeared only in holiday combinations. In season we'd have asparagus, which I liked, sweet corn (Mom always cut her portion off the cob), fresh green beans (which Mom topped, tailed, snapped, and cooked with a piece of bacon). After frozen versions supplanted them, we did not have any canned vegetables other than sweet potatoes, green beans in an emergency, corn out of season, baby beets or sliced beets, and stewed tomatoes. Though I came to love combinatorial tomatoes in almost any form, I did not relish the sweet Del Monte stewed tomatoes which Mom served Dad with cubes of bread to sop up the liquid. I liked beets in all preparations, whole, sliced, julienned, cubed, with or without the sweet-and-sour corn-starch-thickened sauce which made them "Harvard" style, but I don't recall Mom making them from scratch.

Although corn or beets and even lima beans might appear as our starchy vegetable in complement to a green one or Mom would serve canned sweet potatoes baked with marshmallows, brown sugar, and butter, the baked white potato most frequently accompanied a dinner centered by broiled beef. Mom scrubbed and washed russet (Idaho) potatoes and pierced them with a fork in two or three places and baked them for an hour in a 350-degree oven, moving them to a lower rack before broiling the meat. She'd slice them in half lengthwise and place them on our plates in the kitchen, and we'd add our own salt, pepper, and butter at table. I needed no encouragement, only more butter, to eat the skins. A great treat seldom enjoyed was the twice-baked potato. Flossie Lewis often provided them for catered dinner parties, with sour cream, shredded cheddar cheese, and perhaps some onion, garlic powder, or fresh minced scallions—and Dad would eat them.

Salads

Almost all our salads started with iceberg lettuce, which we called "head lettuce," ignoring the many other kinds which grow in heads. Just as I knew no leafy green cooked vegetable other than spinach, so I knew almost no lettuce other than iceberg. Most salad greens did not survive cross country transit before the invention of multi-layered polymer packaging and antioxidizer additives in the 1980s. But the hardy iceberg was reliable, ubiquitous, and affordable by the 1950s. To my parents, whose childhood memories of fresh greens in winter were bounded by white and red cabbage, it was a luxury. Romaine was available out of season by the 1960s, but our family's alternative to iceberg was Boston Bibb, and it was sufficiently dear that I was rarely offered any. Moreover, except in sandwiches where its roles in differentiating layers and varying textures predominated, we didn't so much eat lettuce as eat off it.

Our salads were arrangements of fruits on lettuce leaves: one or two rings of canned pineapple or halves of canned peaches or pears with two or three tablespoons of cottage cheese; canned fruit cocktail or peach slices suspended in Jell-O; very occasionally a Jell-O-based mock tomato aspic of grated carrots and chopped celery; even more rarely a slaw or a carrot-and-raisin salad or "heavenly hash" (mandarin oranges, chopped or miniature marshmallows, chopped nuts, raisins or crushed pineapple, and grated coconut), though these depended upon mayonnaise or heavy cream binders normally on the NPA Index Dietarium Prohibitorum. Almost never would we have a tossed salad—torn pieces of lettuce mixed with thinly sliced cucumbers, grated or finely chopped carrots, sliced radishes, and tomato wedges—though Mom and I enjoyed them with an oil-and-vinegar or a bottled French dressing but omitted or picked out the cucumbers for the same reason we both avoided melon. Perhaps once a year Mom would make Thousand Island dressing and serve it with a wedge of iceberg lettuce: chopped green pimento-stuffed olives, chopped or sieved hardboiled eggs, chopped black olives, bound with Miracle Whip and a couple of tablespoons of ketchup and salt and pepper and paprika; Dad would take a scant tablespoon to our half cups.

Even more than pineapple with cottage cheese on lettuce, Dad liked seeded sectioned oranges. Mom would peel an orange over a bowl to catch the juice. Still able to remember a time in her life when the fruit was so precious that finding one in the toe of her Christmas stocking was a delight, she'd offer me the peel so that with my teeth I could carefully scrape the clinging juice-filled capsules from the bitter white pith.

Our template dinner, then, comprised four elements: meat, vegetable, starchy vegetable, and salad. We almost never had a soup course or a dessert course, because the fruit of our salad stood in for dessert. Bread was always available but not actually planned as part of the meal; rolls or biscuits accompanied party but not family dinners before the advent of convenience preparations. Rarely did our starch choice turn to macaroni, noodles, beans, or rice. While the template did not vary much, its major components did.

Variations: Meats

We enjoyed other broiled meats, especially lamb chops (loin, not shoulder) or ham steaks or occasionally pork chops. We would have small tender roasts of beef, say the sirloin tip. For large gatherings there might be standing rib roasts, still pink in the middle with Dad told to be content with an end slice. Once every couple of years we had a fresh ham, that is, an uncured leg of pork: never had so much tender pork been served in a single slice. On regular occasions when she could plan for leftovers, Mom would roast a whole chicken; affordable separate chicken parts didn't become available in our grocery stores until the 1970s, otherwise our family would have eaten a lot of chicken breast. We didn't eat tougher cuts of meat which require marinating or macerating before quick fatless cooking in thin slices or slow moist cooking in chunks or on the bone. Thus I first encountered Swiss steaks, flank steaks, veal cutlets, London broils, shish kabobs, brisket, pot roasts, short ribs, shanks, beef, pork, lamb, and veal stews outside the home. Ditto cured and smoked meats other than ham. On the other hand, in Mom's kitchen I had calves' liver and meatloaf.

From first bite, I have always found something palatable in liver, even including tougher beef liver held on a steam table. I attribute my liver love to Mother's preparation. While she could broil a piece of calves' liver very acceptably (it's tricky not to overcook it in a broiler), even Dad waived his edict against frying for a piece of her calves' liver twice a month. Mom would open and spread out the butcher paper containing the pound or so she had chosen at Acme. With the tip of a sharp knife she'd cut out any large visible veins or membrane, rinse and dry her hands, sprinkle salt and pepper on both sides, then grab a handful of flour and dust the meat all over, shaking off the excess. Meanwhile in her largest skillet she melted a large dab of butter just to the browning stage, and with every other dinner component ready, she'd lay the pieces of liver in a single layer, watch, turn, watch, and serve. If she were perfect in her timing, and cut a piece right then, the cross section would show the slightest dusky pink and some juices would run. By the time the meat had rested during the two or three minutes before Dad served my plate, the hint of pink would disappear but the juiciness would remain, a crisp outside bite would cover the smooth slightly grainy but mostly pasty texture of the interior, and a rich umami sensation would predominate within the slightly sour and salty iron taste while tongue and hard pallet as much as molars pulverized the meat. If there were bacon in the house, I'd urge her to fry four or five slices and drain away most of the fat before finishing the liver in the same pan. Dad not only endured this preparation; he would eat a strip or two of bacon with his liver. He would not object strenuously to another innovation I learned to request—frying two or three sliced onions in bacon grease before cooking the liver—but he did object to piling the cooked onions on top of the liver, so Mom kept them separate. Lamb kidneys, pâtés, or chopped chicken livers hot or cold or even *foie gras*: they don't compare to Kay Auburn's calves' liver.

I've had better meatloaf than hers. She produced a good one, but she was limited by acceptable ingredients, and she aimed at a low-fat version. Her meatloaf began with one pound of ground round beef steak (90% lean), one small finely chopped onion all evidence of which had to disappear before Dad's appearance, salt, pepper, one egg, and six to eight saltine crackers loosely crumbled. She'd knead these together with her hands vigorously and shape the paste into an ovoid loaf, which she placed on an edged cookie sheet with a single whole bay leaf pressed onto the top, then baked for one hour at 350 degrees. I loved this meatloaf, particularly with ketchup bathing each bite.

Meatloaf and liver nights meant better odds for mashed potatoes. While Dad wouldn't add a pat of butter or use gravy, he loved mashed potatoes enough to lift his ban on its important fatty dairy ingredients. Mashed potatoes always accompanied another favorite meat preparation, city chicken. Sometime in the Depression along the western ridings of the Alleghenies from Binghamton to Cincinnati, butchers pressed inch-and-a-half cubes of pork onto thick four- or five-inch wooden skewers and sold it as a low-cost alternative to chicken, one of which was decidedly not in every pot across America because most of them were being grown, slaughtered, and consumed locally outside of cities. (Perdue and Tyson got into broiler chickens only in the 1940s, and neither distributed beyond their regions until the 1970s. In the 1950s and 1960s, Mom could count on buying a whole stewing chicken or a capon or even a three-pound broiler/fryer most anytime, but she'd have to go to a butcher shop to buy separate chicken parts.) A skewer of city chicken could make a handheld meaty snack the size of a large chicken drumstick, and from Pittsburgh eastward (claims one authority) it was breaded and baked or breaded and deep fried. From Cleveland southwestward the filled skewers were dusted in flour, browned in fat, then braised in broth or water. In Akron, veal cubes alternated with pork, and the braised result was fork-tender white meat with the pan juices forming a nice gravy. We ate it once a month. It was the closest thing to a stew—that is, a braised meat-based dish—that my mother made regularly.

Other than salmon croquettes, which Mom made by picking out the bones and skin from canned salmon and combining the meat with breadcrumbs, egg, and seasoning before pan-frying, I don't remember any fish made at home other than an occasional fish stick dinner after the mid 1950s when Dad was away. We didn't have tuna salad or tuna casserole. I discovered shrimp, crab, and lobster elsewhere and never had a scallop until I ate one on the East Coast. I have no memory of a whole or filleted fish baked, broiled, or pan-fried at home and no memory of tasting clams or oysters, not even in a Campbell soup, except at restaurants. Yet I know that I saw Mother make a creamed seafood Newburg of some kind and load it into her own broad scallop shells and sprinkle it with buttered breadcrumbs and brown it under the broiler, but that must have been for luncheon guests. Since Dad didn't eat most cheeses other than cottage cheese, we rarely had macaroni and cheese or cheese soufflé, though I remember Mother making both just as she had with her mother at Chalmers Place in Chicago twenty years before.

Variations: Composed Dinner Dishes

We had three one-dish meals in at least annual rotation and a fourth (the only baked casserole I remember) that we always ate together annually. Dad associated steamed sauerkraut and pork with his least cherished childhood memories and perhaps his most painful digestive experiences, yet he enjoyed joining Mom and me for her version, which was simplicity itself: two pounds of closely trimmed, lean-as-possible pork spare ribs cut into two- or three-rib pieces, seasoned and covered with a well-rinsed twenty-two-ounce can of sauerkraut, pressure-cooked until the meat fell off the softened bones, eaten over mashed potatoes. I wouldn't choose that preparation today, but my cousins ask me at least once a year to make my version of sauerkraut with brown sugar, caraway seed, onions, and carrots with a less fatty cut of pork well browned before baking covered for three hours, and at least every other year I'll gather smoked pork chops and slab bacon and four or five kinds of sausages to make a wine-infused, sweetened *choucroute* with lots of extra carrots and onions.

Hulda Auburn with thirteen-year-old Norman, 1918. *From the Norman Auburn Papers. Courtesy of Archival Services, University Libraries, The University of Akron*

Another dish in Mom's pressure-cooker repertory was a New England boiled dinner of carrots, potatoes, onions, cabbage, and either a piece of beef brisket or a meaty joint of ham. Corned beef brisket with oven-roasted carrots, potatoes, and onions and steamed cabbage fills that niche in my adult life. And I've certainly moved far away from Mom's chili: a pound of ground round browned then simmered for thirty or forty minutes with a twenty-two-ounce can of tomatoes, a fourteen-ounce can of kidney beans, a cup of chopped celery, a chopped onion, and one or two tablespoons of McCormick chili powder, served over mashed potatoes, which was Mom's childhood preparation.

Every year the last Saturday of July would be Parents' Day at the Manor, and the big trays of "train wreck" of which we partook at the luncheon buffet must have been Betty Clark's version of the Montgomery "macaroni and beef" Kay mentions in her Wawasee letters to Norm. Anyone who had dined at Columbus's well-known restaurant/lunch room on "Johnny Marzetti" would have recognized it: browned ground beef with sautéed onions and green peppers, mixed with chopped canned tomatoes and tomato sauce and seasoned with a bit of basil and oregano, combined with cooked medium broad egg noodles and about one pound of shredded cheese to each pound of noodles, baked one hour in a medium hot oven covered until the last fifteen minutes. Dad ate it only out of politeness, so we didn't make it at home.

Despite her busy schedule as a President's wife, Mother was an active cook, and Dad loved many of the specialties they shared together. Mom's corn pudding used just-picked sweet corn sliced off the cob mixed in eggs whipped with whole milk, butter, and salt baked until the custard set up and browned lightly. That was one of Fanny Montgomery's favorites. Mom watched her mother-in-law Hulda make a creamed spinach, and I wish I could have, too, for I still have many questions about my favorite vegetable preparation. Kay's version depended upon two packages of frozen chopped spinach, cooked in a splash of salted water and drained in a colander. While the spinach cooked she chopped an onion and browned two or three pieces of bacon, set them to drain and crisp up and spooned off much of the fat. Now she sautéed the onion, and when it turned translucent, she sprinkled flour evenly and stirred to coat and cooked, and just before the roux turned brown, she turned the spinach into the skillet, stirred, grated about half a nutmeg over it, crumbled one half the bacon, mixed, tasted and adjusted the seasonings, spooned it into a serving dish, and crumbled the remaining bacon on top. Dad enjoyed this preparation, and he associated it with the dish his mother had made. Today, I can't imagine how Hulda, who died before the wide distribution of frozen food or fresh spinach out of season, made her version, except with canned spinach. We didn't eat spinach that way, although it was certainly part of the Montgomery family offerings.

When the Breadwinner Was Not Home

When Dad was away, Mom's cooking palette expanded to include onions in noticeable quantity, green pepper, garlic, mushrooms, cheeses, and composed one-dish meals of many kinds. She'd whip up curries of leftover lamb, beef, or chicken served on Minute Rice, and they were so good that I was in my forties before I discovered that I could cook a curry from fresh ingredients. She'd make macaroni and cheese or macaroni and beef just for the two of us and for the luncheon leftovers. She gave leftover chicken the same treatment as chipped beef, or she'd use cream instead of milk and a jar of chopped pimentos and fold in beaten egg and top the result with toasted slivered almonds for chicken à la King. She made a Spanish rice with ground beef—meaty, filling, but bland. She'd heat up and doctor with fresh celery and additional water chestnuts canned chop suey and taught me to oven-toast the canned crooked fried wheat sticks La Choy sold as "chow mein noodles" for a delicious sprinkle that I'd reapply after every third or fourth bite. She'd grind up leftover ham including its fat and add breadcrumbs and egg and seasonings and make a ham loaf with pineapple rings baked on top. She taught me how to cook with Campbell's soup, sautéing extra mushrooms (for instance) to add to the green bean casserole with French fried onion topping or baking rice with broccoli, mushroom soup, and cheese or saucing browned ground beef and cubed potatoes and sautéed onions with soup to make a creamy hash that would crisp up on the bottom. She'd whip up an omelet stuffed with onions, green pepper, and chunked ham Western style or with mushrooms and cheese in a French manner.

Dad's being away was also occasion for experimentation with prepared frozen foods, which were beginning to proliferate by the late 1950s. I was eight or so when the first TV dinners appeared. The molded multicompartment aluminum foil trays (developed originally for airline meals) tickled me perhaps more than the food. I could soon be trusted to heat my own if both Mom and Dad were gone at dinner time. A retired Swanson executive once claimed that the 1953 introduction of these TV dinners was a solution to market unsold frozen Christmas turkey, and certainly I remember sliced turkey over stuffing covered by gravy in the large central compartment accompanied by whipped potatoes and cut green beans as one of my favorites. I liked fish sticks or fish fillets accompanied by macaroni and cheese. I enjoyed Swiss steak with mashed potatoes. My only problem with TV dinners from ages ten to thirteen as I shot up in height and added girth was portion size, and it was 1969 before the Hungry Man sizes arrived too late, for I was married and we were cooking our way through Julia Child then.

An age-peer friend of mine teases his ninety-six-year-old mother by saying that the best dish of his youth was her Banquet pot pie. Nothing was perfect about Banquet or Swanson's pot pies. The three or four pieces of beef or turkey always included at least one that was gristly; too often the carrot cubes or peas wouldn't be soft when everything else was hot; the bottom crust was invariably undercooked and pasty (one of them, either Banquet or Swanson, had a bottom crust, and the other didn't) and the top crust would often burn before it browned, and it was never light and flaky like Aunt Betty's pie crust. But I loved them. I loved beef, turkey, and chicken pot pies, perhaps chicken the best. I'd eat two.

Some frozen items first explored during nights when Daddy didn't eat with us made their way into a regular rotation in our template dinner. Mother never deep fried at home or pan fried with more than a quarter inch of oil; we didn't own a fry basket or a draining tray or an oil skimmer or any of the paraphernalia a committed fry cook gathers. But she and I loved French fried potatoes, and when Ore-Ida began marketing fried potato products which could be prepared in the oven, Mom was an early adopter. The novelty and convenience of having something at least as good as reheated leftover restaurant French fries outweighed its inferiority to the fresh products of deep frying. We experimented with the different preparations manufacturers offered, hoping that we'd find more consistent crispness in crinkle cuts or less absorbed oil in steak fries and were disappointed, though we still ate our fill. One product proved good enough to serve to Dad, the compressed large pellets of shredded potatoes called Tater Tots. In those days prior to mandatory nutritional labeling, while the texture and flavor suggested copious fat in the preparation (since nothing but fat can establish crispness and spread flavors so well on the tongue), the effect in digestion was not so obvious, and Tater Tots became an occasional substitute for baked potatoes.

One manufacturer of frozen food gained enthusiastic adoption not only because the products were much to our taste, but also because of its local origin. Stouffer's macaroni and cheese, green beans and spaetzle, and spinach soufflé delivered consistent quality and formed my expectations for each dish. Mom said they were expensive, but she felt she was supporting a local industry. A farm couple in nearby Richfield had opened a coffee shop in the 1920s; their sons had expanded to Cleveland and Chicago and a few other big cities and positioned their restaurants on the top floors of skyscrapers and responded to customers' requests for frozen versions of their signature heartland dishes. While central Ohio's Marzetti family moved more cautiously in marketing, say, their famous boiled sweet-and-sour poppy-seed dressing or their perfect-every-time base for coleslaw, they didn't manage to produce versions of their noodles-and-beef or creamed chicken with cornbread as did the Stouffers's sons for their mother's recipes. Dad particularly liked Stouffer's baked apples: peeled and seeded sections of Jonathans in a thick cinnamon-flavored syrup cooked to a tender-but-still-resistant bite.

Stouffer's baked apples would be a dessert with our template dinner. My preadolescent years coincided Mom's and Dad's middle-age spreads, and so a separate dessert course at home was rare. But Mom made great desserts. She stewed peaches, pears, plums, and apples, and in his last decade Dad loved my turning one of his adult grandchildren's Christmas gifts of boxed pears into peeled halves stewed in sugar and wine, definitely not the way the parson's daughter had made them. At least once every autumn, Mom would transform a half peck of apples into applesauce and enlist me to crank the Foley food mill. She'd bake leftover rice with egg, sugar, and milk into individual ramekins of rice custard, and very occasionally she'd enlist me to stir while she converted freshly cooked rice in slow cooking milk and sugar into rice pudding. She made a bread pudding with eggs and raisins and sometimes made a custard or a hard sauce (one of the few times she cooked with liquor) to complement it. She made sweet crisp and chewy meringue shells to serve under sliced, sugared, and slightly mashed strawberries. She no longer made pies except for holiday feasts; Ames and Dick remembered lots of homemade pies from Cincinnati days. She baked date bars, Tollhouse cookies, oatmeal raisin cookies, and oatmeal chocolate chip cookies fairly often, and she always brought several tins when we went at Christmas to Jonesville. (I did not share her preference for walnuts over pecans in bars and cookies.) Fifty years after enjoying Mom's version at home I encountered floating island in a Jakarta restaurant—a smooth yellow egg-yolk-based custard topped by stiff sweetened egg-white meringue. She made puddings from boxed mixes, glad to not make them from scratch anymore, and she was happy to get more milk into me by means of Junket, a brief-lived commercial mix that made loose fruit-flavored puddings based on rennet-curdled milk. And she loved ice cream, which we bought from Walt the milkman in half-gallon boxes: coffee and mint chocolate chip were her favorites.

SNACKS

Some families regularize between-meal eating by having morning coffee, afternoon tea or pre-dinner cocktails, or mid-to-late evening rituals like the Swensons' pre-bedtime cereal. We did not. I almost never saw Dad eat something except at breakfast, lunch, or dinner. Only later did I learn that he would often take coffee at work midmorning and that most of his suit coats had a small cache of fruit-flavored or butterscotch hard candies. Occasionally I saw him take a half glass of milk and a cookie mid evening, especially when he was writing speeches. Mom, however, regularly nibbled on something between meals, particularly in the evening, and she became my snacking enabler and partner.

Aunt Betty and Aunt Jo accused me of balancing a tall stack of oatmeal chocolate chip cookies cupped underarm and concealed against my body at Christmas as I crept from the kitchen of their Jonesville home up the grand staircase. I think the snack thief of their memory was Dick. Perhaps I later copied him. After homemade oatmeal chocolate chip, Mom's favorite cookie was Hydrox, and hence it became mine. Oreos are no substitute. We usually had graham crackers, sometimes vanilla wafers, Lorna Doones, occasionally fig newtons around. We rarely had ginger snaps, lemon wafers, or coconut crisps. When Archway pioneered larger square soft chewy fruit-filled oatmeal cookies, a kind of crossover to the date bars Mom made in Cincinnati but rarely in Akron, we discovered the standard on which I snacked well into the new century. Mom and Dad welcomed Pepperidge Farms' entry into mass cookie marketing, especially their various short-bread-inspired chocolate-filled sandwiches, which I enjoyed mostly because of their being treated as premium items reserved to the senior members of the household.

It was a mystery to preadolescent me how boxes of candy arrived in the home but never where they were stored—always somewhere in a bookcase in the living room of 344 Merriman Road or the solarium of

856 Mayfair Road, close by where Mom read or watched TV. Why was only dark-chocolate-coated candied orange peel or nut-studded nougat-wrapped crystallized ginger left in the box? Mom took me to Blossom Shop or Mary Coyle's, where I learned that one could specify each piece in a custom-filled box, and I dreamed of my own box with nothing but milk-chocolate-covered caramels and peanut clusters. But I found as much comfort in a Mounds or Almond Joy or Mars bar as in their fresher locally made cousins. Pilferage in Jonesville of Aunt Jo's private supplies introduced me to Buns, three-inch circles of salty Spanish peanuts set in vanilla- or maple-flavored divinity covered in thick milk chocolate. My mother's dental challenges easily surmounted the hard bite of the buttery nut-studded toffee of her favorite Heath bars.

Mom's favorite savory snack was Fritos, followed by potato sticks. But if there were dip in the house, she'd admit potato chips or dunk her Fritos. Dad was no absolute abstainer from a chip or two, if he caught us at it, but mostly he avoided them as he did salted nuts. She countenanced my making popcorn but rarely proposed it, and we never purchased prepared or flavored popcorn, though holiday tins had a way of emptying.

Mother licensed my experimenting with chip dips by having on hand ingredients like cream cheese, cottage cheese, sour cream, and lots of dried herbs and spices and seasonings in her cabinets and by partaking of the results. It was I who probably brought the first Rice Crispy Treat into the house, but other savory commercial cereal-based mélanges proved more popular, particularly Ralston-Purina's Chex mixes baked in the oven with butter and Worcestershire sauce and peanuts. Gift cannisters supplemented oatmeal chocolate chip cookies as holiday offerings.

Savory snacks demand liquid. Dad had coffee at the close of dinner, and he'd sometimes take his cup to the living room while he read the *New York Times* for the previous day (it came by mail a day late) and I waited for him to shoot baskets or play ping pong after he judged his meal to be settled. If he later had a snack, he'd drink milk with a cookie. When Mom had cleaned the kitchen (I would clear the table and rinse and stack the dishwasher, she put away leftovers and wash the pans), she always poured herself a twelve-ounce bottle of Coca-Cola over ice to take to her comfortable chair and ottoman in the solarium where she would smoke and read and sometimes watch television.

I drank milk if I snacked on cookies, but by the time I was ten or so my drink of choice was Coca-Cola. In 1963 I adopted Tab, Coca-Cola's sugar-free product, and I segued to Diet Coke in 1982 when it came on the market, leaving it off only in my sixties. Just as I never drank the last of Dad's milk, so I never took the last of Mom's Cokes. Away from home I tried many other carbonated drinks. I loved the smooth nonacidic undercharged frothy spice of A&W root beer, either in chilled mugs at the drive-in stand or in the wax paper takeaway cylinders filled from a tap. Vernor's, the vanilla-flavored ginger ale from Detroit, pleased me. And I would always snatch cream soda (the bottled version of the fountain vanilla phosphate, but clear and sometimes raspberry flavored) from a picnic tub.

"Eat a piece of fruit" I told my children in the 1970s and 1980s. Sandy's mother Pearl Korman was diagnosed diabetic soon after she gave birth to her only child, and she taught her daughter always to have a bowl of fresh fruit available for snacking. Why wasn't hand fruit regularly available in my childhood home? Since the Spanish American War bananas have been ubiquitous and inexpensive throughout the continental United States. Apples have never been out of season since Red Delicious was hybridized. Grapes, it is true, were still fairly expensive in my childhood, but they were within my mother's food budget as surely as cookies and chips. Pears were defying seasons before Harry and David pioneered mail-order fruit. I can remember when nectarines and tangerines began to appear, and I know that peaches and plums were available winter and spring because Mom would stew them for Dad.

DINING OUT

When I returned to Akron in 1991, I invited my father to join me at a banquet at Tangier's, and he said, "You'll be eating a lot of meals here," which proved true, Tangier's being then the only facility with convenient parking in west Akron that could serve a hot sit-down meal to four hundred or more guests in less than an hour, including speeches. Dad's public responsibilities during his previous forty years in Akron made him a connoisseur of banquet food and service. He and Mom had overseen the logistics to feed three hundred people at a time at the President's Home, and he had expanded the Gardner Student Center in the mid-1960s to include the multipurpose Hilltop Dining Room with facilities open to the public to serve five hundred. Sharing meals in public was an important means for him to do business.

He appreciated restaurants that offered discrete, attentive, prompt service at tables covered with good linen and weighty silverware in unobtrusive, well-lit, quiet atmospheres with menus broad enough to meet his own needs and the usually different tastes of his companions, places well established but not trendy, "rich but not gaudy," costly but not expensive. I ate with him at Morton's in Chicago, Aunt Pitty Pat's Porch in Atlanta, Durgin Park in Boston, Bookbinder's in Philadelphia, Luchow's and the University Club and Keen's Chophouse and the Pierre in New York City, Gage and Tollner's in Brooklyn, Blackie's and the Cosmos Club in Washington, DC, the Fontainebleau and Wolfie's in Miami Beach—only the last was not to his taste. In Akron his favorite was the Akron City Club until during his second marriage he joined the Portage Country Club.

Akron City Club

I think the Akron City Club reminded Norm of the Cincinnati Club, where he arranged for his father to spend part of his retirement. The Akron City Club occupied the top three floors of the Ohio Building at the corner of South Main Street and Church, just down from Bowery and across from Loew's (now the Akron Civic Theater). Dining rooms were on the sixth floor, meeting and game rooms and a grill and a bar were on the seventh, and the eighth was given over the residential rooms. I think Dad became a member as a Presidential perquisite, and I often ate there with him and Mom and their business guests as families. Ward and Marian Keener brought their youngest son, Bobby, whom I would not otherwise have met since he went to Old Trail School while I was at King and Perkins, and to Trinity Lutheran Church while we went to Westminster Presbyterian, and to a Cub Scout den near to Fairlawn Heights while mine was centered around Tallmadge (now Memorial) Parkway and Merriman. Bobby and I became great friends in our preadolescence, roaming the club to play pool on the seventh floor while our parents sipped coffee and arranging to visit there by ourselves and feast in the Women's Dining Room on triple-decker club sandwiches and great piles of crisp French fries and endless fountain Cokes. Whenever our family gathered or out-of-town visitors stayed with us, Dad would propose an evening meal at

Pals Bobby Keener and the author peek into the living room of the President's Home, 1959. *From the author's collection*

the Club, at Mom's instigation, I now suspect. I would need a coat and tie and all other forms of good behavior, and I learned to stand up to greet the people who would pause at our table before we were served or while the adults drank their coffee. And just when it seemed that we were finally leaving, I'd have to maintain my parent-pleasing demeanor while Mom and Dad stopped to chat at other tables or we met folks at the coat room.

At the City Club I enjoyed my first shrimp cocktail, five or six perfectly peeled cold pink two-biters arranged so their tails looped over the edge of a silver-rimmed chambered sherbet cup which incorporated a layer of crushed ice between its inner and outer hemispheres. A lettuce leaf lined the inner cup and was topped with a tablespoon of minced celery and two tablespoons of tomato-chili-horseradish sauce, with four saltines, a wedge of lemon, and a small three-tined seafood fork resting on the service plate. Mom might propose later favors in return for one of my shrimp. Dad never had the shrimp cocktail; he took the beef bouillon or the chicken noodle soup, followed by a tossed green salad with no dressing. Mom would have the cream soup of the day or a seafood bisque with the green salad with

French or Thousand Island dressing. I think I was steered away from club sandwiches at dinner, but I always found something I liked. If it were on the menu, I would enjoy calves' liver with bacon and all the sautéed onions I could desire, and it was here that I had my first mixed grill incorporating a perfect fat still-pink lamb kidney and an unfamiliar sausage that burst at the press of my fork. Dick usually had a steak—strip, sirloin, T-bone, Kansas City, but not filet mignon—purple, please, not red. Mom might have a veal cutlet, breaded and sautéed, or veal scaloppini garnished with lemon butter and capers, or a seafood Newburg on rice. Dad usually had fish, his favorite being Dover sole (though he'd settle for any whitefish), preferably broiled but without the sauce of the day, accompanied by parsley buttered potatoes and peas or whatever hot green vegetable was featured. He'd choose a fruit sherbet, rice pudding, or baked custard for dessert, or very occasionally hot apple pie á la mode, and he'd leave the bottom crust. I looked forward all meal to the hot fudge sundae always available no matter what else was featured. We could have eaten the same meal in a similar but more intimate atmosphere at the Diamond Grille or Sanginetti's or Iacomini's in the 1950s and 1960s, and at the latter two I could have sampled northern Italian cuisine such as I would not encounter until I was an adult.

The Smorgasbord

For several years before I started at the academy, we made a Sunday noon pilgrimage after church to the Smorgasbord in Stow, a twenty-five minute drive across the valley and northern Summit County. It offered a hundred or more selections in the warren of long narrow connected rooms, only a few of the dishes Scandinavian, and Mom helped me expand my food horizons, coaxing me to try something fishy from the many dishes resting on crushed ice on the cold table or something that looked like poultry stuffing but smelled different on the hot table. I loved the dense dark breads or the salted, caraway-seed-studded white rolls and the pale cold chunks of butter and cheeses. We never had onions with our pickled beets, and I rather liked them and the cornichons and the big caper buds with which the beets were garnished. It was certainly the noodles which first attracted me to the Swedish meatballs, but I returned for the meaty mild veal-and-pork texture and the dill-and-sour-cream-laced gravy in which they were served.

Women's City Club

I could always count on a meal to my taste at the Women's City Club on West Exchange Street and Portage Path in a rambling Tudor mansion. We would be invited there as guests both at lunch and at dinner, and my dad's secretary, our family friend Caroline, took just me many times. Here I encountered the sauced dishes Mom rarely made at home—creamed chicken over rice, beef Stroganoff on parsley buttered noodles—and two signature accompaniments: a chambered condiment dish containing three or four appetizer choices from among giant ripe or stuffed green olives, bread-and-butter or watermelon pickles, sweet-and-tangy three-bean salad, pickled beets, cottage cheese, apple sauce, or apple butter, and a bread basket featuring three or four kinds of yeasty soft or hard rolls and always hot corn bread and always warm cinnamon-swirl pecan buns. Caroline would often pick up a take-home box of the sticky buns at the cashier's desk when she settled her bill. Pies and cobblers with ice cream ended most meals, and I rather enjoyed even canned peaches baked with a caramelized flour, cinnamon, butter, and brown sugar crumble more plentiful than the fruit itself.

Downtown Tea Rooms

On many of our shopping trips to O'Neil's or Polsky's, Mom added lunch at their tea rooms. The food was nicely prepared and presented, and it was comfortable to sit for a while after a morning's shopping, but I didn't care too much for, say, a trio of chicken, tuna, and ham salads on lettuce with a fruit garnish and Ritz crackers after a cup of chicken gumbo or clam chowder. I would rather have gotten a hamburger and French fries anywhere, or even to have gone to Kaase's on Mill Street for its creamed chicken in a potato basket (shredded potatoes deep fried in a mold to produce a woven-like brown crispy consumable bowl), especially since there would also be very superior sticky buns to accompany it, and Mom might get some to take home.

Chinese

I can't remember a specific Chinese restaurant which we patronized, but Mom and I did like Chinese food and ate it together when Dad wasn't in the party. By the 1990s when he took many of his evening meals out, Dad would go to China Gourmet at Pershing and West Market (which we called "China Wendy's" because of the building's earlier service to Dave Thomas's Columbus-based hamburger chain) a couple of times a month, ordering chicken almond ding or moo goo gai pan without the mushrooms, but in the 1950s and 1960s he avoided Chinese food. On the coasts and in large cities, sparked by Hawaii's looming statehood in 1959, restaurateurs exploited interest in things Polynesian by dressing entrances with teak gateways and interiors with nets, starfish shells, candles, and wait staff with cotton-print sarongs and leis. Long-established Chinese restaurants acquired coconut shells in which to serve pineapple-and-orange-garnished rum punches and presented their egg rolls and red-glazed spareribs and deep-fried shrimp toast on wooden trenchers centered by small chalices of flaming Sterno as "Pu Pu Platters." I would have made my meal on these finger foods except that they were always packaged with main courses, so I learned about fried rice, lo mein, and the mysterious earthy sour flavor of fermented black beans in shrimp with lobster sauce. Like most of America, for me it would be two more decades before I explored other Chinese regional flavors or any of the wealth of Japanese and southeast Asian cuisines.

Steakhouses and Phelps

When I began to drive in 1962, I discovered sit-down dining on my own budget. I liked Nick Yanko's and its steaks for a fancy date; I'd eat its pilaf as an additional side dish, only discovering in 1990s that its most salient secret was not herbs and spices but a whole stick of butter to one-and-one-half cups of raw rice. I liked the less expensive Brown Derby whose basic eight-ounce steak was always flavorful and dependably cooked to order and whose salads were served in a chilled metal bowl, but whose baked potatoes were steamed in their aluminum-foil cooking wrap. But my most economical discovery was Phelps's.

Phelps's was a neighborhood joint just east of Main and Market and north of the UA campus. Here was good coffee served in thick ten-ounce crockery mugs never allowed to empty. Here was a stratum of society never seen at the Brown Derby, let alone the City Club. Located on the first floor of a frame house on Perkins Street near North Union, Phelps's was entered through a short hallway past a staircase leading upwards, added during a rehab to split the place into apartments. Immediately to the right beyond a door frame two or three rooms had been knocked into one large enough for a six-person lunch counter, a couple of tables, and six booths. The fuggy atmosphere of cooking and cigarette smoke steamed over the windows. Two sturdy women in faded cotton print dresses and half aprons and sensible tie shoes with rolled stockings, one about twenty-five and the other about fifty, served and collected receipts, though only the older one touched the cash register. A skinny tattooed fellow about thirty in a T-shirt with a pack of cigarettes rolled in one sleeve and a white bib apron that could do with some bleach presided over the grill behind the counter and communicated with a kitchen down an aisle past his grill, while near the entrance his twin, twenty or thirty years older, slouched just inside the outer door protecting a glass-fronted case of pint bottles of fortified wine. He took handfuls of coins from folks whom he wouldn't permit past the dining room threshold and gave them bottles in paper bags. Both men were shorter than the women and appeared lighter by ten pounds, but when the father left his post to put the coins in the cash register, it was evident who was in charge. I never had to open my wallet at Phelps's: the silver in my pocket would cover the check. I'd go at seven a.m. before classes for eggs, meat, potatoes, sausage gravy, and toast. I'd find three or four composed dishes ready from 10:00 a.m. to closing at 7:00 p.m.—creamed chicken on biscuits with mashed potatoes, canned peas, applesauce, pork and sauerkraut like Mom's, tender Swiss steak with a thick gravy studded with carrots and celery, and stuffed peppers with tomato sauce. Pie for dessert. And a ten-cent cup of coffee that I'd drain two or three times.

I was so proud of my discovery that I took Mom there. She tripped in wearing her "snow leopard" coat and her twisted gold necklace and before we had finished, she had engaged all the staff in conversation, even the taciturn paterfamilias protecting the place from lapsed Haven of Rest residents, and learned about their people still in West Virginia, still working in the mines that they'd escaped to run their own small business. Had it been purpose-built like the lunchroom in Hopper's "Nighthawks," Phelps's might not have been as attractive to me nor the food and coffee as tasty. It never had a license to serve beer or liquor, as did the rubber-factory lunchrooms like Ido's and New Era, that endured into this century; and it did not have a culinary edge beyond cheap, plentiful, and that coffee.

Win Schuler's

Win Schuler's in Marshall, Michigan, was our destination every year on the last Saturday evening in July. The Manor closed for August, and the thirty boys dispersed to their parents or guardians, and the Clarks and Aunt Jo took a very few days to themselves before it was all hands on deck to make and mend during the only weeks of the year when Betty, Bill, Rob, and Jo could undertake projects that would otherwise disrupt the boys' routine. By five p.m. on Parents' Day the last families had packed and left, and we would climb into three or four cars to drive north for a feast.

Winston Schuler had inherited his father's hotel-based restaurant in the mid 1930s, bought out his brother's interest, and imprinted his name and genial personality upon the collection of interconnected small rooms decorated by fireplaces and what I took to be "Olde English" knick-knacks behind the block-long, half-timber and stucco Tudor façade. It was thirty miles on two-lane roads from Jonesville, but little Marshall stands at the intersection of highways that are today Interstates 94 and 69 connecting Kalamazoo-Battlecreek to Jackson-Ann Arbor-Detroit west to east and Indianapolis-Fort Wayne to Lansing south to north, and without our reservations we would have joined the long line at the door. Win knew Bill, Betty, and Jo by name, and he nodded to Norm and Kay with a smile meant to suggest his recognition of their faces if not his recollection of their names.

Calvin Trillin pilloried that sort of American heartland restaurant which tarted up plain food with continental sauces as "La Maison de la Casa House," and I blush to report that I vaguely recall a "chicken Cordon Bleu" on the Win Schuler's menu—a portion-controlled flattened chicken breast wrapped around a piece of boiled ham and a slice of Swiss cheese and rolled and pressed mechanically into a four-inch cylinder, egg-washed and sprinkled with bread crumbs and flash-fried until mostly cooked then frozen for transport from the Atlanta factory to the Chicago warehouse to the jobber's truck to the kitchen freezer, whence chef popped it into the oven for the suggested fifteen minutes at 475 degrees and splashed some house-made Mornay sauce and sides and fresh parsley onto a plate in return for eighty percent of the price of his average steak. But I also remember thick pieces of herb-crusted prime rib roast, which only a high volume kitchen with a lot of repeat business can afford to have on hand, and slices both rare and well-done arriving simultaneously at our table, and no argument over changing out a too-done slice for one less cooked; steaks still red in the center with natural blackened score marks and crusted deep-brown exteriors achievable only over an eight-hundred degree open-fire grill; two or three kinds of white fish from the four Great Lakes that touch Michigan, perch, pike, or walleye, prepared fried, sautéed, broiled, or even baked to request; and my first rock lobster tail, broiled in the shell and teased out in one piece onto my plate and served with hot clarified butter—it had been frozen for its journey from the warm southern waters in which it spawned, but it was still tender and exotic to my adolescent tastes. And I remember the in-gathering touches: loaves of hot bread on small cutting boards with a broad-bladed serrated knife to cut my own slices, today a commonplace but in the 1950s and 1960s a luxurious novelty; small bowls of meatballs in chunky barbeque sauce; and ramekins of horseradish-and-cheddar cheese spread twenty years before I found it in dairy cases as far south as Arkansas under the moniker "Win Schuler's Bar Scheeze." And I remember the anticipation, the performance, and the two-day post-mortem exaggerations about Rob's and Dick's consumption of yards of beer. Cold pilsner in a bulb-bottomed three-foot-tall glass brought tableside in a wooden trellis as a handle: the trick of drinking the first two feet of the flute portion most any coordinated person could perform, but the finishing of the last sixteen ounces from the bulb without baptizing yourself, well that required a sobriety often banished by the first couple of pints.

There are good *maisons* like Win Schuler's in lots of American towns large and small, but having grown up with Schuler's itself I am apt to idealize it. When I left the small pond of The University of Akron for the great lake of the University of Chicago, I idealized my new instructors, too, among them Gwin J. Kolb, chair of the Department of English and an editor of the *Yale Edition of the Works of Samuel Johnson*. In June of my second year Mr. Kolb invited his doctoral students to join him and Ruth, not at one of Chicago's many great eateries, but to a Dutch treat dinner in Benton Harbor, Michigan, roughly ninety minutes from Hyde Park around the southern crescent of Lake Michigan, to a restaurant that Win Schuler had opened in that resort town. The food was consistently good, he said, but no one he knew outside of Britain had gotten better the physical flavor of an eighteenth-century London tavern such as Dr. Johnson frequented.

TAKE OUT AND CARRY HOME

Mom often said, "We can make that just as good at home." I suppose I may have said that to my children as well. It's not true, of course. It will be ready later, not now, and it won't be "that" but a version of that, and it may be a very pale version indeed because home doesn't have an oven as hot or exactly the same ingredients or a well-vented deep-fat fryer or the mystique surrounding "that" in its commercial form of which we were all enamored. There were four foods we brought home mostly because Mom thought we couldn't make them just as well and also because they were treats to be enjoyed when the Lawgiver and Paymaster wasn't participating: fried chicken, hamburgers, corned beef sandwiches, and pizza.

Pizza

It was 1955, no earlier I think, and Mom and I have driven down Tallmadge Parkway through the valley and up Uhler Avenue to Howard Street to North Main and across what was then called the "high level bridge" into Cuyahoga Falls. We were going to buy pizza. The storefront a couple of blocks north of the State Theatre in the Falls occupied part of the kind of building we would later call a strip mall. To the left just inside the door a counter partitioned a waiting area with a half-dozen chairs from a cash register and work space. Two men in long white bib aprons over white pants and white short-sleeved shirts worked behind the counter and introduced me to performance cuisine. They were dark-haired and olive complexioned, neither particularly tall nor short, clean and neat; their hands were broad, their nails cut close, and they had more than a dusting of flour on their hirsute forearms, aprons, shoes, and sometimes noses and cheeks. One prepared dough for crusts, and the other loaded and placed them in a broad four-door double-deck oven.

The steps of mixing flour, salt, yeast, oil, and water and kneading them into a dough and encouraging a first and second rising had taken place long before we arrived. Our presence occasioned the preparation of the shell for the crust and its loading and baking. We could call ahead—which we did sometimes—but they did not deliver, so we might as well go and watch our pizza being prepared. Mom always came inside with me, and she'd engage the cooks with questions about themselves, their business, and their techniques.

The baker reached into a refrigerator and took into his hands a smooth lump of dough just bigger than his doubled fist and slapped it on a floured surface at his waist behind the counter. He pressed down on it two or three times, flattening and turning until the three-inch sphere expanded into a six-inch circle. Sometimes he'd use a long rolling pin to flatten the sphere. Sometimes he felt something in the dough he didn't like, and he'd double it over half wise, then double again, then push down with his hands or the rolling pin to recreate the circle. He'd flip the circle and sprinkle flour on it and flip it again, sprinkle and press, and about the time the circle was eight inches across he'd slip both his hands underneath and lift it above the surface and toss it higher, up to the level of his chest, imparting some rotation, and catching it as it fell, stretching it outwards, throwing upwards again, and adding to the spin as he tossed it higher than his head, once, twice, three times, expanding its diameter until, as it rose upwards, his right hand grabbed a heavy blackened pan and used it like a cesta to catch the descending disk. When he caught the dough it always just about filled the fourteen-inch pan. Pan and dough he slapped on the floured surface. He smoothed the dough once or twice with both hands until it lapped the edge, then with the fingers of his right hand he crimped the dough at the outer edge of the pan as his left hand rotated the pan until there was a continuous dam perhaps a half-inch tall around the circumference, and then he'd pass the pan to his partner—I'm calling him the cook—on his left.

The cook's work area comprised a two-foot wide table backed by countersunk stainless steel boxes of other ingredients bounded by a large pot of red sauce at the end closest to the floured pastry block and a bin of shredded white cheese on the far side across from the oven. First the cook pulled up a broad, shallow ladle full of the tomato sauce and poured it on the middle of the dough, then with the bottom back of the ladle spread it in expanding circles right up to the fluted dam, as he rotated the pan with his left hand. Sometimes he'd dip out more sauce, but mostly his first estimate spread across the shell to his satisfaction. Then he'd reach over the red-puddled dough into one of the boxes and grab a handful of gray crumbled cooked sausage and cast it like seed on top of the sauce; with his left hand he'd rotate the pan by quarter turns while with his right he'd dribble nickel-sized clumps of the greasy meat. Two handfuls seemed enough, and for our order he'd continue the process with handfuls of chopped squishy canned mushrooms, chopped white onions, and chopped green peppers, then top everything with big handfuls of the white shredded cheese. The cheese would smooth over the pebbled browns, greens, and translucent whites on red like a white nubby crocheted comforter or a thick wet late spring snowfall on risen grass, only partially obscuring the underlying framework.

Now the pizza was ready to bake, less than two minutes since the passing of the dough from baker to cook. Grasping in his right hand the mounded pan of ingredients layered up to the fluted edge and taking two steps toward the oven behind him, with his left hand holding a towel the cook reached to the handle of a middle oven door, pulled it down toward himself, placed the edge of the pan on the flat gray steel surface of the oven, and shaking the pan rotationally with his wrist and using the momentum of his thrust slipped the raw pie off the pan onto the floor of the oven, pulled out the pan, and snapped the door up to close the oven. Now might he reach on top of the oven and grab a long wooden paddle (or "peel"), the flat blade sixteen inches wide and deep, and open the fourth oven down from the top, slip the paddle under a partially cooked pie, and move it up to the second oven. Then he'd check the top oven and perhaps paddle out a fully baked pizza and place paddle and all on another work surface just beyond the dough board and ingredient counter. Balancing the handle on the counter, he'd take a tool like a miniature cross-cut saw with a smooth blade and, grabbing vertical handles at either end, make four rocking cuts, edge to edge, turning the pie into eight triangular segments without separating, then lift the paddle and tip its contents into a flat one-piece covered cardboard box, and tucking in the open flaps, hand us our hot pizza.

I'd hold the box on my legs as Mom drove home, and we'd take the box right to the breakfast nook table with our plates, napkins, bottles of Coke, and glasses of ice. In the twelve-minute drive the pizza had cooled enough to handle. From the predominantly white disk that went into the oven had emerged a thick gooey mosaic of taupes and pinks, greens, whites, and browns, a richly pebbled open-faced sandwich, steaming with the unaccustomed smells of garlic, oregano, basil, and fennel seed. It was some distant cousin of bread, the fluting of the edge turned into a thumb-thick yielding crust, the center firm enough to hold its shape with a supporting finger but soft enough to bite easily with the incisors. The taste was tangy and salty, fatty and meaty and recognizably pork but not like the sage-dominated breakfast links or the marbled spicy salami that I knew. The onions and peppers were still a bit crisp, and the unfamiliar spongy texture of the mushrooms contrasted with the slightly gummy feel of the cheese. It was prepared food made elsewhere, the comfort of a casserole wrapped into the convenience of the hand, and it was utterly different to anything we made at home. The next new food to surprise me as much was my first taco, in California, 1964.

Fried Chicken, Take-Out

I don't remember Kentucky Fried Chicken coming to Akron before 1960, and I don't remember Mom making fried chicken, because she didn't care to try to make it "just as good" at home, and there were good fried chicken sources. The first I remember was "broasted" chicken—more properly, "Broasted," because it's a trademark for a pressure-frying process and the licensed equipment in which to do it. Ours came from a shop on South Portage Path at Dodge Avenue where more than sixty years later someone still advertises it. Crisp outside and moist inside and perhaps with less fat than pan-fried chicken, as claimed, it was pretty good. Harland Sanders built his chain on pressure-frying, though not with the patented Broaster contraption. When KFC came to Akron, it won our allegiance for its more flavorful crust.

But we never gave over the taste we'd developed in the meantime for Barberton chicken. In the enclave city six miles south by southwest of the President's Home, during the Depression a Serbian family who had lost their farm started selling fried chicken dinners in a restaurant they called Belgrade Gardens. They cut their chicken into nine pieces of roughly the same volume to assure even cooking: two drumsticks, two thighs, two wing-end breast pieces, two sternum-end breast pieces, and the back or "chicken ribs." They dusted the pieces lightly with seasoned flour and fried them in lard to form a tight reddish-brown crusted crispy skin over still moist meat. They served the chicken with French fries, a tangy vinegar-based slaw, and what they called "hot sauce," chopped Hungarian-style yellow peppers and tomatoes stewed with rice. The business thrived. Post-war Balkan immigrants and others worked and ate at Belgrade Gardens, then opened their own chicken restaurants. Hopocan Gardens, White House Chicken, and Milich's Village Inn join Belgrade Gardens today in making and selling mostly the same lard-fried product and sides, and Barberton declares itself the "Chicken Capital of the World." We probably wouldn't have taken out from there so often but for Mom's forming a friendship with Ljuba Antov, who worked at Belgrade Gardens.

The Hamburg

Some people believe that Akron's Menches Brothers created the first hamburger about 1865 (and the first ice cream cone in 1904): their descendants think so and print it on their menus today. I have no doubt that Wes Swenson formulated the best "hamburg" of all time. It consists of about 2.8 ounces of 80% lean unseasoned and unadulterated ground beef, pressed into a patty, never frozen, fried and salted by hand to order on a grill top, placed in a toasted and buttered bun, garnished (for "everything") with three dill pickle chips, a single fifth-inch-thick slice of sweet onion, and one-and-a-half teaspoons of regular yellow mustard, wrapped in waxed paper, and served hot by a polite, good-looking curb boy (never a girl until the 1990s) who sprints among the waiting cars whenever he is not carrying a full tray. Of course, there may be a better hamburger; but never a better hamburg.

Our friend Andy Karam years later gave me the term *mealus insomnius* to describe the late adolescent's ten p.m. food needs. On the principle that "if you feed it, it will talk to you," Kay bankrolled most of my midevening trips from 1962, when I could drive, through 1971 to Swenson's to bring home a bag of food before "The Tonight Show" broadcast and chat about my high school or college trials and triumphs.

About 1963 McDonald's opened a drive-up stand at Wallhaven across from Swenson's, and I relaxed my loyalties enough to consume several of their Big Macs ("two all beef patties special sauce lettuce cheese pickle onion on a sesame seed bun") and decided that Swenson's Galley Boy (two beef patties with cheese and a combination of tartar and barbecue sauces) was less bready and more satisfying. At nearly the same time and place Arby's opened its first Akron outlet across from Hardesty Park under the red-and-yellow neon ten-gallon hat, and for a few years Mom found a new favorite in its basic shaved roast beef sandwich, three ounces of tissue-thin slices from flavored beef chunks re-formed sort of like chip-chop ham, held in a hot steamer, and cut to order on demand, served on a soft sesame seed bun and doused with a horseradish-flavored mayonnaise-like white sauce engineered to be stable at room temperature. She and I also liked Arby's potato cake, a three-by-two-by-half-inch rectangle of shredded potatoes and seasonings deep fried to a golden brown and a texture like Ore-Ida's Tater Tots, a concept later to be marketed by McDonald's as their breakfast hash browns.

Lou and Hy's

After Sandy introduced us to it, Lou and Hy's nearly supplanted Swenson's as our late-night favorite. I had just enough Manhattan experience to recognize a full-service Jewish delicatessen but not enough to know that Lou and Hy's was merging the dairy-fish and meat lines in a fashion dependent upon high volume to maintain quality. They seemed to have that traffic when a bunch of us would show up after rehearsal in Kolbe Hall and find seventy or more folks noshing at 10:30 of a weeknight. I came to regard six ounces of shaved corned beef the proper-sized serving, fresh rye bread with plenty of caraway seeds and a good chew to the crust its most comfortable container, yellow mustard the only acceptable condiment, and half-done dill pickles the appropriate savory. From Mom's point of view Lou and Hy's must have represented an unfortunate deviation to the *mealus insomnius*/make-it-talk-to-you pattern, for I tended to eat there and perhaps remember to bring a half corned beef sandwich home for her. Still, there were many occasions when I set off from the President's Home solarium on a round-trip takeout mission for Lou and Hy's corned beef on rye.

Exercise, Sports, and Recreation

One of the last domestic discussions I witnessed between my father and his wife Virginia concerned the treadmill in their third bedroom at the Camelot. Norm was in the hospital in late June 2003, a month after his ninety-eighth birthday, and when he heard that the treadmill had failed that morning, his instructions were clear: replace it now, immediately, before I come home on Monday. Of the exercise options remaining to him in those years, that treadmill was the most important.

It was forty-four years earlier in 1959 that Norm had returned to the President's Home from his doctor's office with a prescription to exercise. His father had died from a heart attack a few months earlier, and now personal physician Dr. Gordon Grant thought that his symptoms pointed to angina, not hiatal hernia, and wanted him to take a pill, take a walk, and take a nap daily. Norm accepted the last two suggestions but resisted the first. And from that day forward, he exercised in some form every day.

FAMILY ATTITUDES TOWARD EXERCISE

When I was a preteen, ours did not seem particularly an athletic family. My mother fended off inquiries about her physical activity with two ripostes, "Whenever the impulse for vigorous exercise overcomes me, I roll over and sleep it off" and "I get plenty of exercise going to my friends' funerals." She didn't like games involving balls or running. She avoided hiking or brisk walking, and I think her feet bothered her some and her varicose-veined legs, too. She had not been athletic in her youth, at school or college, like her sorority sister Blanche Huss or her daughter

"If you can do it in a skirt." Kay takes a ride on Paul Daum's new motorcycle, 1970. *From the author's collection*

Ames. But she still seemed vigorous to me, bustling in the kitchen, climbing stairs, moving around the stores. She took to warm water gleefully, and she knew several swimming strokes. She loved to dance with Dad or any gallant who would ask, and she could make a better and more confident dancer out of almost any partner, and she would dance till her perspiration flowed. She was graceful in movement.

She was usually game to try anything if it could be done in a skirt, and I remember her teaching her granddaughters to use a hula hoop. But she resisted her friend Jane Dunlap's attempts to have her join exercise classes, and she could never master the catch or the throw of a Frisbee. Attacks of bursitis in her shoulders kept her wary of upper-body exercise. Today she would be put on regimens of stretching and aerobics and weight training, given proper shoes, and perhaps have regained a full range of movement and activity, especially if she'd quit the cigarettes; but in the 1960s she wore comfortable flats, elevated her legs when sitting, sat as much as she could, and did not lift anything much heavier than her glass of Coca-Cola on ice.

In contrast to his wife, at earlier times in his life, Dad had pursued vigorous exercise. His father was not only an amateur gymnast but also had walked eight miles a day, two miles each way to work, home for lunch, back to work, and home for supper. For his eighteen years at the University of Cincinnati, Norm walked about forty minutes a day, making three round trips (since he returned to the office after supper) between our Stratford Avenue house and his offices on campus. The presidency of The University of Akron was his first job involving a commute by car, and it was a short eight or nine minutes most days. He appreciated the time savings without noticing the loss of exercise.

Ames and Dick remembered Dad's teaching them or participating in a wide range of sports. Ames made her body athletic with dance, and at Lotspiech School she played soccer, basketball, field hockey. She and Dad walked down the hill from home to play tennis on the public courts. She felt in fact that Dad pushed her sports to compensate for Dick, who was forbidden most contact sports after nephritis crippled his kidneys when he was eight. (But he would be the only Auburn in three generations to letter in a college sport when he played "blocking" fullback on Stu Parry's Zips 1956–1957 and 1957–1958 soccer team.)

HANDBALL AND COURT GAMES

Regular vigorous exercise characterized Dad's Cincinnati years. On his résumé and in interviews during the 1951 transition to Akron, Norm cited handball as a hobby. Ames remembered his playing regularly in Cincinnati, and I remember a dusty canvas bag in the attic at 856 Mayfair Road with a pair of soft leather tie slippers and several sweat-stained gloves, though I never saw him use them.

Handball is a working-class version of squash, and players of either game project an aura of vigor, athleticism, and competitive spirit beyond that of golfers or weekend tennis players. Dad had not gone to war; he was thirty-six and the father of two when the Japanese bombed Pearl Harbor. He wished to appear fit in person, on paper, and by report, as a vigorous athletic handball player. In Cincinnati he could have gotten in several handball matches a week, stealing an hour from the work day with one or more long-time partners to get to a court, change, work up a sweat, shower and dry off, dress, and return to the office.

In Akron he faced two problems: facilities and potential competitors. The University did not have a handball court, so he would have had to leave work and go downtown to the YMCA or east to Goodyear gymnasium, so that a match would involve additional travel time or have to be scheduled before or after work, and he quickly adopted routines for his mornings and evenings with no additional leisure for this kind of interruption. Finding competitors in Akron would have been difficult, too. Here for the first time he was everyone's boss and a public figure, and while many can successfully compartmentalize athletic competition from their off-court peer-suppliant or leader-subordinate business relationships, it takes a very special self confidence in his game and in his business to do so while making new acquaintances. A wicked close handball match with an old friend differs from one with a person he might have to fire or ask for a favor.

That my father was once a pretty good handball player I'm sure, because he was comfortable in other court games. He was a fair tennis player and a good ping-pong player. In tennis, he covered the court economically from both backhand and forehand sides, used topspin and backspin, and had a good drop shot, though he lacked a big or deceptive serve. His serve in ping-pong was better, and his footwork, hand-eye coordination, and court strategy made him competitive with most anyone we knew. I couldn't beat him at either game until I was fifteen and he was fifty-five, and I had the advantage of twenty-twenty vision while he was wearing bifocals, experiencing his first signs of cataracts and glaucoma, and starting to suffer from his bunions.

I always remember ping-pong in the basement. We must have had a table in Cincinnati, and I remember an old one in Akron at 344 Merriman Road and watching Dad and Dick play. Dick became the best of the family and had a wonderful reach and a deceptive paddle stroke so that we couldn't detect the returning ball's trajectory until it had nearly reached the net. (We always believed that Dick became a doctor because of ping-pong: he broke his kneecap on the table at the Phi Delta Theta house, and his subsequent surgery and hospitalization and developing relationship with Dr. Walter Hoyt Jr. led to his switching his major to premed.) When Dad got a three-quarter-size pool table for the basement at the President's Home, he had a portable ping-pong top made for it that stayed set up most of the time. I even remember rare occasions when my mother would take up a paddle as fourth in a doubles match, but mostly I remember coaxing my father to play two out of three no matter who had a reached twenty-one in the first game.

NORM'S PRESCRIPTION TO EXERCISE AND HIS THIRD-BORN

I was a major beneficiary of Dad's prescription to exercise. He used his time to introduce me to many sports and spent more one-on-one time with me than he might have otherwise. In 1959, I was getting to the point where I could provide competitive ping-pong, and I eagerly waited through the half-hour after dinner that Dad reserved for digestion. In better weather we might shoot baskets behind the third garage where Dad had had a backboard and hoop erected above the roll-top door. Weather good enough to shoot baskets was also weather good enough to take a walk. Dad and I always walked Mayfair Road to Delaware to Sunnyside to Ridgecrest and home, about a mile or somewhat under today's thirty-minute prescription for regular cardiovascular exercise. I am sure Dad learned much about my plans and aspirations on these walks, but I don't recall ever setting off intending to seek his permission or his advice until a cold sunny day in late December 1970 when he helped me sort through job offers from Ohio State, the University of Cincinnati, and California State University Los Angeles.

Mom took me or arranged my transportation for Little League baseball when I was nine or ten. I lasted less than one season and played no further organized sports until compelled in boarding school. We owned several baseball gloves and hard- and soft-balls and a couple of bats, and once or twice Dad and I drove to an empty ball field to hit flies and grounders, but mostly we'd play catch on the front lawn where we had a good ninety feet without trees. (The same space, expanding down to the sidewalks and into the street, became our Frisbee pitch.) I loved these sessions and always sought to prolong them. I was amazed when for several evenings in a row Dad would have time to toss the ball; then suddenly that run was over and he'd be too busy again. Later, I figured out that these runs preceded events like an administrators vs. faculty softball contest or his throwing out the first pitch for a Cleveland Indians game.

President Auburn practices his fielding. *Photo by Lou Tobias, from the Norman Auburn Papers. Courtesy of Archival Services, University Libraries, The University of Akron*

I was less happy about one of Dad's favorite forms of summertime household exercise, pruning the bushes. At 344 Merriman Road he had pushed an heirloom hand mower over the small front and back lawns unless he could get Dick to do it. Even at ten, I couldn't handle the drag myself. At the President's Home, University maintenance would mow the grass with power equipment, and our push mower was sold or discarded. But not our hedge clippers and pruning gear. Our back garden was bounded by lilacs and rose-of-Sharon set in pachysandra, and on a nice Saturday afternoon he would put on old clothes and grab a stepladder and clippers and cut off old or injured growth. I was required to pick up his cuttings. So, for an hour or two, a couple of steps up a ladder, manipulating two-foot-long metal clippers, he got good balance training and aerobic upper-body exercise, and I got stoop labor.

Curiously, I took pleasure in a far more vigorous garden-related task. Dad had the tree surgeons leave a large portion of the two elm trees we lost in the late 1950s or early 1960s, and when the twenty-four-inch logs had seasoned for a year or more, he acquired sledgehammers and wedges to split them. A sheltered corner on the southwest of the property became our woodlot, and after he'd taught me to set the wedge with the fifteen-inch five-pound hammer and drive it with the three-foot ten-pound sledge, I'd often work myself when he wasn't around. We put up several cords and burned old elm in the living room and solarium fireplaces for three or four winters.

CAROLINE TEACHES MARK TO GOLF AND BOWL

In the 1950s and 1960s, every one of my pals' fathers (it seemed) played golf. Dad said golf took too much time. But he didn't object when his executive assistant, Caroline Pardee, began taking me with her to Sunnybrook and getting me a few lessons, and he purchased me a starter set of clubs. He took me as well to driving ranges and hit a half bucket of balls to my full bucket. I got to the point where I went out with Uncle Bill and Rob a couple of times and played nine-hole courses with friends when one of us could drive a car. The summer of 1974 after Mother died, Dad and I played nine holes twice or so, neither of us long or accurate or particularly good on the green—and come to think of it, those rounds occurred just about the time that the new widower was courting Mary Thomas, women's golf champion of Portage Country Club.

Caroline also taught me to bowl, and many a winter Saturday afternoon we'd spend in one of the new lanes opening up in Akron's suburbs in the late 1950s and early 1960s. Mom signed me up for a children's league but said I should rent shoes and use the public balls until I'd gained my adult height. Bobby Keener and I would convince one of our mothers to drop us off with enough money to spend a morning bowling and drinking sodas and smoking his dad's or my mom's cigarettes behind the lanes. I followed the fortunes of Dick Weber and other pros, and at the same time as the sport became automated and gentrified, I increased my average to the mid 150s and bragged when I broke 200. Dad didn't usually have the two or three hours an outing took, but I remember going with him once to some lanes downtown on the second floor above a store where the *cra-ack* and *pwok* reverberated off the low ceilings, dust hung in the gloomy smoky air, and I could glimpse the grimy, ropey-armed setters behind the pins. It wasn't until I was forty-five and had returned to Akron that I learned of Dad's regularly taking a break in his Saturday work mornings at Buchtel Hall to roll a line in the Student Center with his colleagues.

RIDING AND SHOOTING

Dad taught me to sit a horse. I enjoyed going trail riding with him once or twice a year. There was a livery in Montrose and some easy paths through meadows and woods where I-77 runs today and a string of reliable mares and geldings for the rental. I can remember being on an amusement park pony before I attended school and riding my dad's saddle on gentle mountain trails in the Colorado Rockies. There may have been a lesson or two in my Cub Scout days, and I had a good head start when Camp Y-Noah brought opportunities to trot and canter, and a trip to the Stanley Hotel in Estes Park included dude riding for me and Mom while Dad attended the Association of Urban Universities meeting which had brought us there.

Dad saw to it that I learned to shoot. It wasn't as soon as I wanted, about the time we moved to Akron and I was cowboy crazy and had the chaps, the holsters, the hat, and the cap guns. It started with archery lessons when I was eleven or twelve to teach me how to aim and respect the power of a projectile. When I'd had a few sessions, Dad joined me in tramping and shooting through an archery course set in meadows and forest near today's Blossom Music Center, and I was surprised that I didn't have to show him how to use a long bow. He must have agreed to my getting a Wham-O slingshot that flung steel ball bearings; not much good came of that, however. While a member of the Air Force ROTC in college, Dick acquired a .22 pistol and rifle. Dad took us out a half-dozen times to plink bottles and cans in a dump near the Botzum sewer plant. In 1983 I needed to prove myself capable of carrying a rifle in an Arkansas deer hunt, and I surprised myself and my Vietnam-veteran sponsor with neat groupings in our practice targets.

MISCELLANEOUS PASTIMES

As a family, we did not pursue the outdoor sports that mimic survival skills—no canoeing, hiking, climbing, sledding, camping, hunting, fishing, or skiing—though I had tried the first four by the time I was thirteen, particularly hiking and rock climbing with Caroline at Nelson Ledges and Virginia Kendall. I learned small-hill sledding, mostly in Jonesville, and I tried skating at the winter shelters of Akron's municipal parks but didn't master. Dick became the first skier in the family when he and Mary took their girls to Colorado for year-end holidays. Had our family taken camping vacations, I might have practiced these and learned other wilderness skills. Mom said camping was fine so long as she could sleep on a bed with sheets within earshot of a flush toilet.

Dad fished and sailed with his father-in-law at Lake Wawasee in northeast Indiana, but the Montgomery family spot was gone by the time I was born, so I learned to fish (and to bird and botanize) with Mary Downing, my Cub Scout den mother. When Dad proved a knowledgeable crew member on Long Island Sound in Tom and Peggy Armstrong's daysailer, I wondered what other athletic skills he might have. Shuffleboard appeared out of the blue one summer in the early 1960s. A University benefactor gathered some male peers for a noontime Saturday face off, and Dad came home from work early and skipped his lunch to join them, mystifying me but gratifying me as well, since it meant a break from pruning.

My folks got me a two-wheeler by the time I was seven; Johnny Swenson taught me how to ride it, and ever after I had an age-appropriate bicycle. Dad didn't have one, or Mom either. About 1966 we got an adult-sized tricycle for Davey; Mom talked UA dean Ken Barker into assembling it. Dad purchased an Exercycle just before we left 856 Mayfair Road, and later he and Virginia had matching street bikes in their Fort Lauderdale home.

SPECTATOR SPORTS

I went with Mom and Dad to most of the Zips football games and with Dad to many of the Zips basketball games. Once or twice a year we traveled by train or car to Ohio Conference games at Ohio Wesleyan, Heidelberg, or Denison. We visited Fenn College in Cleveland for basketball and Wooster and Hiram. I saw Zips baseball with Dad at Firestone

Stadium. But we never went to professional sports contests, so I missed the Browns and the Indians and had moved away by the time the Cavaliers began playing in the Coliseum in Richfield.

Dad had ridden the roller coasters with Ames and Dick at Coney Island in Cincinnati, but it was Mom who took me to Cedar Point soon after it opened and directed me to the roller coaster and nursed what was left afterwards. She took me down to the Armory when Ringling Brothers came to Akron and to Madison Square Garden for three rings of Barnum and Bailey's. She went with me one time to wrestling in the Armory then bankrolled my regular visits with Bobby Keener, picking us up afterwards, overheated, trying out holds on the High Street sidewalk. I still have never been to a professional boxing match.

FAMILY SWIMMING

Swimming was the one regular family recreation of my preadolescent years. And my father had his own pool. He had it before Goodyear CEO Russ DeYoung built his Eaton Road home with outdoor and indoor pools (later to serve as the President's Home under D. J. Guzzetta and William V. Muse). On winter Sunday afternoons after 1954, Dad and Mom and I and perhaps one of my friends would drive to Buchtel Avenue near Union Street, park in a spot reserved in my father's name, and walk to a long two-story grey concrete-faced yellow brick building with several glass-and-metal-framed doors. Dad would select the only one of the doors with an exterior lock, reach into his pocket for his set of keys and open it. Memorial Hall!

We'd enter the huge strangely silent building, open the doors onto the main basketball court, and walk all the way to the back and then through a hatch set flush in the great high movable wall behind the portable stands into the women's gym, running perpendicular to the arena, where we'd split up. Mom went east, and Dad and I west to stairs that led down into tiled space lit by translucent glass block and overhead fluorescent lights, which switched on after Dad unlocked a hidden panel. A painted door led into a locker room, where we'd change into our swimming suits in heavy, wet, warm, chlorine-scented air and move past toilet cubicles and a row of showers to another door that opened into a huge space directly under the women's gym. It was near the deep end of a twenty-five meter pool with three rows of tiled stands on the inside wall and more translucent glass block on the outside wall letting in light to reflect on the still, blue-green water. I'd spring forward to break the surface with my best cannon-ball and recover and dive for the bottom and come up and crawl stroke to the shallow end. Dad would climb down the ladder of the deep end and begin doing slow laps in a stroke of his own devising, sort of a side-breast stroke with a frog rather than scissor kick, his head always above the water. By the time I'd reached the deep end again, Mother would emerge from the women's locker room at the east end, fuss a bit about the temperature of the water and check the adjustment of her swimming cap before easing in and starting a lap or two of breast stroke and back stroke.

We had the pool to ourselves. We never stayed long enough. Once a man in dark blue clothes and a visored cap walked in through the door in the stands, and when my father waved to him he touched his bill and said, "Oh, hello, it's you, Dr. Auburn," and quickly left. When Mom insisted it was time to go, Dad and I would return to our side and shower with soap that he'd brought in a plastic box, dry off with towels we took from varnished wooden boxes built into the walls and dropped in another box and dress, and walk back upstairs to meet Mom, after Dad had shouted to make sure she was done and turned off the switch for the lights. Once or twice when we came we found the locker room or the pool area in disarray from some Saturday activity, and once we arrived when the Athletic Director or a head coach had brought his family to swim. But otherwise, for four or five years, we were alone. By 1960 or so as the University grew and staff was added, the pool was opened to all faculty and students on Sundays, and my folks stopped going. I remember going at other times with Dad to the YMCA pool or with Mom to the Jewish Center on Balch Street, and on warm summer Sundays we might go to the swimming park the Renners operated in Monroe Falls.

Dad was sixty-six when he retired from UA and left the President's Home. He would live for thirty-two years more, and all that time he had one requirement for his Akron living space: it must have an indoor pool available. I swam with him at Fir Hill Towers, Tower 80, and the Camelot. He'd swim mostly about 4:00 p.m. He'd change in his apartment and walk down to the pool in a heavy terrycloth robe and slippers. In his eighties, it took him increasing time to prepare for his swim; he needed to manage hearing aids, lower vision, earplugs, and noseplugs. He rarely used the whirlpool, but he'd often sit in the sauna. Mostly he swam his slow laps, on his side, bottom arm extended forward to cup a handful of water and pull it back to his chest as his top arm returned to his chest to scoop a handful of water and push it back down his side, his head above the water, and his legs coordinated in a sideways frog kick. When he felt he'd done enough, he'd climb the ladder and put on his robe and sit in a chair before going to the sauna which he'd turned on when he entered the pool area. Perhaps once in every three times someone else would be using the pool, and I think he planned his visits for the hours when he was most likely to be alone, for without his hearing aids and his glasses he couldn't communicate very well. He swam for the last time a year or so before he died. I think he'd begun to fear infection and wished to avoid the temperature gradients he had to pass through out of his apartment, onto the elevator, through the basement garage, into the next building, through the hallways, into the pool area, and back again. Besides, the treadmill provided the movement and load that he felt he needed to maintain health.

* * *

Dad was in his late fifties and I about twenty when he walked up every stair of the Washington Monument without pause. He walked for eight or ten hours a day with me through the great castles of Austria and Eastern Europe, the Stalin-era monuments, and the twisting streets of Budapest and Belgrade and still wanted to go out at night for circus or opera or symphony. He carried abdominal fat which he felt unsightly from his forties to his final illness, but he was fit for a man in a sedentary profession with no regular, vigorous, aerobic or body-building pastime. The first proof of any cardiovascular or circulatory disease came when he was ninety-four, and that congestive heart failure was soon controlled with a pacemaker. As Joseph Epstein quipped when he had his heart arteries patched at sixty-seven, heart failure at ninety-four seems a lot like heart success.

He raised me, the last of his children to live at home, with a wide range of experiences in sports and physical and recreational activities from which to make my own life choices. I confess I never learned to ski or to skate, but I never learned to hang-glide, parachute, bungee-jump, or motorcycle, either. I thought I'd spend more time with my own children and teach them more things and provide them more enrichment, and until they were teenagers I had extraordinary flexibility with my time and worked a lot at home. But in fact I spent only a little more time with them than he had with me, and if I increased their range of experience in areas such as family travel, cooking, and theatre, I never saw to such things as archery, shooting, horseback riding, sailing, and skiing.

Bowling (A Reconstruction)

Don Bowles told a story about my father. It was fall 1991, and I had recently returned to The University of Akron. We were having coffee with some other long-time UA faculty and administrators in the Chuckery. I think George Ball was there. Maybe Dick Wright, too.

Don said that in the 1960s, soon after the big addition to the Gardner Student Center had opened, on quiet Saturday mornings the president would combine a coffee break with a bit of bowling. Don took some credit for enabling these trips from Buchtel Hall next door. It was early in his career. He was then purchasing agent. When he told this story a quarter century later, he had been Vice President for Administrative Services under Dom Guzzetta and was finishing his thirty-year career by serving as founding Associate Dean of the College of Polymer Science and Polymer Engineering, working daily with Frank Kelley.

I checked parts of this story with Caroline. She confirmed that she always came to the office on Saturday mornings from 7:30 to 11:45 when my father was in town. Yes, he often went over to the Chuckery for coffee at 10:00 and then slipped down to bowl. No, none of the other "girls" came in on Saturday, so she couldn't leave her desk to get a message to the president. Oh, she remembered this story, all right. Wayne Duff or Jim Banks had made some crack about it. No, she couldn't recall why she'd called to find Dr. Auburn.

> Your dad rolled his first ball in the tenth frame. He bowled last, of course, and the guy before had picked up a spare and struck out. Your dad had 127 coming into the tenth, and he could make 157 if he struck

out all the way or 147 if he picked up a spare, and he was bearing down because he usually rolled only about 120.

When he threw his first in the tenth I thought to myself that it was coming in high on the headpin. And, sure enough, the ball did come in too high and your dad was left with a seven-ten split.

Well, he made some comment I couldn't hear. One of the guys said "You can pick it up, Mr. President," and Wayne said something about that's how things go with a MacGregor design. Wayne wasn't bowling, of course. He was just kibitzing.

Your dad had just finished drying his hands on the blower and was reaching for his ball on the return when the phone behind Chet's desk rang. He'd just gripped the ball and raised it to his chin and was ready to start his four-step crouch-and-slide when Chet called out, "Dr. Auburn, Dr. Auburn! It's Miss Pardee, and she's gotta talk with you right now!"

Your dad didn't quite stop, for he hadn't really got started. He shifted his weight a bit, and he looked back at Chet over his shoulder and said, "Damnit, Chet, tell Caroline I've got only one ball left!"

It got mighty quiet.

I heard a *thropka* ... *thropka* ... *thropka* ..., from the ball return, I thought. Something not fitting right.

George here tried to catch my eye, but I didn't let him.

I could feel the blood rushing up my cheeks, so I held my breath and clenched my teeth, and in managing to avoid looking at George, I locked glances with Wayne, who was suddenly very seriously fiddling with his pipe.

And then Jim caught my eye and I thought I'd lose it, and I heard the ball hit the wood and start rolling.

And Dick was retying his shoe laces with his head ducked practically between his knees, and I thought I'd better call the Brunswick guy to come check the lube on the belts of the return ...

<Oh, my sweet Jesus! "one ball"!>

... and I saw the ball come down the left side of the alley at the gutter edge and kiss the ten pin just enough to knock it across into the seven pin.

Cra-ack plonk!

Then silence, except for that slipping belt.

Your dad stood straight up out of his follow-through and turned around. He stared at each of us carefully for a moment. Then he smiled and said,

"Looks like I still have one ball left.

"Score the spare, Bowles, and I'll try to strike out."

And then he chuckled, turned back to dry his hand and pick up his ball, and we just whooped until we cried ... I thought I'd've died.

Photography

When Dad took up photography, I was happy to have an answer to the question about his hobbies, since nothing else seemed to qualify in the life of this man who worked all the time. Indeed, I think it was many years before I realized that Dad's photography supported his public reporting on foreign travel, and if it was a hobby, it was also a tool to publish his scholarship. Beginning in 1954, Norm and Kay traveled abroad most summers for two to four weeks on University-related study tours. At first they were members of educational delegations organized or countenanced by national higher education associations or governmental bodies like USIA. By the late sixties (and particularly after H. Kenneth Barker joined the University), they were the honorary leaders of University of Akron tours for alumni and friends, "Classrooms Abroad."

They were among the first Akronites to visit the Soviet Union when Nikita Khrushchev took power and encouraged foreign visitors. They entered Outer Mongolia with the first Western visitors since World War II. They visited Africa when Lumumba and Nkrumah ruled post-colonial states and southeast Asia before the Gulf of Tonkin Resolution.

Particularly after Sputnik in 1957, Dad integrated into all his public remarks his experiences as a recent visitor to the Communist states, which were the focus of much Cold War apprehension. And he and Mother both gave slide-illustrated travelogue-lectures throughout northeast Ohio based upon the pictures he took. They were liberal-minded Cold Warriors who believed in furthering international understanding, spreading the gospel of American democracy, and creating

Kay and Norm at the Parthenon, 1968. *From the author's collection*

local and national support for higher education in its quest to produce engineers and rocket scientists, language-trained diplomats, and well-educated ROTC graduates. And Dad made himself a pretty good photographer for these political and education reasons.

I don't believe Dad studied photography formally, but he sought advice from professionals like Lou Tobias (UA's photographer) and the Metzgers (operators of Akron's largest camera and film-processing store). His principal camera was a thirty-five millimeter Leica mechanism with interchangeable lenses for telegraphic and wide-angle and standard effects. After his son-in-law Rusty was posted overseas to Europe, Dad commissioned him to purchase lenses not easily available in the States. He acquired a Minox before Q outfitted James Bond with one, and I remember my apprehensions behind the Iron Curtain when he would surreptitiously snap photographs our Intourist guide had forbidden. He was an early adopter of the Polaroid and lugged the book-sized camera and its bulky film packs on his travels, making friends with the instant images he left in their hands. His Polaroid was the first of his cameras to which I was allowed regular access.

A week or two after they returned from abroad, Dad would bring home one or two dozen amber-yellow boxes of slides, thirty-six to the hinged box in two stacks of eighteen each, numbered 1 to 36 on the side through which he projected the light through the film into the lens. Now the ping-pong table on top of the pool table in the basement would become for a week or two the staging area to select and arrange images. Dad tried working with an illuminated slide tray—sort of like the face of a translucent ziggurat onto which he could place a few dozen slides at a time—but he was more comfortable seeing the images projected onto a screen. By the mid sixties, carousel trays holding 140 slides replaced the rectangular boxes of forty slides which earlier had enabled the speaker to advance through a set without handling each individually. On evenings when he wasn't called away on other University business, my father would be viewing, rejecting, sorting, and arranging slides. Mom would often work with him, and they would reinforce each other's memory of the images.

I don't recall either of them making notes, though sometimes they would write a word or two on the back of the slides, which of course would not be visible to them while they were lecturing. Perhaps there were notes which I never saw: in speaking to large audiences for more than a few minutes, Dad almost always worked from prepared texts, and when I traveled with him, he wrote in a diary every evening and had it transcribed when he came home.

But I think for his travel lectures, the completed set of images was the only guide to his speech. I am sure Mother never wrote out her remarks: while she made extensive marginal notes in her reading and covered sheets of note paper with guiding phrases and numbered points for her book reviews, when I heard her give a slide lecture the spontaneity always seemed genuine, unstudied, and the organization flowed from the arranged images. The presence of those images to provide structure was a good thing in her talks, for otherwise the digressions on people, food, clothing, and objets d'art would lengthen her presentations far longer than Dad's. He marshaled his statistics and pictures of buildings to emphasize the might of our adversaries and the consequent advisability of doubling down on the American investment in higher education; she multiplied anecdote and human nuance to show how much these foreign strangers really were like us and wanted the same things for their children, notwithstanding their being Godless Communists or slaves of the dictators and their ideologies.

The era of the slide-illustrated travel lecture lasted about ten years, I guess, ending around the middle sixties when television won people's evening leisure, lasting perhaps another ten years at Rotary and Kiwanis luncheon meetings before going on hiatus until updated by PowerPoint in the 1990s. Interest in foreign travel in post-World War II Akron was intense. Dad started the "World at Our Door" lecture series at UA, bringing famous travelers and their professionally produced films to paying customers in the 500-seat John S. Knight Auditorium on campus. He and Mom always lectured for free to groups like the Council on World Affairs or the Akron International Institute or the League of Women Voters or the AAUW, Dad doing the evening events and Mom the daytime venues for majority female audiences.

For a time, the Women's City Club offered monthly slide-illustrated travel lectures of which my parents' were just one. Because Akron's Big Four rubber companies operated plantations throughout the tropics, sold tires worldwide, and brought their managers home to their world headquarters, the city had a developed interest in world affairs which such lectures exploited. Akronite Parke Thompson had a new lecture once and sometimes twice a year as he strove to report on his life-list of nations visited, a list that kept expanding with new postcolonial nation-states. Caroline drew large audiences for slide lectures with a naturalist's bent and locations not limited to the superpowers and their satellite states; she reached and reported on Antarctica and the Galapagos Islands, she toured and showed most of the US national parks, she joined National Geographic expeditions, she flipped through twice as many images per lecture, and because she was a middle-aged maiden lady traveling on her own, she projected an aura of exotic independence in the era which produced *The Feminine Mystique*. Caroline also had a network of women friends in the public relations and journalism business, and they faithfully puffed and reported her lectures. (Mother held that she was just imitating her boss and his wife, and Kay didn't feel flattered.) No dinner party at 161 South Union concluded without one of Caroline's slide shows. But, even though Ken Burns's career was just beginning, the public slide travelogue pretty much ceased by the late sixties.

Dad always took the pictures on the travels, and he always took the lead on developing and selecting the slides to show. But otherwise he took few pictures. At family gatherings, it was Uncle Bill and then nephew-in-law Bob Swinehart who filmed the holidays, with Dad occasionally showing off his Polaroid when the technology was new. To document her grandchildren as they came, Mom first used the Polaroid and then acquired a simple Kodak and produced color prints which she sometimes annotated but rarely arranged in albums. She also counted on Dad to have Lou Tobias take formal and informal pictures of the family since so many of our Akron reunions coincided with University-related events. Dad never photographed for simple aesthetic pleasure, except perhaps when he was exploring the capacities of new equipment before a trip. His practice of photography pretty much ended with the last of his UA travels in 1970; his hobby had served its multiple purposes.

Vacations

During our residence in the President's Home, we never took an extended family vacation that did not have some University of Akron purpose. Part of the reason was my father's temperament and emotional resilience, which did not seem to require more than a change of problems to become refreshed, and that only occasionally. Still, there was at least one family vacation that I can recall, and there were lots of trips which other families would describe as vacations.

The first I remember began with a long drive in a dark back seat from Cincinnati to Teddy's Teeth on the eastern slopes of the Rockies near Estes Park, Colorado, where family friend Bud Dean had a cabin. Perhaps we paused at Mammoth Cave, Kentucky, for I remember a walk down wooden staircases in darkness illuminated by bare bulbs on wires and a sense of great black emptiness and lost chances to buy Native American paraphernalia before and after. Dickie and Amesie were with us but not Davey; it was the summer of 1951, I was five, and I think Mother's helper Mary Harris cared for my four-year-old brother. I rode a horse holding onto the pommel ahead of Daddy in the saddle, and we got off to climb through brush up a tall boulder to gain one of three bald summits in a row and look back to the cabin in the trees a mile or more below. This was my father's last family time before starting The University of Akron presidency.

The next vacation I remember was about four years later, 1955 I think, and also took place in Estes Park. It was just me and Dad and Mom. We drove across the Midwest and the Great Plains, this time in a convertible with the top down for part of the trip, and our drive ended as we

Kay and Norm in the Kremlin near St. Basil's Cathedral, 1959. *From the Norman Auburn Papers. Courtesy of Archival Services, University Libraries, The University of Akron*

descended into a valley surrounded by tall peaks where a U-shaped light-colored building which I recalled when I first saw Vienna's Schoenbrunn Palace dominated the scene. It was the Stanley, a resort hotel, where Mom and I went horseback riding, and swam in the outdoor pool, and ate club sandwiches under a high blue sky and I got to stay in our room, eat my own dinner, and watch as much television as I wanted while Dad and Mom dressed up and went to a banquet there in the hotel. It meant little to me that Dad was President of the Association of Urban Universities and that this was their annual summer conference and that he was at work, not on vacation like me.

Other than frequent visits to Jonesville and a couple of trips to New York City, I don't remember much other family travel until 1958. Before I was born there had been a Montgomery family rental cabin at Lake Wawasee in northeast Indiana, to which Big Daddy, Maman, Aunt

Mary, and Aunt Jo retired from the heat of Cincinnati or Chicago during the summers, and my folks had gone frequently enough that my father cited sailing as a hobby on the résumé he prepared in candidating for the Presidency of UA; but the property had passed out of their hands before the end of World War II. In 1954 my parents began a pattern of traveling abroad for two to four weeks during the summer, participating in and later leading higher education study groups.

PRESIDENTIAL TRAVEL ABROAD

Their first trip abroad was in 1954. On a résumé he updated annually well into his high eighties, Dad cited having been to sixty-five countries, and his overseas travels began with the "Sherwood Eddy Seminar Tour of Europe, Summer, 1954" and the "Sherwood Eddy Seminar Tour of Europe (including USSR), Summer, 1956." The "American Seminar" pioneered by Kansas-born Christian-internationalist George Sherwood Eddy (1871–1963) was in its third decade of organizing European tours for political, business, and educational leaders, and Eddy brought local experts and politicians like Marshall Tito into meeting rooms with his three dozen seminarians. I do not know if the US Department of State absorbed the American Seminar, but Dad cites his April–May 1959 trip as a "State Department-sponsored Educational Mission to Survey Higher Education in USSR and satellite nations." July–August 1960 brings his "Third trip to USSR and satellite nations," then a "Fourth trip to USSR and Europe" in October 1962 and a fifth trip to "USSR included in round-the-world educational mission via Outer Mongolia and Far East, June–August, 1963." There was a "Second round-the-world tour, via Afghanistan and India, June–July, 1964" and a "Third round-the-world tour, via Middle East and Southeast Asia and Japan for AID, August, 1965," marking the beginning of his second "sabbatical" year while President of The University of Akron, this one as Special Assistant for University Relations in the Agency for International Development of the U. S. Department of State (1965–66, and continuing as Consultant to 1972). In 1965–66 Dad made AID-sponsored trips to Africa (his third time to the continent, visiting Nigeria, Liberia, Ghana, Kenya, Ethiopia) and South America (Columbia, Ecuador, Peru). Back to his presidency full time and having hired H. Kenneth Barker in part to organize international study tours, Dad traveled round-the-world in 1967, 1968, and 1970, with a Far East study trip in May–June 1969, Europe and South American in August and October 1969, and Africa just as his retirement became effective in summer 1971.

When they went to Europe for the first time in 1954, I spent about ten days of a projected four weeks at Camp Y-Noah south of Akron before pneumonia hospitalized me for a while and left me to recuperate on the couch of the living room at 344 Merriman Road under Ames's anxious care in that summer before her wedding. Well into high school, I remember spending other summers in Jonesville when Mother traveled with Dad (as she almost always did before the AID-sponsored trips).

Travel was my father's graduate study, his brand of scholarship, his growing avenue of service. And that meant that he was too busy during the twenty years of the UA presidency for long family vacations or even for two or three unstructured days at home. There was no family passion for hiking, camping, skiing, sailing, or sea-bathing; I can't remember even day trips to Lake Erie thirty miles to the north or boating on the Portage Lakes ten miles to the south. I remember that Dad and Mom took one recreational vacation about 1966 when they cruised the Great Lakes on a freighter with Dick and Mary, and another in 1973, a beach trip to St. Thomas with Betty, Bill, and Jo at Rob and Jane's condominium.

MARK TRAVELS TO NEW YORK

But I still got to travel far more than most of my peers. My first trip to New York City was in Mom's company, and she was going to a national convention. In Cincinnati she had organized a chapter of United Cerebral Palsy and helped put on a fund-raiser for the statewide association, and in 1953 she had been re-elected Secretary of the national United Cerebral Palsy society. I was a third grader, almost eight, and allowed out of school to further my education with travel. We had a room at the Biltmore, and in between meetings Mom took me on a ferry ride to the Statue of Liberty, a walk through the antiquities galleries of the Metropolitan Museum of Art, and a hansom cab tour of Central Park and restaurant meals with other national officers where I was the only child.

Something about her care plan for me got discombobulated one afternoon, and I was left in our room when she went away. I'd been given a room-service meal, had a book, and had a television—a great novelty, since we didn't have one at home. Perhaps I hadn't understood when she explained her return time or perhaps my sense of time was still rudimentary. Alone in the room, I became frightened. My book didn't hold my attention. The black-and-white pictures of men and women talking on the soap operas held no interest to equal Dave Garraway and J. Fred Muggs on the "Today" show that morning. I wondered how I could use the telephone to summon Mommy, but I had no idea where she was or what number to dial other than UNiversity 4-0458, our home telephone, and I knew she wasn't there. I thought about leaving the room, finding the elevator, and looking for Mommy somewhere below, but I didn't want to talk to the man who operated the elevator and remembered Mommy's instructions not to leave the room because I didn't have a key to get back in and the door would close itself and lock me out.

I went back to the bed and tried to read my book, but I kept thinking that something horrible had happened to Mommy and I was all alone in a place where "344 Merriman Road" would mean nothing even if I could find the right sort of person to tell it to. Finally I heard the most beloved voice say "Markie, I thought I told you to put the chain up" and I grabbed my mother around the waist and cried on her tummy "Mommy, where have you been! Why are you so late? You said you'd be back! I was so scared!" and then it was all right, she claimed she wasn't late hardly at all, only fifteen minutes, and if I were ever scared again and I wanted people around I could always wait for her under the clock, remember the clock in the lobby? the great big living room with chairs and sofas and tables? that she had just been there with some of the other officers chatting away after the meeting, which had run long, and maybe they chatted for twenty minutes or so and if it ever happened again I was just to put myself under the clock, and she'd find me.

I was back in New York four years later to spend a day or two with Dad when he was Acting President of the Council for Financial Aid to Education in 1957–1958, his first "sabbatical" from the UA presidency. I remember his studio apartment somewhere in the east fifties not far from the United Nations, his making our breakfast just exactly as he did in Akron on nearly identical equipment, and our going for dinner at the Sutton Place home of Herman and Caryl Muehlstein. We arrived on an elevator that let us out right into their front hallway, and their apartment spread out with views in all directions. Everything was white and gold—carpets, draperies, sofas, upholstered chairs, wood chairs, the legs of the dining room table, accented silverware, plates, crystal—except for one room which was all books floor to ceiling and leather, all shades of brown, red, and blue, with tiny lights on flexible arched poles that shown powerfully right onto the book in my lap. And I remember Mr. Muehlstein as a dapper, slender, old, old man (he was only 79, but I had known no other aged persons except Granddaddy Auburn) much shorter than Daddy and Caryl—"Call me Caryl, Honey, not 'Mrs. Muehlstein'"—who was bigger than Herman, too, nearly as tall as Daddy, with so much blonde hair around her smiling face, younger than Mommy with big sweeping gestures like Mommy's but much more jewelry, and such petting and kissing of Daddy and me and offering to read me—eleven-year-old me—books.

When I saw "Hello, Dolly" on Broadway two or three years later, I thought Carol Channing was really Caryl Muehlstein until she spoke, and Mommy explained to me that Herman had met Caryl Bergman when she was in the chorus of a Broadway show and had made the only marriage of his life when he was sixty-six and she was twenty-five.

That same year, 1957 into 1958, we spent New Year's Eve with the Muehlsteins at the Fontainebleau in Miami Beach. Dick and Dad had shared driving the University Chevrolet from Akron to southeast Florida. We ate at Wolfie's, my first New York-style delicatessen, and we all spent an evening watching *The Bridge on the River Kwai*, the first time I could remember going to the movies with Dad. Mom had gotten me a powder blue swim set, trunks and cabana shirt, and despite her frequent applications of sun tan lotion I burned my legs badly. I was shocked at the bright red patches with straight edges on the fronts and backs of my thighs and their contrast to the fish-belly-white skin above. I couldn't find a comfortable sleeping position despite the menthol-smelling salve Mom applied, and I was surprised to be shivering late at night when I woke in the dark.

The purpose of this Miami vacation was for Dad to show off some of his family to Herman and Caryl, and Herman wished to entertain us in highest style on America's second-greatest secular feast day, its public Saturnalia. Mom whispered to me that tickets to the Fontainebleau's New Year's Eve dinner cost one hundred dollars apiece: I had much of my birthday and Christmas present money, nearly twenty dollars, a great fortune—most of which I intended to lay out on fireworks on our return drive, so I understood the value of money well enough to expect very fine entertainment indeed.

How disappointed I became, then, as our evening progressed with my rented tuxedo chaffing my sunburned legs and maraschino-cherry-topped ginger ale becoming commonplace and the principal act being Tony Martin crooning songs conspiratorially to the bejeweled, mink-stoled women in their blue bouffant hair-dos. I tired of him soon.

A year later we once again enjoyed New Year's Eve with Herman and Caryl, this time in Manhattan, at the Pierre Hotel, on Fifth Avenue at 61st Street, in the Cotillion Ballroom. Dad and Dick had driven the University Chevrolet to the city. We walked to the Pierre from our hotel about 9:00 p.m., Dick escorting either Terry or Mimi Armstrong (daughters of Mom and Dad's friends from Cincinnati days now living in Phillipsburg, New Jersey, the dream of all four parents being to cement the families' friendship by a marriage in the next generation). And I was escorting Kathy Walker, who had come with us from Akron under Mom's protection. Kathy was the daughter of the pediatrician who had seen me safely through pneumonia in 1954 and measles in 1956, and she was destined to be Sandy's Old Trail School classmate and graduate school roommate and maid of honor when we were married eleven years later.

I remember shrimp cocktail, filet mignon, a flaming dessert, dancing with Kathy so as to make Akron's Mrs. Betty King proud of her tutelage, dancing with Mom, Mom and Dad dancing, and Caryl and Herman dancing—so graceful, both of them, an advertisement for Arthur Murray, images of Ginger Rogers with an aged Fred Astaire. And I remember feline Eartha Kitt singing and shedding pieces of her costume until by 11:45 I couldn't even glance at Kathy without blushing. This would be the last New Year's Eve with Herman; he died three years later, leaving Dad with responsibility for his estate through a foundation.

MARK VISITS HIS GODMOTHER

In summer 1960, Dad and Mom and I drove across Pennsylvania to Tom and Peggy Armstrong's Phillipsburg home, where I was left for two weeks while my parents joined a University study tour to Eastern Europe, meeting at Idlewild Airport in Queens. Neither of their daughters Terry and Mimi was home, so I was Aunt Peggy's only child for the visit. My parents had a couple of days with Tom and Peggy, on one of which Tom took us ocean sailing in a single-masted daysailer and my father distinguished himself as crew. Long lazy days around their pool followed for me with light duties as pool cleaner and as a dependable fourth at bridge in the evenings, a fourteen-year-old holding his own among Tom and Peggy and their friends and adding Jacoby transfers to his store of bidding knowledge.

Four years later I would spend six summer weeks with Aunt Peggy, now divorced from the father of her children and married to Joe Schaefer, a brilliant entrepreneur who shed the mother of his children, sold his company, and moved to Calistoga, California, with Peggy to operate a demonstration dairy farm and profit not from the milk but from the blood lines of his cows. Mom flew out to meet me (I had driven across country in our Impala convertible with Keith Kelly, who had gone to UA for his second college year, lived with us at 856 Mayfair Road, and whom I left with his newly transferred family in Pomona before driving up to the Napa Valley), and after a few days for Peggy and Mom to chat we took more than a week to drive home with stops at Yosemite, Yellowstone, and Mount Rushmore.

MARK TRAVELS ABROAD

In June 1963 when I graduated from Western Reserve Academy, Dad and Mom sent me on a mini Grand Tour with classmate Ron Warner. We flew over and back with a University-sponsored tour, leaving the group after the second day in Edinburgh to wander around Europe on our own with EuRail passes, so that we saw mostly the terminal cities of overnight train journeys (to save on hotels), except for a week in Spain (Ron and I had taken three years of Spanish together and could make our elementary needs understood in that language) and two three-day stays with Ames and Rusty, first in Frankfurt as they packed to change posts and later in Hamburg as they unpacked in their new home—so like my mother, my big sister, to welcome a pair of seventeen-year-old six-foot-four-inch galoots into her life at its busiest time. Then in 1966 Dad took just me with him on a grander tour of Eastern Europe.

'Big galoots' Mark Auburn and Ron Warner prepare to embark for Europe, 1963. *Photo by Lou Tobias, from the Norman Auburn Papers. Courtesy of Archival Services, University Libraries, The University of Akron*

THE PRESIDENT AND HIS SON ABROAD

Dad treated most things in life with the calm concentrated multitasking confidence of a chess Grand Master playing a dozen simultaneous exhibition games. Our trip had the family purpose of assuring parity among his offspring, Dad having taken Ames and Dick on previous trips abroad. It capped his year on partial leave from UA while he served at the State Department working on university R&D overseas, and he could also call it University of Akron business since his reputation as a traveler to the Communist world and its educational institutions was well established with his Board and the Akron public. And he had another secret purpose: he wanted to get a visa to travel to the People's Republic of China, and old hands in the State Department had told him how to try. So we both had things to reveal to one another at the start of our three weeks together, for I had to admit what he had long known, namely that I was an addict to the Montgomery tobacco malady and would be smoking cigarettes in his presence, and he needed to tell me what he hadn't told Mom, that he was likely to leave me in a hotel room in a city behind the Iron Curtain for two or three days at an hour's notice.

Here was his plan. The People's Republic of China had no public and few private diplomatic relations with the United States in 1966, and tensions were especially high because of America's growing involvement in Southeast Asia. Relations between Red China and the Soviet Union were formal but not friendly, and a Westerner was unlikely to be allowed by the Soviet guards to enter the Chinese Embassy in Moscow. China's one close ally in Europe was Albania, the mountainous enclave on the Adriatic, Muslim by tradition, puritan in its Marxist-Leninist-Maoist ideology, technologically underdeveloped, distrustful of all things capitalist or Slavic, and proud of its isolation. Dad thought that if he could get himself into Albania, he could enter the Chinese Embassy in Tirana and there plead his case for an educational visa to mainland China. First, however, he needed to get a visa to enter Albania, whose borders were more tightly sealed against its neighbors Yugoslavia and Greece than its coastline to cigarette and gasoline smugglers from Italy. Now, the USSR would not grant him a visa to visit Albania, nor would Tito's Yugoslavia (which barely tolerated its Albanian minorities in Montenegro and Kosovo), but he thought he had a chance from either Hungary or Romania, and he was prepared to leave his twenty-year-old son alone at the moment his permission was granted.

We traveled in style. We had a local car and driver and an English-speaking guide everywhere—Kiev and Moscow, Warsaw, Prague, Budapest, Bucharest, and Belgrade. Employees of the USSR's Intourist or the satellites' clone tourist agencies were with us most of our waking hours, and Dad hoped they'd report portraits of an apolitical college president sincerely interested in furthering educational ties between his urban university with its great strengths in rubber chemistry and polymer engineering and their institutions of higher education. We wore suits and ties daily, visited the great Stalinist monuments, Party memorials, and universities, and asked politely to see sites off the official paths, like the forest of Babi Yar (subject of Yevtushenko's 1961 poem on the great massacre) or the Jewish cemetery in Prague. We went to opera or circus or theatre or cabaret nightly.

Dad took pictures with his Leica for his lectures and with his Polaroid to leave with officials or people on the street and with his Minox of the objects the guides forbade our recording, and we left ballpoint pens imprinted "University of Akron" and crisp new US one-dollar bills from a supply Dad knew to bring in the hands of drivers, guides, rectors, chancellors, and guards. Despite changing hotels almost daily and rarely encountering foods to Dad's preference, it was an easy trip made easier not just by the private tours but by Dad's regularity of habit. We arose by seven and were in bed by eleven nightly. Dad's jar of peanut butter served his needs every other day or so when he couldn't find anything else to his taste. He taught me to hydrate on beer where water was doubtful (the only time I ever saw him drink beer) and to take every opportunity of a hotel bath and toilet. At his suggestion, and following his own example, I wrote far more in my journal than I had on my tour of western Europe three years earlier, and that autumn I mined it to write weekly color pieces for the *Buchtelite*, "Behind the Iron Curtain" being the series' name. It was my last family vacation and the most continuous time I had ever spent in the company of my father. He didn't get the visa to Albania. He did visit Outer Mongolia before most other Westerners post-World War II, and went on six round-the-world trips before he retired in 1971, and he finally visited the People's Republic of China after President Nixon's opening initiative in 1972.

Cars

In Cincinnati my folks got along with one car. In Akron, even before we moved into the President's Home, they would need two. So, shortly after Mom and I joined Dad and Dickie in October 1951, we went car shopping. We went to Top Motors near the intersection of West Market and Maple Streets across from St. Vincent's Church under the big red neon sign with the dealership's name in letters and a pictograph of the child's toy. Dad was looking for a newer used Hudson, like the one we were driving, and he took us for a ride in one differing in my mind only in color and interior aroma, but we didn't buy it, and I remember some talk about three hundred dollars.

We did get a new car before summer 1952, a two-tone beige and brown Chevrolet convertible. Dad had the University make a family portrait with the top down, himself behind the wheel, Mom in the passenger seat, Dick in the backseat behind Dad, me sitting on the boot, and Ames behind Mom with Davey on her lap. In fact this family car was Mom's, because Dad had a University car, a blue four-door Chevrolet sedan which was changed out every year or two in the fall for the newest blue four-door model. Not until 1965 would he drive a different make or model. Meanwhile, every two years or so Mom would have a new Chevrolet convertible, usually in beige, until fall 1967, when she got an Oldsmobile Cutlass four-door sedan.

Dad's University sedans were either gifts or lease models at favorable rates, I don't know which, from Dave Corbin's City Chevrolet on East Market and Forge Streets near the University. Dad dealt for our family cars

Mark, Ames, Dick, Davey, Kay, and Norm in their new Chevrolet Bel-Air convertible, 1952. *Photo by Lou Tobias, from the Norman Auburn Papers. Courtesy of Archival Services, University Libraries, The University of Akron*

with Paul Martin, Corbin's sales manager, who bought the dealership in 1954 and would become a generous benefactor of UA in the 1990s and 2000s.

A PASSENGER WITH THE PRESIDENT'S SPOUSE

I remember my father as a heavy-footed driver, starting fast from stoplights and cruising in the city at fifteen to twenty percent above speed limits, changing lanes to gain position at the head of traffic but cornering without much lean. Mom was pretty quick, too, but less eager than Dad to head the pack and less focused than Dad because she'd talk and smoke and get distracted at lights but wave gaily to the driver behind whose horn reminded her that the light had changed. I don't remember feeling uncomfortable with Dad driving, but I do remember a couple of times of embarrassment with Mom.

One time was when Mom signaled a right turn but turned left. It seems that the left-hand signal on her Chevrolet was broken, she was being followed closely, and she put on the right-turn signal "to let him know we were turning." The following car took advantage of a clear oncoming path opposite so as not to brake his car when ours appeared to be taking a very slow turn to the right, as Mom's rear signal suggested. He pulled out but had to panic-stop to avoid striking our left front quarter when Mom turned left. Mom explained to me why it was his fault, not hers.

Another time, in the parking lot behind the Acme on West Market Street between North Highland and Conger Avenues at Highland Square, Mom put our car into reverse and moved out of our parking spot at a normal crawl when *cah-rump*! I was all right, Mommy was all right, but when she got out and began interrogating the driver of the injured car with great certainty of her own innocence, I shrank as small as possible. Of course, Dad had to be told about the accident that night and make arrangements to talk to Carl Owens to get it fixed. I didn't witness my parents' exchange, and no one ever asked my recollection of the event. I've always been blessed with good spatial calculations, and one glance at the position of the damage to our car and to the other told me that we had backed into it.

I rode with Mommy for thousands of miles in those Chevrolet convertibles, and that time in the Acme parking lot was the only occasion I heard *cah-rump*! She never had another fender-bender with me in the car. She was never stopped for speeding or for reckless driving. I can't even remember another near miss. I accompanied her across Route 18 to Route 20 to Route 223 into Michigan to M34 and M99 to Jonesville and back at least four and up to six times a year, six-hour two-hundred mile trips each way, reduced to four hours when the Ohio Turnpike opened in 1955, nearly two thousand miles of incident-free annual driving just for those trips. I was driven hither and yon in northeast Ohio by her every day, and we never had an accident and never were stopped. She was a good driver. She overtook rarely on two-lane roads. She signaled her turns and her lane changes, and she didn't drive with the turn signal needlessly blinking. She made full halts at stop signs, she observed the "right-of-way" rotation at four-way stops, and she'd pause to let cars enter highways from blind approaches. And I was the cause of her only traffic citation in Akron.

MY FIRST TICKET

I was fourteen, it was September 1960, and we were returning from dropping Davey off at The Manor. Mom and Betty and Jo had "chewed the fat" until late, then Mom had sat up with Jo (a confirmed night owl and insomniac) until the small hours. We stopped at least twice for Mom to get coffee on the long boring hundred-and-forty-mile turnpike run between the Pioneer and the Route 21 interchanges.

There were no learners' permits in Ohio in 1960, but that didn't stop me. At the Manor I'd been driving the tractor for three years, and I'd driven Rob's car up and down the lanes of the farm property with no problems. I was really fourteen-and-three-quarters, and I now topped 5'10" and had plenty of Western Reserve Academy friends who were already drivers. We'd gotten off the turnpike on Route 21, Brecksville Road, when Mom acceded to the badgering she'd resisted during the long soporific nearly empty stretch of superhighway across the state. We switched seats. I drove smoothly toward home, Brecksville Road changing to Cleveland-Massillon and becoming with a left bend Ghent Road, up to the left turn at Smith (no problem at all: proper signal and pause for oncoming traffic, smooth turn) past Revere Road, Sand Run Road, to the top of Smith Road Hill, and then, a couple hundred yards above the AC&Y railroad crossing, I saw the motorcycle policeman standing at the intersection of Smith with Riverview halting traffic, so that four or five cars were waiting at the stop sign.

I panicked. There was nowhere for me to turn, nowhere for me to stop on the steep hill with deep culverts on either side. When we reached the line of stopped cars, I opened the driver's door and ran around the back and slid into the passenger seat. My action declared our irregularity, and despite her truthful explanation of her fatigue and the pleas about the easy proximity of our destination (in those days without even a traffic light between us and the President's Home), Mom was ticketed.

Over the following weeks Mom got angry at the *Akron Beacon Journal*. First, the paper moved the citation from the terse page-two court-docket listing on the inside to a front-of-section, two-column, hundred-word story on the bottom right headlined something like "Akron U Prexy's Wife Cited." Then, after Mom appeared before the traffic judge, pled guilty, and was fined, the newspaper published those results just as prominently. The newspaper could not make a third story over my appearance before a Juvenile Court traffic referee, those proceedings not being public, or Akron would have been told that I was fined twenty dollars after the referee had learned what my current allowance was and reckoned that four weeks' worth would help seal the lesson and that—far worse—he had declared me ineligible to take my driving test until a full month after my sixteenth birthday, meaning that I missed driving for the entire 1961 holiday season and was absolutely the last person in my class of high school juniors to come of age.

Mom raged against the *Beacon Journal*; she may even have complained to Jack Knight, when he came to the President's Home for dinner. She fulminated against a legal system which required her to go to court twice (she had to accompany me to the referee's office) over a matter which should be within a parent's discretion to judge. Dad said nothing. They both knew that in dozens of Akron homes took place scenes such as Sandy later reported: her father George Korman called to her mother Pearl, who was in the kitchen with Sandy cleaning up after dinner, "Will you look at this! The President's wife let her son drive, and he's only fourteen!"

PRESIDENT AUBURN STRETCHING THE LIMIT

A newspaper story on wrong-doing in the President's family attracted wide readership. So did much else about the family. Dad and Mom understood their public roles, so we drove sensible, middle-class Chevrolets. My parents bet that Kay could be seen in a convertible if it were an otherwise sober, economical make. Eddie Thomas or Ward Keener or Harry Schrank could cruise around in a Cadillac DeVille, and after Russ DeYoung struck a bargain with Chrysler to use Goodyear tires as original equipment, he could sport a succession of luxurious Imperials. But we could not. We were a public college president's family. Dad told me that Dave Towell, the local Cadillac dealer, wanted to give him (that is, the University) a Cadillac, which everyone including Davey knew was America's luxury standard. Dad said that he'd refused more than once. When Dave Towell suggested he take a Cadillac for Mom, he refused that, too.

But Dad succumbed to a different offer from Dave Towell in the summer of 1965. The laws that would make the University state supported in 1967 had been signed and sealed; state assistance had started flowing; there would be no more municipal tax campaigns. He'd been lionized in *Beacon Journal* editorials because "He Gets Things Done." He'd served UA for nearly fifteen years, making him one of the longest presidential servants in the University's ninety-five years, second only to his predecessor Hezzleton Simmons. He was shortly going off on his second working sabbatical, this time to Washington, DC for the State Department, so he'd be driving the University car only on weekends.

And Dave Towell wasn't proposing a Cadillac. He suggested a brand new Oldsmobile model, a Toronado. Dad followed automotive technology. He loved its bright spots. It was the great industry of his life's span, the driver and the measure of consumer confidence. That Hudson we'd brought from Cincinnati was a radical new design, the "step-down" body system produced three years before Detroit's Big Three adopted it. He loved being in the vanguard, and the Toronado was front-wheel drive, nearly the first for an American mass production vehicle. It was spacious enough for six passengers, at 425 cubic inches, the largest motor he'd ever driven, at 211 inches long, longer than any of his Chevy sedans. He took it. (It was blue.) I imagine that he told himself that a University president needed to show leadership and adopt innovation. I think he drove it and successor models for the final six years of his Akron presidency.

Meanwhile, the next car for Mom had to be upgraded from the Bel-Airs when Chevrolet stopped making convertibles in that line. If we wanted a Chevrolet convertible, it had to be an Impala, an immense boat of a car 220 inches long on a 120-plus-inch wheelbase with a 409-cubic-inch motor. Mom always said that her only needs in a car were a top that would go down and a color close to the champagne hair-rinse she used; the Impala was a rag top, but the color had to be white. At least the interior was taupe.

When both the Impala and the Toronado were in the garage of the President's Home, I could barely squeeze between their rear bumpers and the doors, and I had to open the passenger doors on the adjacent sides carefully. Mom had an added complication: she took the side of the garage nearer to the interior door to the kitchen, so she had to park her car at an angle to allow this door to be used. During the next year or two before they sent me to the University of Chicago in it, the Impala became something of a bone of contention between my parents. Mother scraped the garage posts on both sides, and while we all made jokes about her Braille parking methods, she was embarrassed and blamed the size of the Impala. Her next car was a midsized model, the new Oldsmobile Cutlass, smaller than the Impala though larger than most full-sized cars of the twenty-first century. And unfortunately, it didn't come with a convertible top; instead it had a sun roof. At least it was beige.

CARS AFTER THE PRESIDENCY

Dad solved the family's convertible-less status with his first post-presidential purchase: a Cadillac DeVille convertible in white with blue leather (our first leather) interior. Now he could drive a Cadillac; now the family would again have a convertible. If possible, it was larger than the Impala and as overpowered. But it was safe. I nearly rear-ended a stopped semi in 7:00 a.m. fog at the I-76/I-80 split west of Youngstown in it one morning in September 1973 when I drove Mom and a load of household goods to Brooklyn. We were going to set up their apartment on Remsen Street for use during Dad's acting presidency of Brooklyn Polytechnic Institute. Luckily, I escaped on the right shoulder from both the stopped truck in front of me and the one following too close for safety.

Mother's reputation as a driver suffered from more than her garage mishaps. Despite her accident-free driving record, some people felt uncomfortable riding with her because her attention to the road appeared distracted. Deaf from birth in her right ear, as she aged she lost acuity in her left, and by her sixties it would appear to a front-seat passenger with whom she carried on the conversation as she drove that she wasn't paying attention to the road as she turned her eyes and head toward the passenger seat to hear better and to use lip-reading. She was also becoming forgetful about things.

In Brooklyn during autumn 1973, Kay asked Sandy to cash a check for her at a nearby store and gave Sandy her driver's license. The license had expired more than six months before. "Don't tell Daddy II," Mom asked Sandy, using the moniker by which his granddaughter Lucretia had tagged my father, "I'll take care of it." When she went to the License Bureau in Akron, she learned that she would need to retake the driver's exam since her permit was so long out of date. "Why, that doesn't make any sense for someone with nearly forty years driving experience."

In the event, she passed the vision test with her contact lenses, and she got seventy percent of the written test right, but she failed the road test. Mom called Sandy in Columbus one night to tell her about it. The examiner had a pinched mouth and seemed a very sour disappointed person, she said. George Korman had done an interview at the University on Friday, checking the credentials of someone up for a federal appointment, and he stopped at Fir Hill for a cup of coffee and she told him all about it—"But don't say anything to Normy, okay? "—and he told her to be sure to use her own car for the road test.

Dolores took her back the next week, when she was allowed to take the test again. The vision test was the same, she missed only one question on the written test, but again she failed the road test. Now she was worried. She called Sandy: "Yes, I can take it again in two weeks. But if I fail it a third time, I'll have to wait six months. And Daddy II will find out." Sandy asked her if she knew what she hadn't gotten right. "Oh, he said something about one of the turns, how I'd come to a full stop or something." Sandy suggested that she go to AAA and take a driving lesson. Kay was appalled. Sandy explained. "You don't need to take a full course. Just go out with an instructor and tell everything you can remember about the road test." Mom took an AAA lesson, and this time she passed the road test, too. But she didn't like the new picture on the license. Dad never found out.

Having broken through the luxury car ceiling post presidency, Dad next bought a Mercedes 450 SEL "previously owned" saloon. He drove it not even 10,000 miles before he grew tired of expensive repairs. Thereafter until his death in 2003 he always owned some version of the largest Cadillac four-door sedan turnpike cruiser and some version of Oldsmobile's downsized but fully equipped models, the last a Ninety-Eight. (He stopped buying convertibles when Mom died.) He was no longer a public college president; now he was a consultant and a banker, and he rode in whatever American-made luxury car that pleased him.

MARK'S FIRST CARS

When I started at UA in 1963, just as Dick finished medical school and his internship and prepared to be married, I inherited the yellow Volkswagen beetle convertible that he'd been nursing along for several years. I couldn't do much about the rust or the exhaust leaking into the passenger compartment or indeed about anything mechanical, but I had terrycloth seat covers made and polished everything I could reach on this, my first car. By the time it stranded me on the road to Andover so that I missed Dick and Mary's wedding rehearsal (a horrible thing in a Best Man), Dad and Mom had learned the value of my having a dependable car of my own, and Dad bought me a brand new green VW four-door beetle sedan. I was the first person in the family to have seat belts. I drove it throughout college, and Dolores inherited it when I went off to graduate school. I can remember Mom driving both of my VWs and my being surprised that she could handle the standard shift. Where did she learn those skills, I wondered. Duh! For the first half of her driving life there had been no automatic transmissions. She kept to herself her bemusement at the young's preference for a car shaped pretty much like the first ones she and Norm had owned before they modernized with their first Hudson.

Friends

Thousands of people came to the President's Home. Hundreds came more than once. Dozens came monthly and a few even weekly. Amidst this wide acquaintance, only a small number were intimates. Kay's friends were easy for me to identify. If Norm had the kind of friends in whom he confided and from whom he sought consolation, they are unknown to me.

SIBLINGS

My mother was close to her sisters Betty and Jo all their lives. When the three were together, the family of their childhood reconstituted so faithfully that I felt the absent parents (and oldest sister) had but stepped into the next room. Kay's increasing worldliness and wider circle of acquaintance disappeared. Jo's theological bent and scholarly cast struck sparks on Kay's buoyant enthusiasms and travel-broadened cultural prospectives. Betty's quiet commanding "Girls! Now girls!" must have brought their mother or father to mind for only she, the middle child, could quell their arguments at the canasta or bridge table or over an article in *The New Yorker* or about the exact wording of a minor verse in "Amazing Grace," "Dites-Moi," or "Lalla-Rookha."

Each took pride in the others' accomplishments. Betty was acknowledged the expert home cook and the most committed lodge-servant (she was Worthy Grand Matron of Eastern Star in Michigan). Jo's musicianship, gardening, and oil painting expanded beyond her earlier intellectual accomplishments: she had continued taking doctoral courses during

Betty, Jo, and Kay on the court of The Manor, 1953. *From the author's collection*

the 1920s and 1930s from Northwestern University's English faculty beyond her MA until the professors denied her further study on the grounds of her gender. And Jo was prepared to top my mother's praise for *The Group* or for "Bunny" Wilson's piece on the Dead Sea Scrolls or for Walker Percy's novels by introducing her to "archy and mehitabel" or the songs of Tom Lehrer.

I remember only one time when their differing worldly circumstances brought conflict. The Manor in the 1950s and 1960s was a business that couldn't be scaled and was always cash poor. Bill had to take part-time jobs like rural mail delivery to pay their children's tuition to prep school and college. My father and mother always paid the tab for the school-year-ending celebration dinner at Win Schuler's in Marshall, after the Manor children had been picked up for their August vacation and the Clarks and Aunt Jo prepared for a month of make-and-mend-and-paint. At this feast in 1971, my mother sought to solve the problem she had encountered in decorating her new smaller-scale dining room at the Fir Hill apartment to which they were retiring from the President's Home. Betty had inherited their mother's carved rose-back side chairs, and to Kay's eyes, they must be underutilized in Bill and Betty's home. Their only use seemed to be at Thanksgiving and Christmas every other year when the family gathered: surely Betty wouldn't mind loaning them to her? "Good grief, Kay! We like nice things too, you know."

My father, too, had a sibling, his brother Walter. Walter was eight years older, more a mentor than a playmate. While that gap shortened with every decade the brothers lived, geographical separation and their spouses' mutual antipathy forestalled regular family gatherings. Walter and Mildred had moved to Chicago in the early 1920s, and while Ames remembered playing with their children Wally and Corisande on visits home to Cincinnati, I believe that I met Uncle Walter just once. The brothers corresponded, and Norm saved a two-inch thick file of Walter's typed single-space letters. Nothing in that correspondence suggests a maturing of intimacy or a growing mutual dependence. When the two men had retired and remarried in their seventies and eighties, there were cordial couples' visits between Dunedin and Fort Lauderdale. But Walter and his family never came to Akron during our residence in the President's Home.

I cannot tell how close the relationship between my father and his father-in-law was. From welcoming him into the family to arranging the first honorary doctorate, Big Daddy expressed active love for Norm. Norm spent time every summer for nearly a decade at the Lake Wawasee cottage, where he sailed and fished with Big Daddy and Uncle Bill and shared time watching over the children. If it became the intimacy of equals, no evidence remains. (Of course, since Big Daddy died before I was five, I wouldn't have been able to witness it.)

Perhaps there had been special intimacy within his extended birth family. Dad's father had six living brothers and two sisters, and as a result, Dad had many cousins, some of them age peers. I think I met cousins Horace Auburn and Arthur Auburn once or twice, but neither visited our home. And I have no memory of an Auburn family reunion that brought them together. Horace and Arthur were also fellow UC students and Lambda Chi brothers. Dad used his Lambda Chi connections often, I saw, as when he traveled and arranged to meet based upon the ties of fraternity, or when he hired two Lambda Chi brothers away from UC to UA.

But there is no particular Lambda Chi friend or any fellow UC alum of Dad's who showed up sufficiently regularly to be part of our family's life.

CHI OMEGA FRIENDS

But college friends were a part of my mother's life, extending into Akron and elsewhere regularly. Kay maintained close ties to two Chi Omega sisters, Blanche Huss and Peggy Armstrong Schaefer. Blanche was the first Cincinnatian to stay in the President's Home with us. She brought house gifts of favorite regional dishes like goetta or exotic versions of the quotidian like cold-brewed coffee elixir, adding boiling water for the perfect cup. She had Kay's literary bent, and their raised voices would carry from the solarium all the way to the dining room as they disputed the pronunciation of "contumely" (Hamlet's "the oppressor's wrong, the proud man's contumely"). Blanche's son and daughters were contemporaries of Ames and Dick, and when I spent a couple of weeks in her home one summer, Frank Jr. (who was Kay's godson and fourteen years older than I), was very kind to spend time with me and drive me about in his classic roadster.

Blanche had been an athlete as a young woman, and it must have been that vigor which allowed her to adapt to a crippling stroke during one of her pregnancies, before I was born. She walked with a lurch as she pivoted her left hip, and she had limited mobility with her left arm. Blanche's husband Wes (Frank Wesley Huss Sr.) owned and operated movie theatres, and I remember their garage seeming to serve as a warehouse for soft drinks and other concession treats. Blanche's extensive correspondence included a regular stream of consumer complaints which garnered replies and free samples of products from dish soap to candy to wearables. Wes was the first person of my acquaintance to take a daily cocktail. In his den he had built a brass-topped mirrored bar crowded with glasses, bottles, and equipment, which he employed in the rite of preparation—I didn't pay attention to his favorites, but when I saw similar bars on TV's "Bob Cummings Show" or in the movie "Auntie Mame," it reminded me of the one in the rambling Huss country house, with its three acres of cultivated grounds, around which suburban Cincinnati had begun to press.

Peggy Armstrong stood godmother to me at my christening, then moved away from Cincinnati before we did. Mother trusted me with her and her husband Tom in their Phillipsburg, New Jersey, home for a couple of weeks in the summer of 1960. Sometime soon after that visit, Peggy and Tom (the father of their adult daughters Terry and Mimi, both of whom were out of the house when I visited) divorced, and Peggy married Joe Schaefer. Joe had founded an electronics company and been a member of the Young Presidents Organization (YPO). He sold that company, and they remade their lives in California. Already a hobbyist farmer in New Jersey, Joe and Peggy located property in Calistoga, California, to operate a demonstration dairy farm, where I spent six weeks in summer 1964, sleeping in the bunk house with the cowhands. The Schaefers lived in a doublewide trailer while they built a lake and a house beside it. I helped birth a calf, learned to drink beer, and spent precious minute after minute on the office phone late at night (Akron-time) talking and listening to the breathing of my then-fiancée.

I visited the Schaefers again after the house was completed and the dairy farm had become Piney Hill Vineyards, and another time a decade later when a professional meeting brought me to San Francisco. On one of those visits I admired a five-by-four-foot buffalo-hide *wayang-kulit* of the warrior Rama from the Javanese shadow puppet theatre, which Peggy had displayed over the mantel of a fieldstone fireplace, backlit by Christmas lights. My mother had also admired Peggy's tastes, and on one of her round-the-world trips with UA's Classrooms Abroad, she had acquired a pair of *wayang-kulit* shadow puppets which she gave me. When widowed Aunt Peggy closed up the vineyard house in the late 1990s, she called Sandy and me one day to assure that our corresponding address was the same as our shipping address. The next evening by overnight air express came the great Rama.

If Blanche and Kay together were raised voices demanding the floor, Peggy and Kay were two chums whispering confidences in the corner. The intimacy of youth persisted and deepened between the women as distance divided them. Neither was a couple's relationship, though. My father was perfectly cordial with Wes, he enjoyed Tom's company, and when Peg introduced Joe, he courted him: Joe endowed a scholarship at UA in Davey's name to celebrate the opening of the Norman P. Auburn Science and Engineering Center, and I remember that he and Peggy were there for the gala weekend. But I never saw Joe and Norm sharing the closeness of Peggy and Kay.

Kay and Norm receive a check from Joe and Peggy Schaefer, 1968. The Schaefers established the endowed David Bruce Auburn Scholarship in the Community and Technical College. *From the Norman Auburn Papers. Courtesy of Archival Services, University Libraries, The University of Akron*

There may have been couple's relationships in my parents' Cincinnati years, but none endured into the President's Home. Kay had friends, Norm had friends. When I was twelve, I thought Herman Muehlstein my father's best friend, and while the older man genuinely liked and respected Norm and planned many of the details of his estate around the presumption of my father's stewardship, he was closer to Joe Auburn's age, he was childless, and his relationship always had the paternal at base. There were also UA Directors and Trustees with whom Dad seemed close, especially Vince Johnson, Lincoln Gries, Howard Flood, and Ward Keener. I saw Harry Schrank and Norm share confidences about Harry's life unrelated to the relationship of Board Chair and subordinate president. But like the dozens of relationships that Dad formed with men who served on common boards and service projects, even these failed to rise to the intimacy that my mother shared with her sisters, with Blanche and Peggy, and with one other Akronite.

Jane Dunlap. *From the collection of Laurel Dunlap Froehlich*

KAY'S AKRON FRIENDS

Mom formed dozens of relationships springing from her UA duties. Of all the faculty wives who paid court to her, the one that most intrigued her and came closest to moving past the barrier erected to protect the subordinate was Jane Dunlap. Twenty years younger, native of a town just south of Kay's Xenia birthplace, wife of the soon-to-be Head of Theatre, Jane around Kay had a calming presence like Aunt Peggy's. She was a person of eclectic tastes, literate and thoughtful. She was spiritual and reverent without being pious. She wore her Quaker heritage openly but loosely. She worked in advertising and was raising a toddler daughter. My mother almost joined exercise classes with Jane and did read books she wouldn't have found otherwise. The disparity of age and circumstance prevented the growth of this friendship.

No one of the dozens of women by whose side the president's wife served in the University Women's Committee, the PEO, the League of Women Voters, or even the half dozen who labored with Kay to create what would become the Ohio Ballet would have guessed that her most intimate friend was a waitress at Belgrade Gardens, the original Serbian chicken house of Barberton. Ljuba Antov returned from a visit to her native Montenegro on the same steamer that brought Norm and Kay home from their first European trip in 1954. Ljuba was putting her two daughters through college with some help from their father; otherwise, she was a single mother dependent upon a server's salary and tips. They met most often at Ljuba's modest Cape Cod on Kingsley Avenue, midday for Kay which was rising for Ljuba, who worked from 3:00 to midnight. Every year Ljuba coaxed Kay to attend three or four family feasts, which by the Serbian Orthodox calendar fell a week or two after their Presbyterian counterparts, and I usually came along. We visited one married daughter at her home in southeast Chicago when I was in graduate school, and we watched the other court and marry a psychologist of Montenegrin origin and complete her PhD and begin a family and a distinguished career at Kent State University. It was to Ljuba that Kay went for anonymity from the public eye and for the consolation which only an intimate can give. Ljuba had an elemental directness amalgamated with the tested courage and self-confidence of an immigrant. After my mother's sudden death, I visited with her, and as we shared our grief, Ljuba revealed a part of Kay's soul I had but glimpsed.

Most people looking from the outside would have read two of my father's UA subordinates as his intimate friends.

KEN BARKER

Norm met H. Kenneth Barker during his sabbatical year at the US Department of State in 1965–1966. A native of Kentucky with a University of Michigan PhD in educational psychology, Barker came to UA as Special Assistant to the President in 1966. Within a year he was serving simultaneously as Dean of International Studies and Dean of the College of Education (and, when the school calved off Education into its own college, briefly as Dean of Nursing). He had reached traditional retirement age at the start of Bill Muse's presidency, but he served as Special Assistant to the President and as Acting Director of Athletics for Muse, then under the next three presidents continued part-time assignments in Athletics and in Development. His personal and leveraged philanthropic support for athletics, the arts, and especially the Center for Economic

H. Kenneth Barker. *Tel-Buch 1968*

Education, which he had founded in 1975 and which was renamed in his honor when he retired at 79 in 2001, brought millions of dollars to UA.

An experienced traveler, Barker's life list reached eighty-three countries, eighteen more than Norm's. Dad put him in charge of the "Classrooms Abroad" program and traveled with him every summer until he retired from UA. When I came back to the President's Home from graduate study at the University of Chicago in the late 1960s, I found the repeated presence of Dean Barker in my parents' daily lives surprising. There he was in the middle of a weekday morning having a cup of coffee with Kay in the breakfast nook. There he was on a Saturday putting together an adult-sized tricycle for Davey. There he was at the patio door to the kitchen delivering a loaf of banana bread from his wife Libby or dropping off one of his own "American primitive" oil paintings for Dad's study. I had not known anyone so direct, so persistent, and so impervious to discouraging social cues. At the time I didn't understand how useful such a person was to a chief executive whose charisma depended upon maintaining dignified distance and verbal restraint. When, as a three-time vice president, I returned to work for UA in 1991, I had figured it out. Veteran *Beacon Journal* reporter Rick Armon began his November 6, 2014, obituary with "Doors were never closed to Dr. H. Kenneth Barker."

CAROLINE PARDEE

If as an inexperienced young adult I was uncertain about Dean Barker's status in my family, as a preadolescent I had no question about Caroline Pardee's. She was a family friend, like a younger more energetic Aunt Jo or Aunt Blanche, who would spend lots of time with me and not just sit there talking with Mom. It was Caroline who taught me to bowl and to golf, took me hiking and rock climbing, drove me in her Chevrolet convertible across the Cuyahoga Valley bridge on the new Ohio Turnpike, taught me to dine independently of my parents at the Women's City Club or at the lace-covered old-fashioned table in her dining room. Caroline was godmother to my niece Kate (b. 1960), then godmother to our son Ben (b. 1972). When I fled my heritage Presbyterianism in the early 1960s, there was Caroline in the back pew of the church where I landed, the Unitarian-Universalist Church of Akron, once the home congregation of John R. Buchtel.

Caroline was much more than a family friend, and something less. She was a brilliant hire when Dad made her Executive Secretary to the President in February 1953. She was not only talented and experienced, but—unusual for any clerical professional—she was of the same professional social class as her boss. And unusual for a woman, her social stature didn't come from a male partner. She had been Valedictorian of the 1928 class of Central High School on the edge of campus. She had graduated from UA in 1932, and her support of Delta Gamma (which she joined as an undergraduate) became lifelong and cemented relationships through the distaff half of the couples who came to lead and manage many of the key institutions of Akron. She had entered graduate study at Radcliffe College but had had to withdraw when her family's fortunes plummeted in 1932. Her father was a former Probate judge and power in the Summit County Republican party, and Ray Bliss still paid court to her in the 1960s. She had close to a twenty-year work history when my father delegated a close aide to sound her out. In all but name, she was managing an electronics firm on South Main Street. She lived in the 1885 house

Caroline Pardee at her desk in the President's Office, 1963. *From the Norman Auburn Papers. Courtesy of Archival Services, University Libraries, The University of Akron*

adjacent to campus in which she was born (and would die). As a single working woman, after her curtailed graduate study, she networked with others of her gender in Altrusa and the Women's City Club. Her lifetime benefactions to UA exceed my family's.

Bringing someone with so much independent referential power into his inner circle speaks well of President Auburn's self-confidence. She repaid that trust with loyalty and with hard work. Rare was the workday when Caroline arrived later or left earlier than Norm. On nights and weekends, she'd complete tasks unfinished during business hours by the large backroom presidential clerical staff. If she showed up at the President's Home, it was either to pick me up or to bring completed typescripts, express mail, confidential documents, and final event-planning data. She attended all the same UA lectures, performances, and athletic events as the President and his wife, and I would slip away from the President's sideline box at the Rubber Bowl to share her viewpoint from the stands.

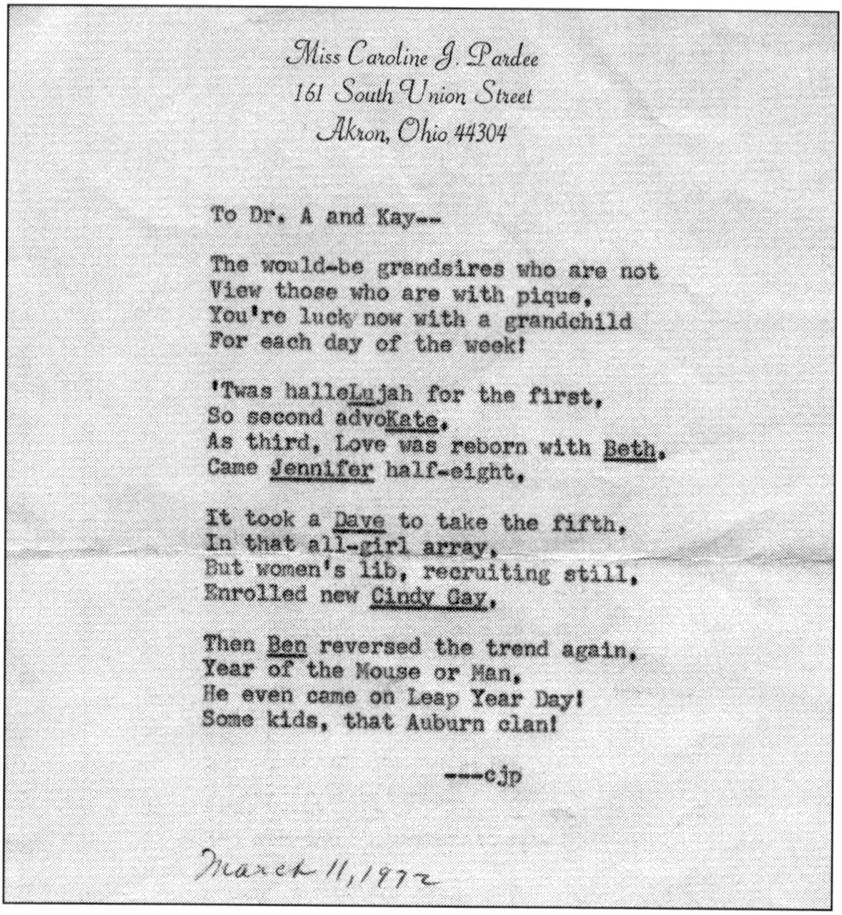

Miss Caroline J. Pardee
161 South Union Street
Akron, Ohio 44304

To Dr. A and Kay--

The would-be grandsires who are not
View those who are with pique,
You're lucky now with a grandchild
For each day of the week!

'Twas halleLujah for the first,
So second advoKate,
As third, Love was reborn with Beth,
Came Jennifer half-eight,

It took a Dave to take the fifth,
In that all-girl array,
But women's lib, recruiting still,
Enrolled new Cindy Gay,

Then Ben reversed the trend again,
Year of the Mouse or Man,
He even came on Leap Year Day!
Some kids, that Auburn clan!

---cjp

March 11, 1972

Caroline's poem to Norm and Kay on the birth of their seventh grandchild, Benjamin Max Joseph Auburn, a fortnight after his arrival. Caroline's occasional verse famously included a new sonnet every Christmas. *From the author's collection*

But my mother expressed occasional jealousy. Caroline had visited as many countries as they had only in imitation, she said. Caroline had this Director or that benefactor to dinner at her house on Union Street only because she knew they were scheduled to come to the President's Home the next month. Perhaps not the classic jealousy of the spouse for the "office wife," nevertheless Kay's occasional grumble seemed very uncharacteristic to me. But I was able to watch the spouse of Norm's second-longest marriage come to express similar discomfort, and for all the twenty-seven years that Virginia and Norm were married, Caroline had no subordinate-supervisor relationship with her former boss. What she had was deep knowledge of Norm's interests and access to information which he almost always relished and the shared memories of eighteen years working together. From Kay's and Virginia's points of view, that constituted an intimacy to which they were not admitted.

Caroline told me and Sandy about a visit she made to my father in the fall of 1974, to Stephens College, where he was serving as acting president. Kay had died in February. Norm had started to date that summer. Caroline was in our Columbus home, and she allowed us to understand that their relationship would not change. For nearly fifty years, she gave him the same oversized birthday card on May 22, then picked it up a few days later to be offered again the next year. She missed May 22, 2003. She was no longer driving herself, she had become less mobile generally, having not complied with knee-replacement rehabilitation and suffering from early dementia. They still talked by telephone once or twice a week, hashing out their opinions about the latest University events. Her caregiver brought her to Norm's funeral, but she didn't come to the Portage Country Club family meal. She died six weeks after him, age 92, the last of his longtime friends.

From the President's Home

Leaving the President's Home

Norm Auburn in Retirement

Dad said he chose the timing of his 1971 retirement from The University of Akron. The Board of Trustees wanted him to remain. As he approached age sixty-five, which had been the mandatory retirement age for his UA predecessor Hezzleton Simmons, they gave him a new five-year contract. Especially through the turbulence of campuses in the late 1960s and the national tragedy of the deaths at Kent State University on May 4, 1970, the trustees took comfort from his experienced leadership.

RELATIONS WITH THE UA BOARDS

He tested the support for his leadership regularly. Whenever Norm showed the offers for which he might leave, they found ways to keep him. In response to an offer whose high salary they could not meet in the current political atmosphere, they had given him an eight-year contract in 1957. The board permitted him to accept two bank board directorships, a practice curtailed for later UA presidents. Against all prior tradition, in the seventeenth year of his presidency, they named the huge new science and engineering center after him. And twice they granted him working sabbaticals, unusual arrangements during which he retained full authority and responsibility of the presidency while spending weekdays in New York City and in Washington, DC, and returning to Akron on weekends to run the university.

Indeed, Norm Auburn is the only UA president, and perhaps the only president of any public American university, to be allowed to serve in two,

The 1968 Auburns assemble to honor their "Living Legend." Davey, Mark, Mary Liz, Dick, Kay, Norm, Ames, Rusty, and in front, left to right, Beth, Kate, and Lu. *Photo by Lou Tobias, from the Norman Auburn Papers. Courtesy of Archival Services, University Libraries, The University of Akron*

year-long, full-time, concurrent positions. In 1957, soon after we moved into the President's Home, my father became Acting President of the Council for Financial Aid to Education. On Monday mornings, first thing, he drove to Akron Canton Airport and boarded a flight to New York City. He usually returned to Akron on Friday evening. Seven years later, in 1965, when I was in my third year at UA and living in the attic suite, he was permitted to serve concurrently as Special Assistant for University Relations in the Agency for International Development of the U. S. Department of State, once again commuting weekly (and traveling overseas frequently).

These two unusual presidential years were "sabbaticals" both because they occurred in roughly the same "seven-on-one-off" pattern as a professor's or minister's career path and also because they served a similar function in my father's professional life. For a professor or a minister, a sabbatical refreshes the spirits and recalibrates the tools of their trades. For my father, the sabbaticals enhanced his capacities as a leader and enlarged his skill set in different more cosmopolitan arenas and expanded his Rolodex in ways useful to Akron and in ways useful to himself. His UA presidency was the longest in the institution's history. But because of the sabbaticals, his presidency might also be viewed not as a continuous twenty years but as three terms of six years or so. Each time when he returned, the appetite for his leadership remained undiminished among those who conveyed the privilege of office. It was a good bargain on both sides of the board-room table. If travel was Norm's scholarship, these two sabbaticals enhanced the value of his leadership to The University of Akron. They also provided the contacts on which he would build his retirement career.

In New York in 1957–1958, Dad deepened his relationship with industrialist and philanthropist Herman Muehlstein. Herman appointed Dad to the board of his eponymous foundation in 1958, and in 1965, three years after Herman's death when that portion of his estate not sequestered to provide for his widow Caryl came to the foundation, Dad assumed the presidency, which he would faithfully execute for thirty-seven years. The Herman Muehlstein Foundation devoted its grants in rough thirds to the United Jewish Appeal Federation of New York, the City University of New York, and The University of Akron. Muehlstein's gifts changed UA. They were the first major private benefactions since the days of Buchtel College. By 2015, that smaller portion of Muehlstein benefactions which were restricted to endowment still constituted close to three percent of all UA endowments. The 275 precious editions of the Muehlstein rare book collection received during his lifetime form the core of The University of Akron's unique holdings in Western humanities, unexpected treasures in a research library more notable for its support of world-class polymer education and inquiry. Dad repaid those debts by his faithful lifelong stewardship of Herman's estate plans, and that service extended long after he'd retired from full-time service at UA.

In Washington, DC, 1965–1966, Dad became a colleague of Alvin C. Eurich. He had probably known Al Eurich when Eurich served as the founding President of the State University of New York and as president of Stanford University and then while he led the educational division of the Ford Foundation in the 1950s and 1960s. But it was from 1965–1966, when Dad worked in DC, that he strengthened his ties to the Academy for Educational Development (AED), which Eurich had co-founded in

1961 with Sidney Tickton. Before retiring from The University of Akron presidency, with his trustees' approval Dad conducted paid consultancies for AED, and he told me that it was Al Eurich who encouraged him to retire in order to pursue the third phase of his higher education career as Senior Vice President for AED and an active "rent-a-president."

Both of these sabbatical jobs impressed the UA directors and confirmed their sense of his national and international stature. The heads of the "Big Three" rubber companies served in person or by deputy on the municipal UA board. So, when it was the former President of General Motors, Alfred P. Sloan, the former Chairman of Standard Oil of New Jersey ("Exxon" to be), Frank Abrams, and the sitting president of US Steel, Irving Olds, who in 1957 sought Dad to be acting president of the Council for Financial Aid to Education, the Akron leaders acquiesced. (It was those three "titans of industry" to whose offer of permanent appointment a year later the Directors replied with an eight-year contract.) When in 1965 Dad explained how the State Department job coordinating international research and development activities of major American universities abroad could benefit Akron's own research programs, the directors listened politely. But when the office of President Lyndon B. Johnson called the Board Chair to explain that this was a presidential appointment which they should expedite, they embraced it. No other UA president has held such important positions while serving the Hilltop, paid or unpaid.

A NEW CAREER PATH

The UA Presidency ended for my father and my mother with different assumptions. Kay was sixty-three, all her able-bodied children were out of the house, off the payroll, and living away from Akron. She had six grandchildren and another on the way, her sisters had eased into retirement as Rob took over the Manor, and she would be happy to see her two most important recent UA projects—E.J. Thomas Performing Arts Hall and the Ohio Ballet—reach completion under other leadership while she watched from her Fir Hill Towers balcony.

Norm was sixty-six. It was getting on to the time for another sabbatical, six years after Washington. The Board wanted him to stay at least another year if not the three remaining on his contract. Certainly, his younger colleague Dom Guzzetta, whom he had made the first Provost of UA, thought that he would stay. Dom couldn't have been happy about not being appointed "acting president" during the State Department assignment, as Dad had been at the University of Cincinnati during President Raymond Walters's service abroad in 1949. So, when it looked as if there would be no retirement for Norm at sixty-five, Dom had gone off to take the presidency of little Marian College north of Indianapolis.

Dad said that Al Eurich had put in the hard sell for his joining AED full time. And Al was just the sort of person to get Norm's agreement, an older male figure whose breadth of power and authority exceeded his own—like Alfred Sloan, like Frank Abrams, like Irving Olds, like Herman Muehlstein. "If I had stayed at Akron," Dad told me, "I'd never have gotten these opportunities." Mom heard his plans and calculated that they wouldn't interfere with helping to raise her grandchildren, and so she expressed her support.

At least one factor in his retirement plans Dad probably didn't share fully with my mother: his sense of long-term financial uncertainty. In those days, a public college president made about twice as much as the highest paid nonmedical professor on staff, not today's ratio of three or four to one. He started UA at $16,000, and he retired twenty years later at $40,000. They had some stocks, including a fair-sized chunk of Proctor & Gamble that Mom had inherited from Maman and Big Daddy, and some savings from the sale of 344 Merriman Road, but they hadn't owned any real estate since 1956 and would soon have to cover much of their living expenses which University housing and a car had greatly reduced. Davey's care would continue to cost about the same as tuition, room, and board at a small private college, which had amounted to close to ten percent of their after-tax income.

Dad could see two pension assets: a flat lifetime consulting fee with The University of Akron of $20,000 a year, which the Board granted together with the title "President Emeritus and Consultant" on the grounds that he had given up an unvested Cincinnati municipal pension to come to Akron; and an Ohio State Teachers Retirement System pension for twenty years' service equaling about forty percent of his final presidential salary, indexed but not assured of meeting inflation, which he would take at a reduced rate based on three lives, his own, Kay's, and Davey's. The STRS pension was safe. A future UA Board or president could put that consultancy in jeopardy at any time, he feared. He had some other income from bank boards, but First National's would end by 1978, because he would age out following his next six-year term, and his tenure with First Federal, though not age-limited, depended upon his energies and banking acumen. He certainly had no reason to believe that he would serve with First Federal for twenty-six years, ending for the last sixteen as Chairman of the Board when it was sold and he was 84, and then going on to serve on the board of the buying bank for another fourteen years, attending his last compensated meeting just fifteen weeks before his death.

No, Dad obsessed (I imagine) about his own father's assets dwindling to nothing. He remembered his father-in-law living in an isolated Michigan town and far too dependent upon the labors of his daughters for his daily bread. He saw his older brother in modest retirement in the Tampa Bay area, content to head the local Friends of the Library for Dunedin. He could see the Vietnam War winding down and another cycle of post-war inflation eating up his savings and his pension income. He had enjoyed living at a level comparable to the Akron rubber executives, but he couldn't afford to buy and maintain a West Akron home like theirs let alone drive the Cadillac he always wanted or travel like he and Mom had under the University's imprimatur. So, from Norm's point of view, he couldn't afford to retire unless he was willing to accept the modest sufficiency of an emeritus professor.

I'm quite certain that my mother didn't see the financial picture as Dad did. It was part of the marital bargain to trust the breadwinner blindly. One March or April evening in 1970 or 1971, as Sandy and Mom watched television in the solarium of the UA President's Home, Dad brought the cover page of my parents' joint federal tax return for Mom's signature. Sandy noticed that he covered the entire form except for the signature line with a sheet of paper which he held in place while Kay inscribed her name. After Norm left she asked her mother-in-law why she would sign without the slightest review of the figures, and Mom said, "Why, Daddy II takes care of all our money."

Kay didn't have her own checkbook until the 1970s, and Dad wrote all family checks on a ledger locked in his desk. Kay never had a general credit card (Diner's Club pioneered the universal credit card in 1950, with American Express following in 1957), though she held store-specific charge plates for O'Neil's and Polsky's, and in the 1960s a brand-specific Sohio charge card. She managed all household groceries and incidentals on a cash basis, with a monthly allowance of $200 through about 1965 and $300 thereafter and irregular applications in person to Norm, whose wallet always held a goodly supply of tens and twenties. This financial dependency seemed old fashioned and condescending to Sandy, whose mother Pearl had always worked outside the home and shared with her husband George in money decisions big and small.

KAY AND NORM'S MARITAL BARGAIN

If the marital bargain allowed Kay to choose ignorance and Norm to assume command for financial affairs, that doesn't fully describe how well it was balanced. In return for dependency, she got her own back. They lived two rhythms together—Dad's regimented, programmed, systematic; Mom's fluid, flexible, spontaneous. Dad's hours admitted no exceptions, Mom's responded to changing circumstances. At table, Dad was Jack to her Mrs. Sprat. She drank and smoked; he tolerated her smoking and sought to disguise his teetotal preference, so he wouldn't appear prissy at cocktail parties. He was neurasthenic, seeking advice over each pang or ache; his sisters-in-law said he was obsessed with dying young to the point of spending reckless sums on life insurance. (But he never complained even of a cold to anyone but intimates: the President of The University of Akron was never ill, and the 1969 operation for his prostate complication was carefully concealed.) Mom pulled up her socks, ignored her symptoms, never took a pill, and consulted the physician only when the bursitis, say, had immobilized her shoulder. Dad was punctual; being tardy ceded a moral ground, a psychological control point, and threatened his self-confidence. Mom was casual, confident that she would be welcomed whenever she arrived (as she was, usually). When I studied psychology and learned about passive aggression, my example came from home, where Mother often forced Dad to wait until he raised his voice and she could say, with reason, "Calm down, Normy. We'll be there in plenty of time," for he was victim to his own anxieties. (And I can report that both his second and his third wives exploited the same insecurities.)

They were a formidable team together. They had shared the ambition to preside at a college at least from the late 1930s, had lost the long odds of its being their alma mater, and had won the chance to start at the top of a smaller one, where their skills and their good luck found them on an up-escalator for twenty years. Norm deferred to Kay's emotional intelligence, particularly in social situations where her charm and quick-witted adjustments won admirers for them both across divides of class, education, and economics. She advanced into the room of strangers and quickly had them contemplating her husband. She led the conversation at table, helping the reticent to shine and the dominant to share. She remembered the names of the children when he could recall only the father's employer. She never blundered when he checked her, and he turned to her for social cues. He explained the strategy, and she planned the party or the longer campaign, say, getting to know the wife until they received the dinner invitation. He sought her advice tactically and operationally. And neither ever criticized the other in public or were heard to utter to one another anything like a command or a reproach.

She understood his strengths and his weaknesses. She sensed his moods of discouragement and was always ready with a word of praise. "I've created a monster!" she'd laugh, when he surfed too high on a wave of success or took himself too seriously. She encouraged her adult children's use of the ironic but loving sobriquet "Living Legend" for him when the Board named the new Science and Engineering Center in his honor in 1968. Dad proved himself professionally adept at managing complicated organizations and pleasing their governors as their confidential agent at all times in his life, from the Cincinnati Consolidated Building Trades Council in the 1930s to the Council for Financial Aid to Education in the 1950s to the office of the Director of the Agency for International Development in the 1960s, but he could not have gained the Presidency of UA or exercised it so successfully without my mother's emotional intelligence and social sense to expand contacts among multiple constituencies, her wide-ranging inquiring mind to enrich his cultural and intellectual horizons, and her gentle, generous, Christian spirit (most of the time) to mitigate his Teutonic tendency toward despotic absolutism and Manichaean dualism in human affairs.

And if they both entered retirement with different expectations, another factor was at play as well. They had aged differently. Kay's vigor was less than before. She couldn't keep up with Norm those last few years, climbing the steps of the world's monuments. Increasingly, she didn't accompany him when he traveled for the State Department or for AED. She still smoked, despite efforts to stop or cut down. He thought she drank too much, and he knew she carried twenty pounds more than she needed. She probably suffered from sleep apnea; her snoring gave meaning to the adjective "stertorous," even "stentorious," and she drifted off in her chair during the afternoon and evening, sometimes even in company. She resisted friendly invitations to join nature walks or yoga groups, bragging that she got enough exercise attending her friends' funerals.

Norm agreed with her about family: he loved the children and grandchildren and all their bright prospects, and he loved being surrounded by them in the family portraits he arranged to have made whenever many were together, and he loved visiting their homes for quick trips and helping them out with gifts of money. But his future was still professional. There were consultancies and maybe there were even other college presidencies. Family considerations were foremost, of course, but what could be better for the family than assuring an inheritance through the sweat of his brow as he, everyone's breadwinner, always had? And for this work, he really didn't need Kay's help except at the occasional formal dinner or annual meeting cocktail party.

Their life rhythms had always differed, but now their life cycles grew out of harmony. Except for his prostate scare in 1969 and in spite of his pessimistic assessment of his longevity, my father grew increasingly younger for his age. My mother craved retirement; she did not need a fresh challenge to wake up enthused by a new morning, and she did not need the accolades of strangers. I remember the novels and memoirs of Vladimir Nabokov and Marcel Proust—slow, ruminative works, spun out of the past remembered more than the future contemplated—being important to her in these years, while Dad sought the excitement of nudging people into analyzing rather than reacting to their problems and the pleasure of entering rooms surrounded by the aura of authority which a sizeable fee casts upon its recipient. She wanted to put her feet up and enjoy the fruits of a family well raised; he wanted new horizons, new people, new problems.

RETIREMENT FOR THE PRESIDENTIAL COUPLE

So they left the President's Home. Dad and Mom had worked in 1970, before construction, with the developer of Fir Hill Towers, being built near the UA campus across from the Lambda Chi chapter and the Hower mansion and adjacent to what was then the University Club, and they'd adjusted the templates for a pair of adjoining apartments on the top floor, facing toward the Hilltop, turning one into a three-bedroom, two living-room, two-bathroom aerie and the other into a snug one-bedroom apartment. Mom and Dad took the bigger place, and housekeeper-companion Dolores would live in the smaller one across the hall in consideration for continuing to look after them. (As a university employee, Dolores was reassigned from the President's Home to student residence halls; she managed her UA employment so as to be available to them after hours.) Having lived for years with furnishings many of which had always, after all, belonged to the University, they negotiated the purchase of some, even including carpeting; a Steinway upright studio piano was the most expensive single piece. They acquired furniture, for instance, a new dining room table and two bedroom suites to replace personal items whose large proportions wouldn't work in the smaller rooms. They had bookcases roughed, planked, and painted in the apartment for their shared collection. They put some things in storage. They moved.

The first two years of my father's retirement brought little alteration to his habits. The Akron office he visited daily wasn't in Buchtel but in West Hall, adjacent to the Law School on Wolf Ledges, with a secure three-room suite on the southwest corner including a spacious room with three book-case-lined walls and one bay of three windows in front of which he placed his desk, so that natural light fell over his shoulders. Adjacent was a fair-sized clerical office, though without a direct communication door, sharing the window wall, with built-in files, and in the interior off a common short hallway a private half-bath lavatory. Dad hired his own secretarial support, I gather. In the middle 1990s, he told me that he considered himself fortunate that his immediate successor president Dom Guzzetta did not choose to require any duties of the "President Emeritus and Consultant." By the time the next president William V. Muse became well established, Dad was asked to serve in 1989 as Honorary Co-Chair of "Heritage and Vision," the first major capital campaign since "Challenge Seventy," which had funded E. J. Thomas Performing Arts Hall. Thirteenth UA President Peggy Gordon Elliott beginning in 1992 invited him to join the commencement stage parties three times a year, a tradition that continued up until his final illness. And fifteenth UA President Luis Proenza in 2001 leveraged two of his titles, President Emeritus and Consultant, and President of the Herman Muehlstein Foundation, to accelerate the final payout of the latter and direct it toward purposes tangential to Herman's previous gifts.

I'm not sure what AED contracts Norm worked on from 1971–1972 and 1972–1973. I do remember his speaking around this time of the National Fire Academy (that evolved into a US Department of Commerce contract) and of a school I'd never heard of called St. Norbert's College in Wisconsin and of public Northeast Missouri State University in Kirksville. The last place was to become a national leader in assessment-based pedagogy; it earned the designation as Missouri's statewide public liberal arts university, and later it was renamed Truman State University, shedding the parochial "directional" designation. Later, Dad told me how interlocking personal and political relationships enabled much change and growth: President Charles McClain with whom he worked at Northeast Missouri was good friends with the state's young attorney general, John Ashcroft, who would become governor, senator, and US Attorney General.

Norm and Kay found time to travel over Christmas 1972 to East and West Germany using Ames and Rusty's home in Berlin as their base. In spring 1973 they joined Kay's sisters at Jane and Rob's condominium in St. Thomas, Virgin Islands, a rare vacation without a purpose. Dad was tickled by the ocean-side hamburger kiosk whose chef refused to serve ketchup with his sandwiches, and for years he would repeat the explanation "ketchup kills" as a punchline whenever condiments were mentioned. Mom told me she had been surprised at losing her breath and confidence in swimming from shore to an anchored raft. A year later I was to remember this incident, but at the time I didn't notice how unusual it was for her to complain.

The big professional news of spring 1973 developed rapidly, as would eight other opportunities in Norm's post-UA career: Brooklyn Polytechnic Institute needed an acting president. And, as my mother put it, "Barkis is willin.'" (In *David Copperfield*, coach-driver Mr. Barkis courts

David's childhood nurse Clara Peggotty with this description of his readiness to marry.) The task was to run this private engineering school while it accomplished a mission-saving merger with New York University and attracted a permanent leader. It included responsibilities for home entertaining in a to-be-furnished Remsen Street brownstone apartment near the Brooklyn Esplanade. I think Mother was invigorated by the challenge. Kay managed to enlist Sandy and me to leave our toddler sons with the other separately to make solo trips with her to the city to comb antique shops and furnishing stores for complete decorations.

There was a lot of commuting between Akron and Brooklyn that fall. Dad had two bank boards and their attendant committees to balance, and one last big project of his UA presidency marked its full completion. In October 1973, E. J. Thomas Performing Arts Hall celebrated its grand opening. (Only family insiders knew that the earliest glimmers of this structure occurred over the breakfast nook table at 856 Mayfair Road. Kay had joined four other prominent Akron women to attract choreographer Heinz Poll and his life partner designer Tom Skelton to establish a school called the Chamber Ballet, which would train dancers for a nascent Ohio Ballet and dance, where? "Well, not in the Akron Armory, Normy. We've got to build them a first-class space!") UA President Dom Guzzetta, who had helped raise the money for E.J., graciously asked Norm to speak at the gala inaugural. At Christmas, much of the family gathered in Jonesville.

On Wednesday morning, February 13, 1974, my mother awoke in Fir Hill Towers and told my father that she wouldn't be flying with him to Brooklyn at 9:30 that morning. She had the flu. As he followed his morning routine and Dolores came from across the hall to help them organize for their planned departure, she died quietly in her bed. She was three months short of her sixty-sixth birthday. An autopsy confirmed that her heart had been damaged from earlier silent attacks.

She was eulogized on Friday in a packed Westminister Presbyterian Church. Newspapers throughout Ohio and in New York City recorded her passing with stories and obituaries. In the *Akron Beacon Journal* for February 15, 1974, society writer Betty Jaycox capped twenty-two years of reporting on Kay with a sweet tribute:

> In the life of the University of Akron and in the city itself, few women have made the lasting impact that Kathleen Auburn, affectionately called "Kay," has left behind her.
>
> Wife and daughter of a college president, she was never eclipsed, not even by the prominence of her husband, Dr. Norman P. Auburn, president emeritus of Akron U. Her life-long work for cerebral palsy was inspired by the tragic affliction of their youngest son. On both the local and state level her dedication to ameliorating the dread disorder has done much toward drawing public attention to the problem.
>
> She gave speeches around the area on the world-wide travels she shared with her husband, turning over all stipends to cerebral palsy.
>
> Kay was like a skyrocket on a dark night, lighting the lives of others with the fire of her vibrant personality. She will be missed.

She was buried that Saturday morning in Cincinnati's Spring Grove Cemetery next to the graves of her mother and father and older sister Mary, in the Lane Theological Seminary section.

Back at Fir Hill Towers with all her children present except Davey, my father oversaw a sober, business-like parceling out of my mother's personal possessions. (He remembered the ill will generated by the haphazard distribution of his mother's treasures.) Within another day or two, we began to disperse, Ames and family to Berlin, Dick and his girls to Munster, Indiana, and Sandy and I and the boys to Columbus. There was little time for sharing our distress. I had lost the uncritical adoration of a loving mother, and my grief was intensified by the shock of my father's desolation, though it was hardly apparent to those outside the intimacy of the family and obscured effectively by the demands of his Akron and New York City professional responsibilities. Perhaps they were a salutary distraction. When Dad said to me a few months later that he suspected he would marry again sometime, I took his statement as an affirmation of life, not a repudiation of grief. For I remembered that Mom always said she would expect Norm to re-marry and that his re-marriage would affirm the strength of their own almost forty-four-year partnership.

NORM WITHOUT KAY: A NEW LIFE BEGINS

The rest of spring 1974 was packed for Norm. Brooklyn Polytechnic took the first step of three in a merger with New York University later that spring, becoming the "Polytechnic Institute of New York." Being the second former UA president to serve Brooklyn Poly brought the kind of historical resonance which my father—an avid reader of history and biography—deeply appreciated: Parke Rexford Kolbe, last president of Buchtel College and founding president of the municipal University of Akron 1913 to 1925, presided at Brooklyn Polytechnic from 1925 to 1932. (The two had met in 1956, when Norm assumed the presidency of the Association of Urban Universities and Dr. Kolbe, a co-founder of the organization, gave the keynote address.)

I'm not certain about the timing between the conclusion of this job and the beginning of the next, but by August 1974 Dad had moved into the red-brick Georgian colonial presidential residence on the campus of Stephens College in Columbia, Missouri. If there was a remote logic to appointing a retired twenty-year veteran of an urban public university with strong technical and research programs to a private engineering school in urban Brooklyn, finding a similar connection to his appropriateness to lead a private liberal arts women's college, particularly the sort which maintains stables where young ladies may board their horses, seems a reach. He approached the new challenge with professionalism which obscured the pain he felt to return to a gracious president's home so resembling 856 Mayfair Road without the life partner of forty-four years who had always complemented him. Ames left her husband and her three teenage daughters and her invalid widowed mother-in-law in Berlin to help Dad decorate and open this President's home with a fancy reception.

During his first two acting presidencies, Norm developed a pattern resembling in many ways the practices of his two working sabbaticals. He returned to Akron with great regularity. In 1972, he was re-elected to the board of First National Bank for his last six-year term. In 1973, he was elected Chairman of the Board of First Federal Savings and Loan, a position he would hold until First Federal was acquired by Charter One Bank in 1989. (In the 1960s and 1970s, banking laws differentiated the spheres of business of the two kinds of organizations sufficiently so as not to cause conflicts of interest for directors.) As a director, his presence was required, and his compensation based upon attendance, at full board and committee meetings. He hinted once that the cost of travel sometimes exceeded the compensation. He believed that the long-term reward of faithful service exceeded all short-term difficulties, and it was engrained by long habit to "present the body" as Kay had lectured him from the earliest times in their relationship, using Montgomery-family shorthand. From New York, presenting the body meant at least an airplane commute. From Columbia, it was three planes or a ten-hour drive. In 1971, he had accepted appointment as a trustee of the University of Dayton, becoming one of the first members not under vows to the Society of Mary, not even a Roman Catholic. Somehow, he kept his appointments with that board as well. For Christmas 1974, he returned to Germany, to Ames and Rusty's home in Berlin, which he and Kay had visited the year before.

But before that, by fall 1974, Norm was dating. He brought two different widows to our Columbus home on Ohio State football weekends, one the mother of an Old Trail School classmate of Sandy's, the other a friend from their young married days in Cincinnati. To Ames in Berlin, he showed a wallet keepsake photograph of an Akron divorcée, Virginia Kirk, whom he had brought to Ames's home in the Philippines in 1967 when she and he and Kay were traveling around the world with UA's "Classrooms Abroad." He invited at least two other Akron women to visit him at Stephens College, the second of those being Mary Thomas, the widow of a Firestone executive who lived in the generous modern French provincial house she and her late husband Robert had built on Delaware Avenue, about a block from the President's Home. When the Stephens College assignment wrapped up, he returned to Akron, invited his children to visit at Mary's home, and in early Fall 1975 at a dinner at Portage Country Club, announced their engagement. She was the club women's golf champion and a regular at duplicate bridge, pastimes for which he had no passion and little skill. They married privately soon after the new year 1976.

Early that new year Norm traveled twice to Saudi Arabia in pursuit of an AED contract to build a nation-sponsored university. He went by himself in February and in April. And by late spring, the marriage between Norm and Mary had been dissolved by mutual agreement—"as if it never happened," Dad told me. He did not record it on his résumé or in any of his many professional biographies, like *Who's Who in America*. He had kept the Fir Hill Towers apartment, and to that he returned. Shortly after the new year 1977, he and Virginia Kirk married privately in Florida, where she kept a condominium apartment. They took an extended round-the-world tour. In Akron he gave up his Fir Hill Towers apartment and she gave up her Fir Hill Towers apartment, and together they moved into Tower Eighty on North Portage Path and then a couple of years later to the Camelot, on the site once occupied by Old Trail School, where in their second home and the twenty-seventh year of their marriage he would die at age ninety-eight.

SECOND PARTNERSHIP

Virginia was highly supportive of Norm's higher education career, and shortly after their wedding he resumed his rent-a-president adventure. The Saudi Arabia contract never materialized. But later in 1977, plans were made to move into the President's home at the private liberal arts women's Cedar Crest College, in Allentown, Pennsylvania. In 1978, they moved to the acting presidency of Union College in Schenectady, New York, which brought with it the concurrent acting chancellorship of Union University in Albany, New York (a governance arrangement designed to share responsibilities for two very different kinds of higher educational enterprises, a distinguished almost Ivy-League-level liberal arts college, and a graduate center and medical school).

Union College celebrated Norm's service by awarding him the DCL, Doctor of Civil Law. It was his eighth honorary doctorate. He spoke of Union as a place whose intellectual distinction impressed him. He was able to host distinguished lecturers there—Harold Wilson, Isaac Asimov, C.P. Snow, Cicely Tyson. And it was at Union College that Virginia helped him undertake a significant shift in his wardrobe to richer fabrics and textures, still off-the-rack rather than bespoke, but of higher quality without ostentation; that happened because he noticed that men in upstate New York, even in New York's state capital, were wearing sport coats rather than suits for daytime work responsibilities, and he had few sport coats beyond blue and camel blazers.

Norm hadn't had responsibility for a medical school since he was at the University of Cincinnati. He did as Interim Chancellor of Union University. He had been unsuccessful in gaining for UA either an Akron location or a sole UA sponsorship for the lately formed institution which became the Northeast Ohio Universities College of Medicine in Rootstown. Presiding at Union brought another secret pleasure which he only, and almost no one else then living, could appreciate. Walter Langsam,

C. P. Snow and Acting President Norm Auburn at Union College, 1979. It was the second time my father conferred an honorary degree upon Lord Snow, the first being at UA in 1968. *From the author's collection*

whom the directors of UC had chosen as president in 1955 over him, snatching from him and Kay the prize they then most appreciated, had taught at Union during the Depression.

When Norm completed installing a permanent leader at Union College, the next assignment brought him into his first time as a Senior Vice President and Provost of Widener University in Chester, Pennsylvania, about fifteen miles equidistant between Philadelphia and Wilmington, Delaware, along the northwest bank of the Delaware River. Widener has the special complexity of operating in two states, and its law school is the only one in Delaware. They lived in a University-owned townhouse, and the two-year appointment soon stretched into a third, from fall 1979 to spring 1982. Virginia helped Norm rediscover the joys of watching baseball by exercising University-owned season tickets to the Phillies.

The Widener University job might have lasted yet another year, but they were called to the acting presidency of little Salem College, a Seventh-Day Baptist liberal arts school with nursing and teacher education missions, in Salem, West Virginia, for 1982–1983. Dad's Cincinnati boyhood among many Appalachian émigrés and Virginia's southeast Ohio roots made them feel at home. Salem College was a beneficiary of the Charles Worthington Benedum Foundation, headquartered in Pittsburgh and devoted to the support of human development throughout West Virginia and southwestern Pennsylvania. As the acting presidency drew to a close, Norm was tapped to coordinate a Benedum Foundation Study Project headquartered fifty miles northeast at West Virginia University, in Morgantown.

In his role with Benedum at WVU, Dad met a thirty-nine-year-old first-time college president, formerly WVU's law dean, named E. Gordon Gee. When the Benedum study concluded, President Gee asked seventy-nine-year-old Norman Auburn to stay at West Virginia University as Executive Assistant to the President, an assignment that stretched from 1984 to 1986, when Gee left to become president of the University of Colorado.

Throughout the first ten years of their marriage, Virginia served as "first lady" to Norm in those acting presidencies. She brought an outgoing personality and strategies to help people talk about themselves (she had worked in guidance counseling) and an appreciation of the good and expensive things in life, and when pressed to speak of herself, she drew from a large fund of experience as a world traveler. Indeed, she and my father always said they had first met on a University of Akron-sponsored "Classrooms Abroad" trip. Twelve years his junior, she was vigorous and enjoyed relatively good health into her mid-seventies.

Good health and vigor made not just these higher education assignments possible. They also permitted the banking career, upon which maintenance of a comfortable lifestyle and establishment of an estate sufficient to support his disabled child depended. While from 1978 onward Dad had only the one bank directorship at First Federal Savings and Loan to consider, he was Chairman of the Board, and he needed in-person meetings to fulfill his responsibilities and assure his continued leadership. The calculus of time, distance, and expense most often dictated travel by car: 380 miles from Allentown, 480 from Schenectady, 410 from Chester, 195 from Salem, 180 from Morgantown. Virginia was the primary driver. Norm could arrange the bank committee meetings to coordinate with the bank board meetings, and he could load his college presidency schedules into three or four days one week followed by six or seven days the next. But that would work only if Virginia expended the energy to drive: subsidies for air travel, probably a part of the employment agreements for his New York and Washington, DC, sabbaticals during his University of Akron service, couldn't be loaded fairly into the AED contracts under which he served these institutions. So, they piled up the hours and miles in big soft-riding turnpike cruisers, Oldsmobile Ninety Eights or Cadillac Sedans de Ville.

Through all this higher education work, all this banking, all this commuting, during these first ten years of marriage, they also traveled abroad extensively, not just once but sometimes three times a year. Their honeymoon was Norm's seventh round-the-world tour, this one via South Africa, southern and southeast Asia, and the People's Republic of China. In 1978 and 1979, while serving Cedar Crest and Union Colleges, cruises to the Caribbean; to the Mediterranean; and to the Baltic. While at Widener, Europe on the ground; Colombia, Ecuador, and the Galapagos; Cuba and Mexico; Spain and Morocco. After Salem College and before the conclusion of work for President Gee at West Virginia University in 1986, Japan, Hong Kong, and the PRC; another Caribbean cruise; a trip to the UK; on the ground in Germany, eastern Europe, Turkey, and the Soviet Union; and back to Great Britain again.

From 1986–1987, Virginia got him to spend more time at their twelfth-story ocean-view condo in Fort Lauderdale. As long as they could travel—which meant for most of the first twenty-five years of their marriage—they would spend as much as five months a year there. Norm always argued for more time in Akron, and he had his bank responsibilities to plead and, latterly, University of Akron assignments. Plus, they became comfortable with spending the money to fly between their homes, making the 1,200-mile driving trip only before and after northern winter. As they settled into this pattern, suspiciously resembling retirement, there was one more surprise.

Official portrait of the Acting President of Lincoln University of Missouri, 1987. *Photo by Wright Studio, from the author's collection*

In 1987–1988, at age eighty-two, Norm was elected Acting President of Lincoln University in Jefferson City, Missouri. His consulting work at what is now Truman State University and his service eleven years earlier at Stephens College in Columbia had made him a familiar figure in the state. But this was his first hands-on experience with a Historically Black University, the 1895 land-grant of Missouri. When I visited him in 1987, he told me in a circumspect fashion of the usual kinds of fractures in the faculty and between the campus and its curators, which he had confronted and worked to relieve in six presidencies. He also said that the 670-mile commute to Akron was proving difficult.

Dad served no more full-time rent-a-presidencies after Lincoln University. He continued to AED as Senior Vice President after the death of Al Eurich in 1987, well into the 1990s. Through an AED contract, for instance, he guided a team of retired presidents in vetting Ohio State's upper administration for Gordon Gee during his transition from Boulder to

Columbus. He outlived Eurich's AED co-founder, his friend Sid Tickton. When he came back to Akron in 1988, UA President Bill Muse put him to work—this "President Emeritus and Consultant" whose substitute pension could look like a sinecure as the reasons for its establishment faded into history—on a major fund-raising campaign. And the most important event of his banking career happened at the end of August 1989.

The banking laws which had permitted Norm to serve both First National Bank and First Federal Savings and Loan in the 1960s and 1970s were changing in the 1980s, and savings-and-loan businesses were moving into areas earlier reserved for banks. This movement made consolidation attractive, and a well-run profitable local network of savings and loan offices like First Federal of Akron saw its shareholder value poised to increase greatly through a sale. Charter One of Cleveland, which got its start in 1934 serving eastside Czech immigrants, was continuing to expand. It went public in 1988. As part of ten acquisitions that decade, in 1989 Charter One bought First Federal. Directors of First Federal were compensated for their equity shares, of course, and that compensation was sufficiently beyond a simple translation of First Federal stock into Charter One stock that it earned their approval. The terms of the sale negotiated by First Federal's Board included two seats on the board of Charter One, which the Chairman of the First Federal Board and the CEO of First Federal assumed. At age eighty-four, banker Norman P. Auburn began service as a Director of Charter One. The acceleration of bank mergers and acquisitions in the banking industry continued. By 2001, Charter One operated in Ohio, Michigan, Illinois, New York, Massachusetts, and Vermont with assets of more than $35 billion, and by 2002 only 34% of its business was in mortgages (the mainstay of the old savings and loans), which had constituted nearly 75% as recently as five years earlier. Norm went to his last meeting (now as "Director Emeritus," but still paid and expected to participate in discussions) in March 2003, the year he turned 98, four months before he died.

Norm's and Virginia's families aboard *Celebrity Horizon* for his eighty-fifth birthday, June 1990. *From the author's collection*

Norm and Virginia with their children and grandchildren at the Chautauqua Institution, New York, July 1995, Norm's ninetieth birthday. *From the author's collection*

Survivors of Norm Auburn, following his funeral, July 26, 2003. Photo by John Ashley, *from the author's collection*

Davey

One member of our family never lived in the President's Home, though he did visit often. To understand my mother Kay, you need to meet her youngest child. To understand my father Norm, to understand his special burden and one motivation for extending his professional career, you should meet my brother Davey.

My sister Ames remembers that our thirty-nine-year-old mother Kay looked radiantly beautiful in the spring of 1947 when she was pregnant with Davey. Ames herself was fourteen-and-a-half that May, Dick was ten, and I was a seventeen-month-old toddler. Later, Mother spoke of realizing Davey's physical limitations for the first time when she felt the rigidity of his little body in the bassinet. She would darkly hint at some irregularity in the modern "twilight sleep" anesthesia employed during his birth. His labor and birth contrasted vividly with my own easy one, which had occurred just six or seven hours after interrupting an evening of song and drinks and cigarettes around the piano and which brought relief to our fortyish parents, who had endured four miscarriages before they greeted the long-awaited third child.

Mother and Dad made the fourth child so that I would have an age-peer sibling. Ames says that Davey and I were inseparable there at 2822 Stratford Avenue in Cincinnati. But my infant memories in that large bungalow are of delicious solitary hours lying on the carpet in my father's first-floor study listening to the radio and of playing beneath a cherry tree on the front lawn and of crossing Stratford Avenue to a construction site where I would help strong-muscled Ray form the courses of bricks

David Bruce Auburn, 1995, age forty-eight. *From the author's collection*

and mortar and eat a sandwich with him when he paused in his work. And maybe Davey was there, on the hip of Mary Harris, Mother's girl-of-all-work, but I don't remember. Certainly Mary helped me cross the street to watch Ray, whom she married shortly after we left Cincinnati.

The October I was five and Davey was four, we moved to Akron, and it was there at 344 Merriman Road that Davey brought me the corpse of Junior. Junior was a white mouse, *my* white mouse, and he lived in a small wire-and-wood cage kept in the dining room. I brought him his food and water and changed the wood shavings on the floor of his cage after carefully unlatching the small door and grabbing Junior to prevent his escape, and Davey must have imitated me, but his grasp was too strong, and Junior died of excessive love. It was the first death of a living warm-blooded creature which either of us had experienced, and perhaps Davey learned then the mantra, "Junior in heaven? Oh, no," which he lived long enough to have to repeat, with changes of name, about parents, aunts and an uncle, friends, a nephew, a brother. But not about the immortal "Petey Lamb." We ate Petey, but Petey was immortal because Davey gave his name to nearly every pale white or pastel four-legged stuffed animal that subsequently came his way. They all were "Petey Lamb" thereafter.

Davey and I shared a bedroom on Merriman Road while we lived there, and later we slept in the same back bedroom at 856 Mayfair Road when he was home at Christmas and Easter and for the month of August. When I was permitted to set my own bedtime, I would delay until after he went to sleep. Davey composed himself for sleep this way: he would lie on his right side with his left arm tucked under his right ear and his right thumb in his mouth, and he would rock his body back and forth in rhythm with a hymn or song he would sing. His hearing loss seemed greater beyond his thirties, but he had a good memory for music, and he never forgot a song lyric. To a martial air like "Onward Christian Soldiers" he'd rock the springs and mattress and even bang the headboard against the wall, and often in the small hours of morning I'd awake to "banners flow" followed by silence and several measures of rocking, a barely audible voiced phrase, more rocking, then a final triumphant "cross of Jesus, Going on before."

The last time I slept with Davey was about 2001 in our home in Fairlawn. From his forties onward, Davey found it uncomfortable to sleep away from Jonesville's Montgomery House, The Manor's group home where he lived from 1977 until his death in 2009. He'd be fine during the day, but in the early morning hours something often awoke him. When he stayed with us in Columbus or Jonesboro or Fort Wayne, we tried him in the guest room, until he fell down the stairs during the night, then on a pallet in our bedroom, which resulted in three people awakening at 2:00 or 3:00, and finally in Sandy's place in our king-sized bed, which seemed to provide him as much comfort as he could find outside his own room. At fifty-four, he still rocked and sang to himself, though much less energetically than when he was younger.

All but the first five of Davey's sixty-two years were lived under the care of The Manor. My mother's decision to send Davey there was very difficult for her. The physical limitations from Davey's cerebral palsy were apparent early, but she held out hope that the accompanying intellectual disability was only developmental until Davey was five. Moving to a strange new city, and without options to enroll him in the public schools in those years, she became certain that he needed institutional care. She investigated a state facility at Applecreek, thirty-five miles from Akron, but it depressed her. Once, she told Ames in despair, she thought the only way to prevent Davey's life being passed in sterile regimentation was to take him with her in the car and drive over a cliff.

Jonesville was a long day's drive in those pre-turnpike days, nearly as far away to the mind as Chicago or New York. But at The Manor was the love and care which her sisters Jo and Betty and brother-in-law Bill provided, and there Davey would have two new older siblings in his cousins Janey and Rob as well as the companionship of the thirty other boys. Mother knew that Davey was happy at The Manor, but when a child's happiness depends upon being separated from his mother, there is much heartache.

Because Aunt Jo devoted many hours to Davey, indeed became his surrogate mother, he could recognize the letters of the alphabet and even scrawl his name. I never heard or saw him read a page of prose with an understanding of its narrative, but having been born to a family of readers, Davey became one after his own fashion, happily leafing through books and magazines even after his near-sightedness made it difficult for him to see any type smaller than sixteen-points. Like our brother Dick, he needed to hold a book or magazine while he watched television, and he would often call for a pen or pencil as if to fill in a crossword puzzle while his favorite "Road Runner" cartoon blared away. If a bathroom were supplied with a magazine rack, his trips would stretch past the half-hour mark. If he discovered no magazines were available after he'd reached an intimate posture, he would summon me to supply them. He laughed with delighted incredulity when I showed him a book written by his nephew: "Markie, that's me! That's my book!" when I pointed out "David Auburn" on the title page, and he turned each page to find the "David Auburns" incorporated in the running page headers. It was a magic I couldn't explain to his satisfaction, the way his name kept showing up during his last decade in magazines and books and on a huge poster in his bedroom.

Davey was differently abled from most of us in surprising ways. He had superior senses of direction and spatial orientation. He would often wish a drive around Hillsdale County to last longer, and he would know even a dozen miles away when the car's vector had been directed back toward Jonesville. We spent many hours driving around Akron in our teens, and years later, no matter who our companion, he would announce

Uncle Davey with his namesake, the playwright David Auburn, 2000. *From the author's collection*

our proximity to the home of some former girlfriend we had once visited. If I happened to drive past the street on which Sandy's parents George and Pearl Korman lived, he would demand that I "turn here, Markie!" long after they'd sold up and moved to Arizona. Sandy, our David, Ben, and I moved to Arkansas from Columbus in 1983, and Rob, Jane, Jocie, and Eric brought Davey for Christmas. When Rob hit I-80 and turned west rather than east, Davey asked him, "Where going, Mr. Rob?" Rob told him to Mark and Sandy's. Davey was sure we still lived in Columbus, so he replied, "Wrong way, Mr. Rob." For eleven hours, whenever he noticed unfamiliar scenery he would ask the destination, be told, and then announce with absolute certainty, "Wrong way, Mr. Rob." The four Clarks arrived a bit shell-shocked by Davey's litany, and Davey looked at our new home and asked me, "That you house, Markie?" I said, "Yes," and all he replied was "How you, Markie?"

If Davey's senses of direction and spatial orientation were more acute than some, so too his sense of humor outstripped that of many better abled people. He couldn't always follow the intricacies of verbal narrative, and his appreciation of simple word play was rudimentary. But he loved physical absurdities and aberrations, particularly pratfalls and the incongruous in movies. In 2008, he laughed at the bumbling swollen cartoon humans on the cruiseship space-ark of *Wall-E*. In 2007, he chuckled most of the way through *Ratatouille*, immensely amused at a rat secretly directing human activities in a restaurant kitchen. And he would laugh till the tears flowed at Hollywood scenes of car crashes. Others in the audience felt concern for Matt Damon in his subcompact maneuvering at high speed down the wrong lane of a superhighway with huge Mercedes saloons in pursuit, but Davey knew this was an absurd premise, a senseless waste of fuel and metal, a contravention of man's civil laws, a violation of nature's rules of inertia and gravity, and he would howl "Funny! Oh, Markie, that funny!" His voiced recognition of the absurdities of such scenes disturbed strangers who didn't share his reasonable perspective. When Sandy and I were dating, we finally chose to take him to drive-in movies where he could laugh as much as he wanted.

His sense of humor, particularly for the absurd, was better than most; and it was more good natured, too. He loved to tease and to be teased, but he understood the limits of teasing. With his younger nieces and nephews, he would play the missing nose game, nipping their noses between the second knuckles of his curved index and middle fingers and then displaying the captured nose with his thumb. He would coax them to look at an imaginary bird, then try to steal a treat while they gazed off to where he had directed their attention. I think Uncle Bill taught him the missing nose game, and I confess to teaching him "look-at-the-bird." In fact, I confess to teasing him a lot. To various pokes and misdirections, he'd respond with laughter—"Oh, no, Markie!" and imitation, then mild irritation—"Ow! You, Boy!"—or fake aggression—"All right, you Boy! Mm-m-m-mouth!" meaning "I'll hit you in the mouth," which he never did more than threaten. The last stage was fake or even genuine aggrievement—"Stop it the teasing!"—joined with an appeal to someone nearby—"Miss Jane, Markie teasing!" This last response happened particularly when I sat out of reach and had made a face or crossed my eyes to break his demeanor and couldn't be accused of a physical poke or the theft of some goodie from his plate. When he thought the teasing had violated good humor, he might declare "Markie cheating! You cheating" in place of "Markie teasing."

Good humor is more than what we call a sense of humor. Good humor also describes essential disposition. Unlike the bulk of mankind, Davey never carried a grudge; he was genuinely good humored. It was not that he forgot the cause of pain. He was just as able as the rest of us to avoid what hurt, and maybe he was better because he rarely overindulged in food or drink. He avoided those who proved malicious, but there were very few such people in his life, and he always forgave neglect or inconsiderate treatment. When Davey saw me, no matter how long my absence or how recent my insult, he greeted me with the same sunny enthusiasm as if I had only gone to the next room.

Davey had three or four conversational gambits which he used at more or less appropriate times. Cars were a favorite subject, and those of interest were divided into two classes. Large luxury sedans were all "Cadillacs," and two-seat roadsters were "cute cars." A great treat was to ride in some Cadillac or Cadillac-like car while calling out the appearances of Volkswagen Beetles or Chrysler PTs or MINI Coopers as "cute cars." A ride in Miss Jane's MGB—a veritable cute car—was a special event. My large Chrysler LHS entered his life in 2001 but didn't quite qualify as a "Cadillac" in his estimation, and I tried to raise his appreciation by popping the trunk with the keyless entry system without showing him the connection between the trunk lid's sudden opening and my hidden controller, and while he was suitably mystified, even delighted, it didn't promote my car to Cadillac status.

It was hard for my mother to drive Davey back to The Manor after a visit to Akron. As a preteen, Davey could sadden her with tears and plaintive repetitions of "No home today!" By his forties and fifties, he made a conversation starter out of his separation anxiety. "No home today," he would say an hour or two after arriving at our house. "Home tomorrow" (meaning some remote moment later than now), he would announce. I could tell how well his visit was going by the frequency with which he returned to this topic, and when it disappeared after a couple of days, I knew that we needed to get him back to Montgomery House soon. By his late fifties, when the pleasant stimulation of his grandnephews and nieces had turned fatiguing, he even got to the point of asking to go home, and I saw how he was aging.

"No home today." Kay and Mark return Davey to The Manor, 1958. *From the author's collection*

Family, particularly absent family, was a conversational gambit more favored than discussion of his departure. He would recite the catalogues, wanting confirmation that they were complete. "Kiki, Mary, Dindy, Dennifer" (the Richard P. Auburns), "Ame, Rutt-y, Lu, Beth, Kate" (the M. L. Latta Jr. family), "Mr. Rob, Miss Jane, Eric, Jothee" (the Robert M. Clarks), "Dandy, Mark, David, Genilman," "Jane, Cottie, Clarkie, Marthie" (Jane Clark Swinehart and her children), and then "Daddy, Mommy, Dolores, Ari." This last name was somewhat out of place. "Dolores" certainly belonged there. Dolores White was Davey's caregiver in Akron, our mother's helper from 1958 until Kay's death in 1974, even Davey's and my adoptive older sister. But "Ari" was "Aristotle Onassis," a Lhasa Apso lapdog my mother acquired in her late fifties. Now, Davey would usually acknowledge that fact: "Ari's just a dog," he would say in a puzzled fashion. Dolores thinks this comment arose when she and Davey drove Norm and Kay to the airport, and Kay carried her fluffy companion aboard the plane with her, but didn't offer to take Davey. According to Dolores, saying "Ari's just a dog," expressed his sense of displacement.

Davey's fourth conversational gambit still puzzles me. He would use it in two situations. In one he seemed to want to enliven a dull exchange with

Dolores cuddles Davey at her LaBelle Avenue home, 2001. *From the author's collection*

something shocking and spectacular. In the other situation he was offering an example of chaos sprung loose upon his world and seeking assurance that normality would return. In both, paragraph would succeed paragraph with almost nothing verbally intelligible but with the perfect rhythm and intonation of narrative; he might even look away or roll his eyes upward, but I still felt grasped by the lapel and forced to listen. And then the payoff would come in the first clear words: "ambooyanth!" and "Dr. Biddle!" He'd pause and wait for my response. Well, I figured that an ambulance coming to The Manor or Montgomery House was a pretty special event, and I was so used to Davey's not being able to hear the sound of the letter S and substituting the letter B for P or D for T, that I thought this one more retelling of an exciting story of one of his housemates being taken away in an ambulance to the hospital. In fact, I asked him the first or second time if "Dr. Biddle" meant hospital, and he always said, "Yes. Dr. Biddle." Or sometimes he'd use his all-purpose superlative—"That's two!"—as in a REAL ambulance or a REAL hospital, or so I thought. I had it wrong, it turns out. Dr. Biddle is an eye specialist who lives in the century home just east of Mont-

Norm cuddles Davey, Fir Hill Towers, 1972. *From the author's collection*

gomery House. Whether he's regularly visited by ambulances I don't know. And as far as my missing the point of his story every time, I suspect Davey would have said, "I don't care, Mr. Markie, I don't care."

It's restful, being with the pure of heart. Hanging out with Davey usually brought that comfort and peace.

My father never spoke his feelings about Davey to me. Norm spent much of his life as a public figure, and Davey appears in the family portraits designed for public occasions, like the picture of the six of us in the Chevrolet convertible shortly after we moved to Akron or the grouping, with children-in-law and grandbabies, at the opening of the Auburn Science and Engineering Center seventeen years later. After our mother died and Dad remarried, I'm not aware that Davey again visited him in Akron except when he'd come to stay with Sandy and me. But for more than two decades Norm took the drive to Jonesville to see Davey once or twice every year well into his mid nineties, until he was no longer capable of the long car trips. He made a canny provision in his estate plan which guaranteed Davey's maintenance in the event of withdrawal of federal SSI support or the dissolution of The Manor, so that Ames, Dick, and I and our families need not assume the burden. Davey loved him, even when neither of them could hear the other nor see much, either. Rob and Jane brought Davey to Akron for Norm's funeral in 2003, and Davey said to me, "Daddy in heaven, Markie? Oh, no!"

Sandy and I were in Bali, Indonesia, in April 2009 when Fred Prasser contacted us about Davey's hospitalization and sudden surgery. No one we know was more capable than Fred of assuring Davey's well being, except the man whom Fred succeeded in leading The Manor, namely Rob Clark. Because of Rob, and Fred, Davey lived many years, even decades, longer than his childhood pediatricians and specialists predicted, and because of the Clarks and Fred, he lived a happy life. So when Fred called us on the far side of the world, from which even our immediate return would be too late, all we asked was that someone familiar be with Davey during his ordeal. Davey's housemother, Brenda Templeton, was there, and so Davey saw and talked with his "Mom" when he awoke after surgery and before he went quietly into his final sleep.

We held a memorial service to honor Davey on July 11, 2009, in the First Presbyterian Church of Jonesville, the church where our grandfather R. Ames Montgomery preached the last sermons of his fifty-four years as a Presbyterian minister and where Davey himself was for many years a regular congregant. At that occasion I couldn't help reminding everyone of the Communion Service there thirty years before when Davey's young cousins had to be chastised for undue levity during the Sacrament: Davey's mouth must have been dry when he took a piece of bread, for he chewed it vigorously and loudly, loudly but still below his hearing threshold, for minutes on end it seemed, making more appreciative smacks and gummings than a starving Bedouin welcomed to a meal at a strange oasis, and the giggles of his cousins rippled up and down the pew behind and beside Davey and caused their elders serious embarrassment, as well as concern that they too might break up. At the memorial service, it also seemed appropriate to declare, in a statement he might have made, "Davey in heaven? Oh, . . . yes!"

DAVID BRUCE AUBURN, 61, of Jonesville, Michigan, died April 7 [2009] after a brief illness. Preceded in death by his mother Kathleen, his nephew Benjamin, his father Norman, and his brother Dr. Richard, he is survived by his sister Ames M. Latta of Rockville, Maryland, his brother Mark (Sandy) of Akron, Ohio, his sister-in-law Mary of Naples, Florida, his cousin Jane Swinehart of Reston, Virginia, his cousin and guardian Robert M. Clark (Jane) of Onstead, Michigan, and Vieques, Puerto Rico, his nephew David (Frances Rosenfeld) of New York City, his nieces Lucretia Tyckoski (James) of Bethesda, Maryland, Kathleen Hofherr (Dan) of Vienna, Virginia, Elizabeth Renalds of Fairfax, Virginia, Jennifer Van Metre (Evan) of Atlanta, and Cynthia of Chicago, five second cousins, eight grandnephews and nieces, and his friend Dolores White of Akron.

Born May 25, 1947, in Cincinnati, Davey moved to Akron with his family in 1951. In 1952 Davey matriculated at The Manor in Jonesville, Michigan, a residential care facility for special-needs children operated by his mother's sisters Josephine Montgomery and Elizabeth Clark (William). In 1977, Robert Clark (then President of The Manor) created Montgomery House, the group home in which Davey resided with several of his Manor classmates until his death. Davey's sunny nature, generous spirit, and unfailing sense of humor enriched all who knew him.

A Celebration of Life was held at the First Presbyterian Church of Jonesville (300 E. Chicago), at 3:00 p.m., Saturday, July 11, 2009. The family thanks Brenda Templeton, Davey's housemother, and Fred Prasser, President & CEO of The Manor, for their loving care of their brother, cousin, uncle, and friend.

Index of Principal Persons

About the Author

Photo by Michael Chritton. Courtesy of the *Akron Beacon Journal*

Mark Auburn was educated at King Elementary School, Simon Perkins Junior High School, and Western Reserve Academy. He became the third of Norm and Kay's children to graduate from UA in 1967. After completing a PhD at the University of Chicago in 1971, he taught and administered at Ohio State University, followed by appointments as dean or vice president at Arkansas State University, the University of Arkansas System, and Indiana University-Purdue University at Fort Wayne. In 1991, he returned to UA as Senior Vice President and Provost for President William V. Muse. He served in other administrative roles under Presidents Elliott, Ruebel, and Proenza, retiring in 2006.

Mark met Sandy Korman (BA, '67; MA, '68; PhD, Ohio State, '78) on the stage in Kolbe Hall where they performed under the direction of Professor James F. Dunlap in "The Wonderful Tang," summer 1965 Children's Theatre Workshop. They married in 1969.